GRANTA

4

Editor: Bill Buford
Executive Editor: Pete de Bolla
Design: Chris Hyde
Editorial Assistants: Cathryn Gwynn, Robin Shellow, and
Michael Hofmann
Editorial Board: Malcolm Bradbury, Elaine Feinstein, Ian Hamilton,
Leonard Michaels, Fay Weldon
U.S. Editor: Jonathan Levi, 3A, 25 Claremont Ave., New York,
N.Y. 10027

Editorial Correspondence: Granta, Box 666, King's College,
Cambridge CB2 1ST. (0223) 315290.
All manuscripts are welcome but must be accompanied by a stamped,
self-addressed envelope or they cannot be returned.

Subscriptions: For individuals, £6.50 for four issues; for institutions,
£9.50 for four issues. For foreign subscriptions, add £3.00 per year for
postage. Single copies available for £2.50 including postage.

Granta gratefully acknowledges the assistance of the Eastern Arts
Association.

Special thanks to John Dugdale and Paul Evans.

Cover: Chris Hyde.
Cover illustration: One of the *One Hundred Views of Fujiyama*
by Hokusai, reprinted with permission of the British Museum.

ISSN 0017-3232

CONTENTS

HONORARY PATRONS

Prof. A. Alimard
J. K. Aronson
J. T. Bains
J. Berryman
Harold Campbell
Martin Caton
W. J. Chapman
Dr F. W. Cook
Martin Cook
Hugh Cooke
A. M. Davey
Sue Davies
Rev. Dr Harry Escott
P. Faulkner
Christoqher J. Furniss
W. Garland
F. Gawthrop
E. I. Goswami
John Goulding
Andrew Graham-Yooll
Dr Susan Gregory
Tony Häfliger
Dr A. A. Hampton
Lawrence Holden
Derek Horton
G. G. Howe
Linda Hutchinson
C. Lanning
Patrick Lyons
Dr Nicholas Mann

Glenn Mascord
John Matson
Bel Mooney
M. Moore
Keith Norman
Alan Pardoe
D. M. Parnell
Graham Pilcher
Robert M. Pollett
Dr M. von Riefenstahl
Alister Ross
Rugby School
T. Russell-Cobb
P. Sandys-Wunsch
V. W. Shiel
John Skelton
T. R. J. Stockting
P. G. J. Summers
Steve Surmon
Rev. R. A. Swallow
Ann and Anthony Thwaite
Mr and Mrs A. G. Tuite
J. D. Turner
A. Vaughan
Fred Watson
T. Weinert
D. J. Westwood
C. A. Williams
Robert Wilson
Lesley Wright
Prof. M. Zavarzadeh

GRANTA

GUY DAVENPORT
FIFTY-SEVEN VIEWS
OF FUJIYAMA

Months, days, eternity's sojourners. Years that unfold from the cherry in flower to rice thick in the flat fields to the gingko suddenly gold the first day of frost to the red fox across the snow. The sampan pilot from Shiogama to Ishinomaki, the postman galloping from Kyoto to Ogaki, what do they travel but time? Our great journey is through the years, even when we doze by the brazier. Clouds move on the winds. We long to travel with them. For I, Basho, am a traveller. No sooner, last autumn, did I get home from a fine journey along the coast, take the broom to the cobwebs in my neglected house on the Sumida River, see the New Year in, watch the wolves slinking down from the hills shoulder deep in white drifts, look in wonder all over again, as every spring, at the mist on the marshes, than I was ready to set out through the gate at Shirakawa. I stitched up the slits and rips in my trousers, hitched a new chin strap to my hat, rubbed my legs with burnt wormwood leaves, which puts vigour into the muscles, and thought all the while of the moon rising full over Matsushima, what a sight that would be when I got there and could gaze on it.

●

We set out, she and I, a fine late summer day, happy in the heft and chink of our gear. We had provender for a fortnight in the wilderness along the Vermont Trail, which we took up on a path through an orchard abandoned years ago, where in generous morning light busy with cabbage butterflies and the green blink of grasshoppers an old pear tree still as frisky and crisp as a girl stood with authority among dark unpruned wine-saps gone wild, and prodigal sprawling zinnias, sweet peas, and hollyhocks that had once been some honest farmwife's flowers and garden grown from seeds that came in Shaker packets from upstate New York or even Ohio, now blooming tall and profuse in sedge and thistle all the way to the tamaracks of the forest edge, all in that elective concert by which the lion's fellowship makes the mimosa spread. This trail was blazed back in the century's teens by a knickerbockered and tweed-capped comitatus from Yale, carrying on a tradition from Raphael Pumpelly and Percy Wallace and Steele MacKaye, from Thoreau and Burroughs: a journey with no purpose but to be in the wilderness, to be in its silence, to be together deep among its trees and valleys and heights.

•

Having, with great luck, sold my house by the river, thereby casting myself adrift, so to speak, from obligations and responsibilities, I moved in for awhile with my friend and patron, the merchant Sampu, himself a poet. *Bright flash makes me blink: spring field, farmer's spade.* But before I went I brushed a poem for my old doorpost. *Others now will sing high in peach blossom time behind this door wild grass blocks.* And at dawn I set out, more of night still in the sky than day, as much by moonlight fading as by sunlight arriving, the twenty-seventh of March. I could just make out the dim outline of Fuji and the thin white cherry blossoms of Ueno and Yanaka. Farewell, Fiji! Farewell, cherry blossoms! Friends had got up early to see me off, indeed to go with me for the first leg of the journey by boat, as far as Senju. It was not until they left me that I felt, with a jump of my heart, the three hundred miles I was proposing to go. Water stood in my eyes. I looked at my friends and the neat clusters of houses at Senju as if through rain. *Fish and bird regret that springtime is so brief.* This was my parting poem. My friends took copies, and watched till I was out of sight.

•

On the beach at Sounion. Tar and seaweed shift in the spent collapse and slide of shirred green water just beyond our toes. We had been to see Byron's name carved with a penknife on a column of Poseidon's temple. Homer mentions this cape in the Iliad, perhaps all of Attika that he knew. It was here that the redstone *kouros* was excavated who stands in Athens by the javelin-hurling Zeus. We lie in Greek light. The silence is musical: the restlessness of the Ionian, the click of pebbles pushed by the seawash. There is no other sound. *I am Hermes. I stand by the grey sea-shingle and wait in the windy wood where three roads meet.* A poem? From the *Anthology*. Wet eyelashes, lens of water in navel. Another. *To Priapos, god of gardens and friend to travelers, Damon the farmer laid on this altar, with a prayer that his trees and body be hale of limb for yet awhile, a pomegranate glossy bright, a skippet of figs dried in the sun, a cluster of grapes, half red, half green, a mellow quince, a walnut splitting from its husk, a cucumber wrapped in flowers and leaves, and a jar of olives golden ripe.*

●

All that March day I walked with a wondering sadness. I would see the north, but would I, at my age, ever return? My hair would grow whiter on the long journey. It was already Genroku, the second year thereof, and I would turn forty-five on the way. My shoulders were sore with my pack when I came to Soka, a village, at the end of the day. Travel light! I have always intended to, and my pack with its paper overcoat, cotton bath robe, neither of which were much in a heavy rain, my notebook, ink block, and brushes, would have been light enough except for gifts my friends loaded me with at parting, and my own unessential one thing and another which I cannot throw away because my heart is silly. We went, Sora and I, to see the sacred place of Muro-no-Yashima, Ko-no-Hana Sakuya Hime, the goddess of flowering trees. There is another shrine to her on the lower slopes of Fuji. When she was with child, Ninigi-no-Mikoto her husband would not believe that she was pregnant by a god. She locked herself into a room, set fire to it, and in the flames gave birth to Hohodemi-no-Mikoto, the fire-born noble. Here poets write of the smoke, and the peasants do not eat a speckled fish called *konoshiro*.

•

We set out, she and I, like Basho on the narrow road to the deep north from his house on the Sumida where he could not stay for thinking of the road, of the red gate at Shirakawa, of the full moon over the islands of Matsushima, he and Kawai Sogoro in their paper coats, journey proud in *wabi zumai*, thinking of wasps in the cedar close of an inn, chrysanthemums touched by the first mountain frost. A few years before, Minoru Hara and I had climbed Chocorua to find a single lady slipper on a carpet of pine needles, to which he bowed, Chocorua that Ezra Pound remembered in the concentration camp at Pisa, fusing it with Tai Shan in his imagination, Chocorua where Jessie Whitehead lived with her pet porcupines and bear, Chocorua where William James died, Thoreau's Chocorua that he strolled up laughing that people used the word *climb* of its easy slopes. We set out into the deuteronomic mountains Charles Ives rings against *The Rockstrewn Hills Join in the People's Outdoor Meeting* with the chime of iron on iron, sabre, bell, and hammer, bugle and mess kit, ram-rod and spur, remembering how congenial and incantatory music led the caissons over the Potomac to Shiloh.

●

I spent the night of March thirtieth at Gozaemon the Honest's Inn at Nikko Mountain. Such was my landlord's name, which he made much of, assuring me that I would sleep out of harm's way on his grass pillows. When a stranger so advertises his honesty, you take more care than ever, but this innkeeper was as good as his name. There was no more guile in him than in Buddha the merciful, and Confucius would have approved of his scrupulousness and manners. Next day, April first, we climbed Nikko, Mountain of the Sun's Brilliance. The sainted Kobo Daishi named it and built the temple on it a thousand years ago. Its holiness is beyond words to describe. You can see its benevolence in every field round about. In it I wrote: *New leaves, with what holy wonder do I watch the sunlight on your green.* Through the mist we could just make out Mount Kurokami from the temple on Nikko. The snow on its slopes belies its name, Black-Haired Mountain. Sora wrote: *I arrived at Kurokami with my hair shorn, in new clean summer clothes.* Sora, whose name is Kawai Sogoro, used to chop wood and draw water for me. We were neighbours. I aroused his curiosity and made him a student of scenery. He too wanted to travel to see Matsushima in its beauty, and serene Kisagata.

●

Crickets creaking trills so loud we had to raise our voices, even on the beach down from the cycladic wall under the yellow spongy dry scrub with spiky stars of flowers. It is, he said, as if the light were noisy, all of it Heraclitus' little fine particles cheeping away, madly counting each other. *Thotheka! entheka! thekaksi! ikosieksi! khilioi! Ena thio tris tessera!* Hair of the family of hay, torso of the family of dog, testicles of the family of Ionian pebbles, glans of the family plum. Give us another poem, here by the fountain-pen-bluc-ink sea. *To Apollo of the Lykoreans Evnomos of Lokris gives this cricket of bronze. Know that, matched against Parthis in the finals for the harp, his strings rang keen under the pick until one of them snapped. But the prancing melody missed never a beat: a cricket sprang onto the harp and sounded the missing note in a perfection of harmony. For this sweet miracle, O godly son of Leto, Evnomos places this little singer on your altar.* From the *Anthology.* So it's Apollo and not Heraclitus running these nattering hoppergrasses and their katydid aunts and crickcrack uncles? And salty kneed old Poseidon singing along from the sea.

●

So Sora, to be worthy of the beauty of the world, shaved his head the day we departed, and donned a wandering priest's black robe, and took yet a third name, Sogo, which means Enlightened, for the road. When he wrote his haiku for Mount Kurokami, he was not merely describing his visit but dedicating himself to the sacredness of perception. We climbed higher above the shrine. We found the waterfall. It is a hundred feet high, splashing into a pool of darkest green. Urami-no-Taki is its name, See from Inside, for you can climb among the rocks and get in behind it. I wrote: *From a silent cave I saw the waterfall, summer's first grand sight for me.* I had a friend at Kurobane in Nasu County. To get there you cross a wide grassy moor for many's the mile, following a path. We kept our eyes on a village in the distance as a landmark, but night came on and rain began to pelt down before we could get there. We spent the night at a farmer's hut along the way. Next day we saw a farmer with a horse, which we asked the loan of. The paths over the moor, he said, are like a great net. You will soon get lost at the crossroads. But the horse will know the way. Let him decide which path to take.

•

These were the hills whose elegiac autumns Ives summons with bronze Brahms as a ground for Lee standing in his stirrups as he crossed the Mason and Dixon Line while a band of Moravian cornets alto, tenor, and baritone, an E-flat Helicon Bass Horn, drums battle and snare, strutted out the cake-walk dash of *Dixie*. The rebels danced in rank and gave a loud *huzzah!* These are the everlasting hills that stand from dawn time to red men to French hunter to Calvinist boot to rumours from farm to village that the bands played waltzes and polkas under the guns at Gettysburg when the cannonade was at its fiercest. We trod these hills because we loved them and because we loved each other, and because in them we might feel that consonance of hazard and intent which was the way Ives heard and Cézanne saw, the *moiré* of sound in the studio at West Redding where a Yale baseball cap sat on a bust of Wagner, the *moiré* of light in the quarries and pines at Bibémus. What tone of things might we not involve ourselves in the gathering of in these hills? With each step we left one world and walked into another.

•

I mounted the farmer's horse, Sora walked beside us. Two little children ran behind us. One was a girl named Kasane. Sora was delighted with her name, which means *many petalled.* He wrote: *Your name fits you, O Kasane, and fits the double carnation in its richness of petals!* When we reached the village, we sent the horse back by itself, with a tip knotted into the saddle sash. My friend the samurai Joboji Takakatsu, the steward of a lord, was surprised to see me, and we renewed our friendship and we could not have enough of each other's talk. Our happy conversations saw the sun across the country sky and wore the lantern dim way past moonrise. We walked in the outskirts of the town, saw an old academy for dog hunters—that cruel and unseemly sport was of short duration in ancient times—and paid our respects to the tomb of the lady Tamamo, a fox who took human shape. It was on this grave that the samurai archer Yoichi prayed before he shot a fan, at a great distance, from the mast of a drifting boat. Her grave is far out on the moor of grass, and is as lonely a place as you can imagine. The wind travelling through the grass! The silence! It was dark when we returned.

●

Leaves not opposite on a stem arrange themselves in two, five, eight, or thirteen rows. If the leaves in order of height up the stem be connected by a thread wound round the stem, then between any two successive leaves in a row the thread winds round the stem once if the leaves are in two or three rows, twice if in five rows, thrice if in eight, five if in thirteen. That is, two successive leaves on the stem will be at such a distance that if there are two rows, the second leaf will be halfway round the stem; if three rows, the second leaf will be one third of the way around; if five, the second will be two fifths of the way around; if eight, three eighths; if thirteen, five thirteenths. These are Fibonacci progressions in phyllotactic arrangement. The organic law of vegetable growth is the surd towards which the series one half, one third, two fifths, three eighths, and so on, approximates. Professor T. C. Hilgard sought for the germ of phyllotaxis in the numerical genesis of cells, the computation of which demonstrates Fibonacci progressions in time.

●

Guy Davenport

The tomb of En-no-Gyoja, founder of the Shugen sect, who nine hundred years ago used to preach everywhere in humble clogs, is in Komyoji Temple. My friend Joboji took me to visit it. In full summer, in the mountains, I bowed before the clogshod saint's tall image to be blessed in my travels. Unganji the Zen temple is nearby. Here the hermit Buccho, my old Zen master at Edo, lived out his life in solitude. I remember that he once wrote a poem in pine charcoal on a rock in front of his hut. *I would leave this little place, with its five feet of grass this way, five feet of grass that way, except that it keeps me dry when it rains.* We were joined by some young worshippers on the way. Their bright chatter made the climb seem no time at all. The temple is in a wood of cedars and pine, and the way there is narrow, mossy, and wet. There is a gate and a bridge. Though it was April, the air was very cold. Buccho's hut is behind the temple, a small box of a house under a big rock. I sensed the holiness of the place. I might have been at Yuan-miao's cave or Fa-yun's cliff. I made up this poem and left it there on a post: *Even the woodpeckers have not dared touch this little house.*

•

The first thing to go when you walk into the wilderness is time. You eat when you are hungry, rest when you are tired. You fill a moment to its brim. At a ford shoaling over rocks we doffed our packs, took off our boots and jeans, and waded in our shirt-tails for the childishness of it. Creek-washed feet, she said, as God intended. We dried in the sun on a boulder as warm as a dying stove, and fribbled and monkeyed with each other, priming for later. Jim Dandy! she said, and purred, but we geared up and pushed on, through Winslow Homer glades and dapple and tones that rose as if horn-heralded across sunny fields and greendark woods and tempers now lost except for the stubborn masks of their autochthony, Ives imitating a trumpet on the piano for Nikolai Slonimsky and hearing at Waterbury gavottes his father had played during the artillery barrage at Chancellorsville, Apollinaire hanging a N'tomo mask of the Bambara on his wall beside Picassos and Laurencins, Gaudier drawing Siberian wolves in the London Zoo, tempers with lost coordinates, for essences survive by chance allegiances and griefs: the harness chains on the caissons moving towards Seven Pines, dissonance and valence.

●

We ended our visit at Kurobane. I had asked of my host that he show me the way to Sessho-seki, the famous killing stone which slew birds and bugs that lit on it. He lent me a horse and guide. The guide shyly asked me, once we were out on the road, to compose a poem for him, and so delighted was I with the surprise of his request, that I wrote: *Let us leave the road and go across the moors, the better to hear that cuckoo*. The killing stone was no mystery. It is beside a hot spring that gives off a deadly gas. Around it the ground was covered with dead butterflies and bees. Then I found the very willow about which Saigyo wrote in his *Shin Kokin Shu: In the shade of this willow lying kindly on the grass and on the stream as clear as glass, we rest awhile on the way to the far north*. The willow is near the village Ashino, where I had been told I would find it, and we too, like Saigyo, rested in its shade. *Only when the girls nearby had finished planting rice in a square of their paddy did I leave the famous willow's shade*. Then, after many days of walking without seeing a soul, we reached the Shirakawa boundary gate, the true beginning of the road north. I felt a peace come over me, felt anxiety drop away. I remembered the sweet excitement of travellers before me.

●

All of that again, he said, I long to see all of that again, the villages of the Pyrenées, Pau, the roads. O Lord, to smell French coffee again all mixed in with the smell of the earth, brandy, hay. Some of it will have changed, not all. The French peasant goes on forever. I asked if indeed there was any chance, any likelihood, that he could go. His smile was a resigned irony. Who knows, he said, that Saint Anthony didn't take the streetcar into Alexandria? There hasn't been a desert father in centuries and centuries, and there's considerable confusion as to the rules of the game. He indicated a field to our left, beyond the wood of white oak and sweetgum where we were walking, a field of wheat stubble. That's where I asked Joan Baez to take off her shoes and stockings so that I could see a woman's feet again. She was so lovely against the spring wheat. Back in the hermitage we ate goat's cheese and salted peanuts, and sipped whiskey from jelly glasses. On his table lay letters from Nicanor Parrá and Marguerite Yourcenar. He held the whiskey bottle up to the cold bright Kentucky sunlight blazing through the window. And then out to the privy, where he kicked the door with his hobnail boot, to shoo off the black snake who was usually inside. *Out! Out! You old son of a bitch! You can come back later.*

●

Guy Davenport

The great gate at Shirakawa, where the North begins, is one of the
three largest checkpoints in all the kingdom. All poets who have
passed through it have made a poem of the event. I approached it
along a road overhung with dark trees. It was already autumn here;
and winds troubled the branches above me. The unohana was still in
bloom beside the road, and their profuse white blossoms met those of
the blackberry brambles in the ditch. You would think an early snow
had speckled all the underwood. Kiyosuke tells us in the *Fukuro Zoshi*
that in ancient times no one went through this gate except in his finest
clothes. Because of this Sora wrote: *A garland of white unohana
flowers around my head, I passed through Shirakawa Gate, the only
finery I could command.* We crossed the Abukuma River and walked
north with the Aizu cliffs on our right, and villages on our left, Iwaki,
Soma, Miharu. Over the mountains beyond them, we knew, were the
counties Hitachi and Shimotsuke. We found the Shadow Pond, where
all shadows cast on it are exact of outline. The day was overcast,
however, and we saw only the grey sky mirrored in it. At Sukagawa I
visited the poet Tokyu, who holds a government post there.

●

Dissonance chiming with order, strict physical law in its dance with hazard, valences as weightless as light bonding an *aperitif à la gentiane* Suze, a newspaper, carafe, ace of Clubs, stummel. And in a shatter and jig of scialytic prismfall quiet women, Hortense Cézanne among her geraniums, Gertrude Stein resting her elbows on her knees like a washerwoman, Madame Ginoux, of Arles, reader of novels, sitting in a black dress against a yellow wall, a portrait painted by Vincent in three quarters of an hour, quiet women at the centre of houses, and by the pipe, carafe, and newspaper on the tabletop men with a new inwardness of mind, an inwardness for listening to green silence, to watch tones and brilliances and subtleties of light, dawn, noon, and dusk, Étienne Louis Malus walking at sunset in the gardens of the Palais du Luxembourg, seeing how twice refracted level light was polarized by the palace windows, alert to remember what we would see and hold and share. From fields of yellow sedge to undergrowth of wild ferns tall as our shoulders, from slippery paths Indian file through trees to bear walks along black beaver ponds we set out to see the great rocks rolled into Vermont by glaciers ten thousand years ago.

●

Tokyu, once we were at the tea bowl, asked with what emotion I had passed through the great gate at Shirakawa. So taken had I been by the landscape, I admitted, and with memories of former poets and their emotions, that I composed few *haiku* of my own. The only one I would keep was: *The first poetry I found in the far north was the worksongs of the rice farmers.* We made three books of linked *haiku* beginning with this poem. Outside this provincial town on the postroad there was a venerable chestnut tree under which a priest lived. In the presence of that tree I could feel that I was in the mountain forests where the poet Saigyo gathered nuts. I wrote these words then and there: *O holy chestnut tree, the Chinese write your name with the character for* tree *below that of* west, *the direction of all things holy.* Gyoki the priest of the common people in the Nara period had a chestnut walkingstick, and the ridgepole of his house was chestnut. And I wrote this *haiku: Worldly men pass by the chestnut in bloom by the roof.* We ended our visit with Tokyu. We came to the renowned Asaka Hills and their many lakes. The katsumi iris, I knew, would be in bloom, and we left the high road to go see them.

●

Sequoia Langsdorfii is found in the Cretaceous of both British Columbia and Greenland, and *Gingko polymorpha* in the former of these localities. *Cinnamomum Scheuchzeri* occurs in the Dakota group of Western Kansas as well as at Fort Ellis. Sir William Dawson detects in strata regarded as Laramie by Professor G. M. Dawson, of the Geological Survey of Canada, a form which he considers to be allied to *Quercus antiqua*, Newby., from Rio Dolores, Utah, in strata positively declared to be the equivalent of the Dakota group. Besides these cases there are several in which the same species occurs in the Eocene and the Cretaceous, though wanting in the Laramie. *Cinnamomum Sezannense*, of the Paleocene of Sézanne and Gelinden, was found by Heer, not only in the upper Cretaceous of Patoot, but in the Cenomanian of Atane, in Greenland. *Myrtophyllum cryptoneuron* is common to the Paleocene of Gelinden and the Senonian of Westphalia, and the same is true of *Dewalquea Gelindensis. Sterculia variabilis* is another case of a Sézanne species occuring in the upper Cretaceous of Greenland, and Heer rediscovers in this same Senonian bed the Eocene plant *Sapotacites reticulatus* which he described in the Sachs-Thüringen lignite beds.

•

But not a single *katsumi* iris could we find. No one we asked, moreover, had ever heard of them. Night was coming on, and we made haste to have a quick look at the *Kurozuka* cave by taking a shortcut at Nihonmatsu. We spent the night at Fukushima. Next day I stopped at Shinobu village to see the stone where *shinobu-zuri* cloth used to be dyed. It is a composite stone with an amazing facet smooth as glass of many different minerals and quartz. The stone used to be far up the mountain, I was told by a child, but the many tourists who came to see it trampled the crops on the way, so the villagers brought it down to the square. I wrote: *Now only the nimble hands of girls planting rice give us an idea of the ancient dyers at their work.* We crossed by ferry at Tsuki-no-wa—Ring around the Moon!—and came to Se-no-ue, a post town. There is a field nearby, with a hill named Maruyama in it: on this hill are the ruins of the warrior Sato's house. I wept to see the broken gate at the foot of the hill. A temple stands in the neighbourhood with the graves of the Sato family in its grounds. I felt that I was in China at the tombstone of Yang Hu, which no person of cultivation has ever visited without weeping.

●

Through forests of sweetgum and hickory rising to larch, meadows of fern and thistle, we came toward the end of a day to an old mill of the kind I had known at Price's Shoals in South Carolina, wagons and mules under its elms, dogs asleep in the shade beneath the wagons, chickens and ducks maundering about. This New England country mill was, however, of brick, with tall windows, but with the same wide doors and ample loading platforms. It was a day in which we had lost time. I interrupted our singing along a logging road to say that my watch had stopped. So had hers, she said, or the map was cockeyed, or night comes earlier in this part of New Hampshire than anywhere else in the Republic. Clouds and a long rain had kept most of the day in twilight. A new rain was setting in for the night. But there was the mill, and we were saved from another night of wet such as we had endured the second night out. Tentless, we had slept in our bedrolls zipped together into one on a slope of deep ferns and waked to find ourselves as wet as if we had slept in a creek. The map showed shelter ahead, which we had expected to reach. But there had been the strange advancement of the day in defiance of my watch, which had stopped hours ago and started up again. What luck, to chance on this old mill.

●

In the temple I saw, after tea with the priests, the sword of Yoshitsune and the haversack of his loyal servant Benkei. It was the Feast Day of Boys and the Iris. *Show with pride*, I wrote of the arms in the temple, *the warrior's sword, his companion's pack on the first of May.* We went on and spent the night at Iisuka, having had a bath in a hot spring beforehand. Our inn was dirty, lampless, and the beds were pallets of straw on an earthen floor. There were fleas in the pallets, mosquitoes in the room. A fierce storm came up in the night. The roof leaked. All of this brought on an attack of fever and chills, and I was miserable and afraid of dying next day. I rode awhile and walked awhile, weak and in pain. We got as far as the gate into County Okido. I passed the castles at Abumizuri and Shiroishi. I'd wanted to see the tomb of Sanekata, one of the Fujiwara, a poet and exile, but the road there was all mud after the rains, and the tomb was overgrown with grass, I was told, and hard to find. We spent the night at Iwanuma. *How far to Kasajima and is this river of mud the road to take?*

•

Our packs off, the sleeping bags laid out and zipped together, supper in the pan, we could listen to the rain in that windy old mill, hugging our luck and each other. Packrats in little white pants, and spiders, and lizards, no doubt, I said, and we will make friends with them all. Her hair had lost the spring of its curls and stuck rakishly to her forehead and cheeks, the way I had first seen it as she climbed from a swimming pool in the Poconos. What are you talking about? she asked. She searched my eyes with a smiling and questioning look. I thought by such comic inquisitiveness that our luck was hard to believe. The mill there, Sweetheart, I repeated, pointing. A grand old New England water mill, dry as a chip and as substantial as Calvin's *Institutes*. She looked at the mill, at me again, and her mouth fell open. The stone steps to the door rose from a thicket of bramble we would have to climb across with care. There was something of the Florentine in all these old brick mills. Their Tuscan flavour came from architectural manuals issued by Scotch engineering firms that had listened to Ruskin and believed him when he said there was truth in Italian proportions and justice in Italian windows.

●

With what joy I found the Takekuma pine, double-trunked, just as the olden poets said. When Noin made his second visit to this tree, it had been cut down for bridge pilings by some upstart of a government official. It has been replanted over the years, it always grows back the same, always the most beautiful of pines. I was seeing it in its thousandth year. When I set out on my journey the poet Kyohaku had written: *Do not neglect to see the pine at Takekuma amid late spring cherry blossoms in the far north.* And for him, as an answer, I wrote: *We saw cherry blossoms together, you and I, three months ago. Now I have come to the double pine in all its grandeur.* On the fourth of May we arrived at Sendai across the Natori River, the day one throws iris leaves on the roof for good health. We put up at an inn. I sought out the painter Kaemon, who showed me the clover fields of Miyagino, the hills of Tamada, Yokono, and Tsutsuji-ga-oka, all white with rhododendron in bloom, the pine wood of Konoshita, where at noon it seems to be night, and where it is so damp you feel the need of an umbrella. He also showed me the shrines of Yakushido and Tenjin. A painter is the best of guides.

●

The Bay of Spezia, mulberry groves, sheds where the silkworms fatten, but here, the sun in golden sheets and slats on the floor, young Revely's study was all Archimedes and Sicily, or a tabletop by Holbein with instruments in brass and walnut, calipers, rules, maps, calculations in silverpoint and red ink. Under a map in French colours, slate blues and provincial yellows, poppy reds, cabbage greens, a sepia line from Genua across the Lunae Portus to Pisa, there sat in harmonic disarray a wooden bowl of quicksilver (a cup of Tuscan moonlight, a dish for gnomes to sup down in the iron roots of mountains where the earthquake demons swill lava and munch gold), cogged wheels, a screw propeller, drawings of frigates, steamboats, a machinery of gears and levers coloured blue and yellow, lighthouses with cyclopean lamps, plans of harbours and moorings, a lump of rosin, a china cup full of ink, a half-burnt match, a box of watercolours, a block of ivory, a volume of Laplace, a book of conic sections, spherics, logarithms, Saunderson's *Algebra*, Simms' *Trigonometry*, and most beautiful of all this Archimagian gear, tilted in its fine calibrations, gleaming index and glass, the newly unpacked theodolite.

•

Guy Davenport

When we parted, the painter Kaemon gave me drawings of
Matsushima and Shiogama and two pairs of sandals of straw with iris-
purple straps. *I walk in iris blossoms, it seems, so rich the blue of my
sandal laces.* He also gave me drawings to guide my way along the
Narrow Road to the Deep North. At Ichikawa I found the tall
inscribed stone of Tsubo-no-ishibumi. The characters were legible
through lichen and moss. Taga Castle was built on this site the first
year of Jinki by order of General Ono-no-Azumabito, Governor of the
Far North by decree of the Emperor, rebuilt in the sixth year of
Tempyohoji by Emi-no-Asakari, Governor General of the Provinces
East and North. This stone is 965 years old. Mountains break and fall,
rivers shift their beds, highways grow up in grass, rocks sink into the
earth, trees wither with age, and yet this stone has stood from ancient
times. I wept to see it, and knelt before its presence, very happy and
very sad. We went on across the Noda-no-tamagawa River to the pine
forest of Sue-no-matsuyama, where there is a temple and graveyard
that gave me melancholy thoughts of the death that must end all our
lives, whatever be our love of the world.

●

I could imagine the inside: spiderwebs and dog droppings, the inevitable Mason jar and flattened crump of overalls that one always found in abandoned buildings, a newspaper gone brown and some enigma of a utensil that turned out to be the handle of a meat grinder or meal sifter or mangle gearing. I anticipated rills of ancient flour in the seams of sills, the flat smell of mildewed wheat, the quick smell of wet brick. Mill? she said. Her smile was strangely goofy. She took me by the sleeve. What mill? Then I stood dumb and cold. There was no mill. Ahead of us was the edge of a wood, nothing more. The dusk thickened as we looked at each other in the rain. We went on, stubbornly. We knew better than to follow a blazed trail by dark. We hoped that the campsite with shelter marked on the map was just on the other side of the wood before us. It was not yet wholly dark. Were it not a rainy day, we might plausibly have an hour's half light yet: plenty of time to nip through the wood, get to the shelter, and be dry for the night. You say you saw an old mill? Underfoot there were rocks and roots again. We longed for the easy tread of the logging road.

●

We came to Shiogama just as the curfew bell was tolling, the darkening sky completely cloudless, the island of Magaki-ga-shima already but a shadow in a sea that was white with moonlight. We could hear the fishermen counting their take. How lonely it is to enter a town at dusk! We heard a blind singer chanting the rustic folksongs of the north. Next day, we worshipped at the Myojin Shrine of Shiogama, a handsome building. The way to it is paved, the fence around it is painted vermillion. It pleased me that the powers of the gods are so honoured here in the Deep North, and I made a sincere obeisance at the altar. An ancient lantern burns near the altar to keep alive the memory of Izumi-no-Saburo, that gallant warrior of five hundred years ago. In the afternoon we took a boat to Matsushima, two miles out. Everyone knows that these are the most beautiful islands in all Japan. I would add that they rival Tungting Hu in Hunan and Si Hu in Chekiang. These islands are our China. Every pine branch is perfect. They have the grace of women walking, and so perfectly are the islands placed that Heaven's serenity is apparent everywhere.

●

Ezra Pound came down the *salita* through the olive grove, white mane jouncing as he stepped his cane with precision stride by long stride. He wore a cream sports jacket, a blue shirt with open collar, pleated white slacks, brown socks and espadrilles. The speckled boney fingers of his left hand pinched a panama by the brim. The way was strewn with hard green olives torn from their branches by a storm the week before. *Shocking waste,* Miss Rudge said, *and yet it seems to happen year after year, and somehow there's always an olive crop, isn't there, Ezra?* Then, over her shoulder, she asked me if I knew the Spanish for *romance. Ezra wants to know, and can't remember. As in* mediaeval romance? I ask, startled. *Romanthé, I think.* Novela *would be a later word.* Relato, *perhaps. Ezra,* she called ahead, *would that be right? No!* he said, a quiver of doubt in his voice. Romancero, I said, *is a word Mr Pound himself has used of Spanish balladry.* Romancero, *Ezra?* Miss Rudge said cheerfully. Single file was the rule on the *salita.* He always went first, up or down, steep and rough as it was. *Not the word,* he said, without looking back.

●

Ojima, though called an island, is a narrow strip of land. Ungo, the shinto priest, lived here in his retirement. We were shown the rock where he liked to sit for hours. We saw small houses among the pines, blue smoke from their chimneys, the red moon rising beyond them. My room at the inn overlooked the bay and the islands. A great wind howled, and clouds scudded at a gallop across the moon; nevertheless, I kept my windows open, for I had that wonderful feeling that only travellers know: that this was a different world from any I had known before. Different winds, a different moon, an alien sea. Sora, too, felt the peculiarity of the place and the moment, and wrote: *Flute-tongued cuckoo, you must long for the heron's wings of silver to fly from island to island at Matsushima.* So fine was my emotion that I could not sleep. I got out my notebook and read again the poems my friends gave me when I set out, about these islands: a poem by Sodo in Chinese, a *waka* by Dr Hara Anteki, *haiku* by the samurai Dakushi and Sampu. Being at Matsushima made the poems much richer, and the poems made Matsushima a finer experience.

●

We juggled in debate whether we should doss down then and there in leafmuck and boulder rubble, or, heartened by the thin light we found in clearings, suppose that the failure of the day was more raindusk than the beginning of night, and push on. We found at least an arm of the lake on the map in a quarter of an hour. It was a spillway which we had to cross on a footlog. Rabbitfoot, I said, and don't look down. We got across more in dismay at the unfairness of a footlog to deal with in failing light and drizzle than with any skill with footlogs. What a miserable mean thing to do, she said, putting a blithering log to balance across with both of us winded and wet and you seeing hotels. The rain had settled in to stay. We had fair going for awhile and then we came upon swamp. There was no question of camping in water that came over our shoe tops. I broke out a flashlight, she held onto my pack so as not to get lost from me, and we nosed our way through ferns and huckleberries, sinking up to our shins in mud. I think I'm scared, she said. Of what? Nothing in particular. Of everything. I'm scared, I said, if for no other reason than that I don't know where we are.

•

We set out for Hiraizumi on the twelfth, our immediate plans being to visit the Aneha Pine and Odae Bridge. Our way was along a woodcutter's path in the mountains, as lonely and quiet a trail as I have ever trod. By some inattention to my instructions I lost my way and came instead to Ishinomaki, a port in a bay where we saw a hundred ships. The air was thick with smoke from chimneys. What a busy place! They seemed to know nothing of putting up travellers on foot, or of the art of looking at scenery. So we had to make do with shoddy quarters for the night. We left next day by a road that went I knew not whither. It took us past a ford on the Sode, the meadows of Obuchi, and the grasslands of Mano. We followed the river and came at last to Hiraizumi, having wandered a good twenty miles out of our way. We looked with melancholy on the ruins of the Fujiwara estate, now so many rice paddies. We found Yasuhira's abandoned house to the north of the Koromo-ga-seki gate. Though the grandeur of the Fujiwara lasted three generations only, their achievements will be remembered forever, and looking on the ruins of their castles and lands I wept that such glory has come to nothing, and covered my face with my hat.

●

In July I saw several cuckoos skimming over a large pond; and found, after some observation, that they were feeding on the *libellulae*, or dragon-flies, some of which they caught as they settled on the weeds, and some as they were on the wing. Notwithstanding what Linnaeus says, I cannot be induced to believe that they are birds of prey. A countryman told me that he had found a young fern-owl in the nest of a small bird on the ground; and that it was fed by the little bird. I went to see this extraordinary phenomenon, and found that it was a young cuckoo hatched in the nest of a titlark; it was become vastly too big for its nest. The dupe of a dam appeared at a distance, hovering about with meat in its mouth, and expressing the greatest solicitude. Ray remarks, that birds of the *gallinae* order, as cocks and hens, partridges and pheasants, are *pulveratrices*, such as dust themselves, using that method of cleansing their feathers, and ridding themselves of their vermin. As far as I can observe, many birds that wash themselves would never dust; but here I find myself mistaken; for common house-sparrows are great *pulveratrices*, being frequently seen grovelling and wallowing in dusty roads; and yet they are great washers. Does not the skylark dust?

●

Tall grass grows over the dreams of an ancient aristocracy. Look there! Did I not see Yoshitsune's servant Kanefusa in the white blur of the unohana flowers? But not all was gone. The temples remain, with their statues and tombs and sutras. *Dry in the rains of May, the Hikari Do keeps its gold and gloom for a thousand years.* We reached Cape Ogoru next day, and the little island of Mizu in the river. Onward, we came to the Dewa border, where the guards questioned us so long and so suspiciously (they rarely see foot travellers even in the best of weather) that we got a late start. Dusk caught us on the mountain road and we had to stay the night with a toll-keeper, and were lucky to find even his hut in so desolate a place. *Fleas and lice bit us, and all night a horse pissed beside my mat.* The toll-keeper said that many mountains lay between us and Dewa. I was most surely apt to get lost and perish. He knew a stout young man who would consent to be our guide, a strapping fellow with a sword and oak staff. He was indeed necessary: the way was an overgrown wilderness. Black clouds just above our heads darkened the thick underwood of bamboo.

•

Where we are, she said, is slogging our way by flashlight through a New England swamp up to our butts in goo and I'm so tired I could give up and howl. The important thing to understand, I said, is that we aren't on the trail. We were, I think, she said, when we got off into this. We couldn't be far off it. Off the trail, she said in something of a snit, is off the trail. And there's something wrong with my knees. They're shaking. We're probably walking into the lake that stupid log back there went over an outlet of. I turned and gave her as thorough an inspection as I could under the circumstances. She was dead tired, she was wet, and her knees did indeed shake. Lovely knees, but they were cold and splashed with mud. I slipped her pack off and fitted it across my chest, accoutred front and back like a paratrooper. We went on, the flashlight beam finding nothing ahead but bushes in water, a swamp of ferns. There was a rudimentary trail, it seemed. At least someone had put down logs in the more succulent places. It is the trail, I insisted. A yelp from behind, a disgusted and slowly articulated *Jiminy!* and while I was helping her up, sobs. Don't cry, Sweetheart! It rolled. The motherless log rolled when I stepped on it.

•

In Obanazawa I visited the merchant poet Seifu, who had often stopped on business trips to see me in Edo. He was full of sympathy for our hard way across the mountains, and made up for it with a splendid hospitality. Sora was entranced by the silkworm nurseries, and wrote: *Come out, toad, and let me see you: I hear your got-a-duck got-a-duck under the silkworm house.* And: *The silkworm workers are dressed like ancient gods.* We climbed to the quiet temple of Ryushakuji, famous for being in so remote and peaceful a site. The late afternoon sun was still on it, and on the great rocks around it, when we arrived, and shown golden in the oaks and pines that have stood there for hundreds of years. The very ground seemed to be eternity, a velvet of moss. I felt the holiness of the place in my bones; my spirit partook of it with each bow that I made to the shrines in the silent rocks. *Silence as whole as time. The only sound is crickets.* Our next plan was to go down the Mogami River by boat, and while we were waiting for one to take us, the local poets at Oishida sought me out and asked me to show them how to make linked verses, of which they had heard but did not know the technique. With great pleasure I made a whole book for them.

●

Could she stand? She thought so. It hurt, but she could stand. I shone the flashlight as far as I could ahead. Treetops! Treetops ahead, Samwise. Higher ground, don't you think that means? She limped frighteningly. We shloshed on. I could tell how miserable she was from her silence. We were slowly getting onto firmer ground. I studied her again by flashlight. She was a very tired girl with a sprained ankle or the nearest thing to it. I was getting my second wind, and put it to good use by heaving her onto my hip. She held to my neck, kissing my ear in gratitude. By coupling my hands under her behind, I could carry her to high ground if it was near enough. We reached forest, with roots to slip on and rocks to stumble over. The flashlight found a reasonably level place. I cleared trash from it while she held the light. We spread our tarpaulin, unrolled and zipped together the sleeping bags. It was our pride that we were hiking without a tent, though at that moment we longed for one. We undressed in the rain, stuffing our damp clothes into our packs. At least they wouldn't get any wetter. We slipped naked into the sleeping bag. Too tired to shiver, she said. She got dried peaches and apples from her pack, and we chewed them, lying on our elbows, looking out into the dark.

•

The Mogami River flows down from the mountains through Yamagata Province, with many treacherous rapids along the way, and enters the sea at Sakata. We went down the river in a farmer's old-timey rice boat, our hearts in our mouths. We saw Shiraito-no-take, the Silver-Stringed Waterfall, half-hidden by thick bamboo, and the temple of Sennindo. Because the river was high and rough, I wrote: *On all the rains of May in one river, I tossed along down the swift Mogami.* I was glad to get ashore. On the third of June we climbed Haguro Mountain and were granted an audience with Egaku the high priest, who treated us with civility and put us up in a cabin. Next day, in the Great Hall with the high priest, I wrote: *This valley is sacred. The sweet wind smells of snow.* On the fifth we saw the Gongen Shrine, of uncertain date. It may be the shrine Fujiwara-no-Tokihira in the *Rites and Ceremonies* says is on Mount Sato in Dewa, confusing the Chinese for *Sato* and *Kuro, Haguro* being a variant of *Kuro.* Here they teach Total Meditation as the Tendai sect understands it, and the Freedom of the Spirit and Enlightenment, teaching as pure as moonlight and as sweet as a single lantern in pitch dark.

●

He and Bruni, the watercolour painter, you know, they were the closest of friends, used to argue God something terrible. He was an atheist, Tatlin, and Bruni was a very Russian believer. It terrified me as a child. Tatlin would take us to swim in the river in the spring, and he wore no icon around his neck and didn't cross himself before diving in. He was wonderful with children, a grown-up who knew how to play with us without condescending, but with other people he was self-centered, vain about his singing voice. Pasternak, now, had no way with children at all. He didn't even see them. Tatlin made his own lute, a replica of a traditional Slavic lute such as blind singers had, strolling from village to village. Especially in the south. What did Tatlin look like? O, he was lanky, as you say, skinny. He had slate-grey eyes, very jolly eyes that had a way of going dead and silvery when he fell into a brown study. His hair was, how shall I put it, a grey blond. When he sang the blind singers' songs he made his eyes look blind, rolled back, unseeing. The voice was between baritone and bass. He was not educated, you know. He lived in the bell tower of a monastery.

•

On Haguro Mountain there are hundreds of small houses where priests meditate in strictest discipline, and will meditate, to keep this place holy, as long as there are people on the earth. On the eighth we climbed Mount Gassan. I had a paper rope around my shoulders, and a shawl of white cotton on my head. For eight miles we strove upward, through the clouds, which were like a fog around us, over rocks slick with ice, through snow. When we came to the top, in full sunlight, I was out of breath and frozen. How glorious the sight! We spent the night there, on beds of leaves. On the way down next day we came to the smithy where Gassan used to make his famous swords, tempering them in the cold mountain stream. His swords were made of his devotion to his craft and of the divine power latent in the mountain. Near here I saw a late-blooming cherry in the snow. I cannot speak of all I saw, but this cherry will stand for all, determined as it was, however late, however unseasonable, to bring its beauty into the world. Egaku, when I returned, asked me to make poems of my pilgrimage to this sacred mountain.

●

Bedded down in dark and rain, we felt both a wonderful security, warm and dry in our bed, and a sharp awareness that we didn't know where in the world we were. That swamp grew there since they printed the map, she said. I feel, I said, as if we were all alone in the middle of a wood as big as Vermont. We could be six feet from the lake, or on the merest island of trees in the world's biggest swamp. I don't care where we are, she said. We're here, we're dry, we're not in that swamp. We hugged awhile, and then lay on our backs to distribute the rock weight of our exhaustion, a hand on each other's tummy for sympathy and fellowship. You saw a mill? she said. A fine old water mill, of red brick, about a hundred years old, I suppose. As plain as day. I said that I was both glad and a bit frightened to have seen it, a superimposition of desire on reality. The first ghost I'd ever seen, if a mill can be a ghost. If it had been real, we would have had a hot supper, with coffee, and could have set up house, and got laid, twice running, after a wonderful long time of toning things up beforehand, with porcupines standing on their hind legs and looking through the windows. But she was asleep.

•

How cold the white sickle moon above the dark valleys of Mount Haguro. How many clouds had gathered and broken apart before we could see the silent moon above Mount Gassan. Because I could not speak of Mount Yudono, I wet my sleeves with tears. *Tears stood in my eyes*, Sora wrote, *as I walked over the coins at Yudono, along the sacred way.* Next day we came to Tsuru-ga-oka Castle, where the warrior Nagayama Shigeyuki welcomed me and Zushi Sakichi, who had accompanied us from Haguro. We wrote a book of linked verse together. We returned to our boat and went down the river Sakata. Here we were the guests of Dr Fugyoku. I wrote: *Cool of the evening in the winds crisscrossing the beach at Fukuura, and twilight: but the tip of Mount Atsumi was still bright with the sun. Deep into the estuary of Mogami River the summer sun has quenched its fire.* By now my fund of natural beauty was bountiful, yet I could not rest until I had seen Lake Kisagata. To get there I walked ten miles along a path, over rocky hills, down to sandy beaches and up again. The sun was touching the horizon when I arrived. Mount Chokai was hidden in fog.

●

We woke next morning to find that we were no more than twenty yards from the campsite we were trying to reach. Golly, she said, looking out of the sleeping bag. A black lake lay in a cedar wood whose greenish dark made its shores seem noonbright in early morning. We rose naked and put out clothes on bushes in the sun. She spied blueberries for our mush. I managed to get wood ash in our coffee, and we had to eat with the one spoon, as mine had got lost. The lake was too brackish to swim in, so we stood in the shallows and soaped each other, dancing from the chill of the water. I was rinsing her back with handfuls of water poured over her shoulders when I saw a popeyed man gaping at us from beyond our breakfast fire. His face was scholarly and bespectacled and he wore a Boy Scout uniform. The staff in his hand gave him a Biblical air. He was warning away his troop with a backward hand. Hi! she hailed him. We're just getting off some grime from the trail. We got lost in the rain last night and came here through the swamp. We'll give you time, he said with a grin. Oh for Pete's sake, said she, proceeding to soap up my back. We're just people. They've seen people, haven't they?

●

If the halflight and the rain were so beautiful at Kisagata, how lovely the lake would be in good weather. Next day was indeed brilliant, I sailed across the lake, stopping at the mere rock of an island where the monk Noin once meditated. On the far shore we found the ancient cherry tree of Saigyo's poem, in which he compares its blossoms to the froth on waves. From the large hall of the temple Kanmanjuji you can see the whole lake, and beyond it Mount Chokai like a pillar supporting Heaven, and the gate of Muyamuya faintly in the west, the highway to Akita in the east, and Shiogoshi in the north, where the lake meets the breakers of the ocean. Only two lakes are so beautiful: Matsushima is the other. But whereas Matsushima is gay and joyful, Kisagata is grave and religious, as if some sorrow underlay its charm. *Silk tree blossoming in the monotonous rain at Kisagata, you are like the Lady Seishi in her sorrow. On the wet beach at Shiogoshi the herons strut in the sea's edge. Some sweetmeat not known elsewhere is probably sold at Kisagata on the feast days.* Teiji has a poem about Kisagata: *In the evening the fishermen sit and rest in their doorways.* Sora wrote of the ospreys: *Does God tell them how to build their nests higher than the tide?*

●

I loved her for her brashness. Her seventeen-year-old body, in all the larger and speculative senses aesthetic and biological, was something to see. It was Spartan, it was Corinthian: hale of limb, firmnesses continuing into softnesses, softnesses into firmnesses. There was a little boy's stance in the clean porpoise curve of calf, a tummy flat and grooved. Corinth asserted itself in hips and breasts, in the denim blue of her eyes, the ruck of her upper lip, in the pert girlishness of her nose. We aren't proud, she said. I can't recommend the pond here, as it's full of leaf trash from several geological epochs back. The blueberries over there on that spit are delicious. By this time there were Boy Scout eyes over the scoutmaster's shoulders. We went back to our stretch of the beach, dried in the sun while making more coffee, and fished shirts from our packs in deference to our neighbours. It was further along the trail that day that we found in a lean-to a pair of Jockey shorts, size small, stuck full of porcupine quills. One of our Boy Scouts', she said. Do you suppose he was in or out of them when Brother Porky took a rolling dive?

●

Leaving Sakata, we set out on the hundred-and-thirty-mile road to the county seat of Kaga Province. Clouds gathered over the mountains on the Hokuriku Road, down which we had to go, and clouds gathered in my heart at the thought of the distance. We walked through the Nezu Gate into Echigo, we walked through the Ichiburi Gate into Ecchu. We were nine days on the road. The weather was wet and hot all the way, and my malaria acted up and made the going harder. *The sixth of July, the nights are changing, and tomorrow the Weaver Star and the Shepherd Star cross the Milky Way together.* At Ichiburi I was kept awake by two Geisha in the next room. They had been visiting the Ise Shrine with an old man, who was going home the next day, and they were plying him with silly things to say to all their friends. How frivolous and empty their lives! And next day they tried to attach themselves to us, pleading that they were pilgrims. I was stern with them, for they were making a mock of religion, but as soon as I had shooed them away my heart welled with pity. Beyond the forty-eight shoals of the Kurobe, we came to the village of Nago and asked to see the famous wistaria of Tako.

●

Hephaistiskos, our Renault bought in Paris, who had slept in a stable in Villefranche, kicked a spring outside Tarbes, and spent the night under the great chestnut tree in the square at Montignac, under palms at Menton and under pines at Ravenna, was hoisted onto the foredeck of the *Kriti* at Venice for a voyage down the Adriatic to Athens. We had no such firm arrangements for a berth. Along with two Parisian typists of witty comeliness, two German cyclists blond, brown, and obsequious, a trio of English consisting of a psychiatrist and her two lovers, the one an Oxford undergraduate, the other the Liberal Member from Bath, and a seasoned traveller from Alton, Illinois, a Mrs Brown, we were billeted on the aft deck, in the open air, with cots to sleep on. All the cabins were taken by Aztecs. *Mexican Rotary and their wives*, explained the lady psychiatrist, who had Greek and who had interviewed the Captain, leaving a flea in his ear. The sporting bartender had shouted to us over the Greek band, in a kind of English, that it was ever the way of the pirate who owned this ship to sell all the tickets he could, let the passengers survive by their wits. *It's only a week. No say drachma, say thrakmé.*

●

The wistaria of Tako, I was told, was five lonely miles up the coast, with no house of any sort nearby or along the way. Discouraged, I went on into Kaga Province. *Mist over the rice fields, below me the mutinous waves.* I crossed the Unohanayama Mountains, the Kurikara-dani Valley, and came on the fifteenth of July to Kanazawa. Here the merchant Kasho from Osaka asked me to stay with him at his inn. There used to live in Kanazawa a poet named Issho, whose verse was known over all Japan. He had died the year before. I went to his grave with his brother, and wrote there: *Give some sign, O silent tomb of my friend, if you can hear my lament and the gusts of autumn wind joining my grief.* At a hermit's house: *This autumn day is cold, let us slice cucumbers and mad-apples and call them dinner.* On the road: *The sun is red and heedless of time, but the wind knows how cold it is, O red is the sun!* At Komtasu, Dwarf Pine: *The right name for this place, Dwarf Pine, wind combs the clover and makes waves in the grass.* At the shrine at Tada I saw the samurai Sanemori's helmet and the embroidered shirt he wore under his armour.

•

The Liberal Member from Bath, the Oxford undergraduate name of Gerald, and the lady British psychiatrist demonstrated the Greek folkdances played by the band. *A Crimean Field Hospital*, I said of our cots and thin blankets set up as our dormitory on the fantail of the *Kriti. Exactly!* said the Liberal Member from Bath, accepting us thereby. *Rather jolly, don't you think?* The Parisian typists chittered and giggled. *Pas de la retraite! Que nous soyons en famille.* Mrs Brown of Alton tucked a blanket under her chin and undressed with her back to the Adriatic. The Parisian typists came to her aid, and they became a trio, with their cots together, like the English. They stripped to lace bras and panties, causing the Liberal Member from Bath to say, *O well, there's nothing else for it, is there?* The German boys undressed pedantically to pissburnt briefs of ultracontemporary conciseness. We followed suit, nothing daunted, and the Liberal Member from Bath did everybody one better, and took off every stitch, a magnified infant, chubby of knee, paunchy, with random swirls and tufts of ginger hair. The Parisian typists squealed. The Germans looked at him with keen slit eyes. He was surely overstepping a bound.

•

Sanemori's helmet was decorated with swirls of chrysanthemums across the visor and earflaps; a vermilion dragon formed the crest, between two great horns. When Sanemori died and the helmet was enshrined, Kiso Yoshinaka wrote a poem and sent it by Higuchi-no-Jiro: *With what wonder do I hear a cricket chirping inside an empty helmet.* The snowy summit of Shirane Mountain was visible all the way to the Nata Shrine, which the Emperor Kazan built to the Goddess of Mercy Kannon. The garden here was of rocks and pines. *The rocks are white at the Rock Temple, but the autumn wind is whiter.* At the hot spring nearby, where I bathed: *Washed in the steaming waters at Yamanaka, do I need also to pick chrysanthemums?* I was told by the innkeeper that it was here that Teishitsu realized his humiliating deficiencies as a poet, and began to study under Teitoku when he returned to Kyoto. Alas, while we were here, my companion Sora began to have a pain in his stomach, and left to go to his kinpeople in Nagashima. He wrote a farewell poem: *No matter if I fall on the road, I will fall among flowers.*

●

The Liberal Member from Bath had indeed overstepped a bound in taking off all his clothes on the fantail of the *Kriti*. Just as the lady psychiatrist was urging her other lover, the Oxford undergraduate, to join him in cheeking these outrageous foreigners for booking us passages and then deploying us out here under the sky in what the American archaeologists so aptly dub the Crimean Field Hospital, the Captain of the ship, together with the Steward, made their way through a tumult of pointing Mexican Rotarians and arrived in our midst whirling their arms. The Liberal Member stared at them pop-eyed. *What's the Pirate King saying? Who can understand the blighter?* He says you must put on your clothes, I offered. He says you are an affront to morals and an insult to decency. *He does, does he?* said the lady psychiatrist. *Gerald dear! Off with your undershorts.* She then, with help from Gerald dear and the Liberal Member, set out on a speech in Greek which we realized with an exchange of glances was a patchwork of Homeric phrases, more or less syntactical on the psychiatrist's part, but formulaic from her chorus, so that her *what an overweening hatefulness has crossed the barrier of thy teeth* was seconded by Gerald dear's *when that rosyfingered dawn had shed her beams over mortals and immortals together.*

●

When Sora left me, because of his illness, I felt both his sadness and mine, and wrote: *Let the dew fade the words on my hat, Two Pilgrims Travelling Together*. When I stayed at the Zenshoji Temple, they gave me a poem of Sora's that he had left there for me: *All night I heard the autumn wind in the hills above the shrine*. I too listened to the wind that night, grieving for my companion. Next morning I attended services, ate with the priests, and was leaving when a young monk ran after me with ink block, brush, and paper, begging for a poem. I wrote: *For your kindness I should have swept the willow leaves from the garden*. Such was my sweet confusion at being asked for a poem that I left with my sandals untied. I rented a boat at Yoshizaki and rowed out to see the pine of Shiogoshi. The beauty of its setting is best caught in Saigyo's poem: *urging the wind against the salt sea, the Shiogoshi pine sheds moonlight from its branches*. At Kanazawa I had been joined by the poet Hokushi, who walked with me as far as the Tenryuji Temple in Matsuoka, far further than he had meant to go.

●

We notice the ugliness of the Hellenistic and Roman style of Greek lettering as compared to the Archaic. Small columns of marble lying about that look as if they might have been grave markers. The Tower of the Winds with its curious figures that look Baroque: a few columns left standing, forming a corner of the street. This sort of ruin is actually what is most prevalent, especially at the theatres and at Eleusis, dismantled Roman ruins built on top of the Greek. An excavation trench near the church with a large urn only half dug out, under an olive tree. More piles of marble, looking very unorderly and as if the archaeologist had never been there: no attempt to order, classify, straighten. Little indication of street levels, except around the standing columns, these being straight shafts of marble, rather than sections fitted together. The Greek snails. We photographed a snailshell in your hand held beside a piece of marble ornament. What a motif. The pattern on the snails much more closely resembling the Geometric and Cycladic jars. The snails are caught by the sun as they climb a column and cooked there in their shells, which cling to the stone. Their spiral design is a chestnut brown band separated from a charcoal band by a thin white line.

●

It was only three miles to Fukui. The way, however, was dark, as I had started thither after supper. The poet Tosai lived there, whom I had known in Edo ten years before. As soon as I arrived I asked for him. A citizen directed me, and as soon as I found a house charmingly neglected, fenced around by a profusion of gourd vines, moonflowers, wild cockscomb kneedeep, and goosefoot blocking the way to the front door, I knew this was Tosai's home and no other's. I knocked. A woman answered, saying that Tokai was down town somewhere. I was delighted that he had taken a wife, and told him so with glee when I routed him out of a wine-shop later. I stayed with him for three days. When I departed, saying that I wanted to see the full moon over Tsuruga, he decided to come with me, tucking up his house kimono as his only concession to the road. The peak of Shirane gave way to that of Hina. At Asamuzu Bridge we saw the reeds of Tamae in bloom. With the first migrating geese in the sky above me, I entered Tsuruga on the fourteenth. The moon was to be full the next night. We went to the Myojin Shrine of Kei, which honours the soul of the Emperor Chuai, bringing, as is the custom, a handful of white sand for the courtyard.

●

Most of them are plants that are abundantly represented in nearly all the more recent deposits, such as *Taxodium Europaeum*, found all the way from the Middle Bagshot of Bournemouth to the Pliocene of Meximieux, *Ficus liliaefolia, Laurus primigenia*, and *Cinnamomum lanceolatum*, abundant in nearly all the Oligocene and Miocene beds of Europe. *Quercus chlorophylla* occurs in the Mississippi Tertiary as well as at Skopau in Sachs-Thüringen, and is also abundant in the Miocene, and *Ficus tiliaefolia* is found in the Green River formation at Florrisant, Colorado. The two species of hazel, and also the sensitive fern from the Fort Union deposits regarded by Dr Newberry as identical with the living forms, must be specifically so referred until fruits or other parts are found to show the contrary. Forms of the Gingko tree occur not only in the Fort Union beds, but in the lower Laramie beds at Point of Rocks, Wyoming Territory, which differ inappreciably except in size of leaf from the living species. A few Laramie forms occur in Cretaceous strata.

●

This was a custom begun by the priest Yugyo, so that at the full of the moon the area before the shrine would be as white as frost. *The pure full moon shown on Yugyo the Bishop's sand.* But on the night of the fifteenth it rained. *But for the fickle weather of the north I would have seen the full moon in autumn.* The sixteenth, however, was fine, and I went shell-gathering on the beach. A man named Tenya came with me and his servants with a picnic. We savoured the loneliness of the long beaches. *Autumn comes to the sea, and the beach is more desolate than that at Suma. Clover petals blown into the sea roll up with fine pink shells in the waves.* I asked Tosai to write an account of our day's excursion and to deposit it at the temple for other pilgrims. My friend Rotsu met me when I returned, and went with me to Mino Province. We rode into Ogaki on horseback, and we were met by Sora. At Joko's house we were welcomed by Zensen, Keiko, and many other friends who acted as if I had returned from the dead. On the sixth of September I left for the shrine at Ise, though I was still tired from my journey to the far north. *Tight clam shells fall open in the autumn, just as I, no sooner made comfortable than I feel the call of the road.* Friends, goodbye!

●

GRANTA

BRIGID BROPHY
THE ECONOMICS OF
SELF-CENSORSHIP

Which would you rather be: good or published? That is the dilemma that 'the crisis in publishing' has begun to press on British writers. Those ardent afternoons of adolescence, when aspirant writers wondered if they would ever produce anything good enough to be published, have turned into the small-hours disquiet of professional writers wondering if they can bring themselves to write anything bad enough.

The dilemma is not, of course, put explicitly. In talking to writers, publishers have long used a coded language, in which, for instance, 'We'll leave you free on that one' means 'I don't like the sound of your next book, so my option will now apply to the one after.' Recently I have sensed an extension of the code. 'Several of us here in the office were not wholly convinced by the characterization in Chapter Twelve' now means 'We think it a marvellous book, but a realistic first printing would be 750 and we'd rather put our money into a better bet.'

Often enough, code is not needed. The message has been conveyed by the fame of the crisis. Suppose you are a novelist whose most recent book failed to cover its advance. Your publisher doesn't brandish its failure at you, though neither does he go out of his way to explain to you, should you be ignorant of the economics of publishing, that failing to cover your advance is not necessarily the same as morally owing him money. In any case you know that he will mention the failure, regretfully, when you show him your next book and he offers you a lower advance than the one before. Suppose now your imagination is seized and fired by a new novel unlike any of your earlier ones: surrealist, say, or linguistically innovative or 'sensitive' in a mode that has been out of use these twenty years. The thing becomes a matter of tact between you and your publisher. You don't want to be rebuffed or to put him in a position where he has to rebuff you. Anyway, there's the electricity bill to pay and the children's duffel coats to buy. You decide to take up the banal and middle-brow idea for a novel that has been lying around in your mind for years and failing to excite you into writing it. Thus without a word spoken does crisis make cowards of us all and a dreariness of 'contemporary English writing'.

The traditional response of a publisher to a financial or economic problem is to urge a writer to accept a lower royalty. The grandmother's footsteps of the approaching crisis became audible five or six years ago when writers began receiving such symptomatic requests as that they shouldn't insist on mounting the next royalty step when a reprint would entitle them to do so. They acquiesced, of course, because the alternative was no reprint.

The publisher's absolute freedom not to reprint or not to publish at all is the threat that keeps writers subservient. It is probably true, though it has been queried by disillusioned writers, that publishers want to make money. But no law of economics or psychology compels them to extract all the profit that could be extracted from any particular book. The writer's livelihood depends on the successful exploitation of his particular books. The publisher, however, always has plenty to choose from, and he may well choose to put all his cash and effort, both of which are scarce commodities, into exploiting the three biggest profit-makers on his list, letting such profits as he might have made from the other ninety-seven go ha..g. No writer can ever be sure of being one of the three rather than the ninety-seven, with the result that all writers are on the junior side in a relationship whose essence is expressed by the option clause, which appears in almost all publishing contracts that are not governed by a Minimum Terms Agreement between the Writers' Guild and the publishing house, and which binds the writer but not the publisher. Publishers habitually maintain that the option clause is never enforced; but I am one writer, and I know a couple of others, who have had to pay cash for their freedom from it.

Copyright law propounds the misleading fantasy that it is the writer who is the capitalist, the owner of a piece of 'intellectual property', who licenses the publisher to exploit his property, on which he then draws 'royalties' for all the world as though it were an oil well. Common parlance knows that the truth is the other way about. It is the publisher who 'accepts' or 'rejects' the manuscript. If he accepts, the writer has to bargain for the terms from his junior position. Even the rich and best-selling writer has only limited bargaining power, because there is only a small number of firms able to pay the advance his bestsellerdom should command and at the same time competent to publish his particular type of book with tolerable efficiency. Less-than-best-selling writers, having invested a year's or more work in the book together with a year's or more living expenses, are in such urgent need of money down that they accept the first offer, being unable to afford to waste more time, and risk everything, by going in search of a better offer that may never turn up.

Even the copyright itself is not invulnerable. The 1956 Act, which is still in operation, makes the artist (unless he happens to be an employee in certain circumstances) the first owner of the copyright in his own work. The Act does not proceed, however, on the lines of West German law, which provides for the artist to bequeath his copyright but makes it inalienable from him during his lifetime, or even of French law, which makes the 'moral' aspect of the copyright inalienable, giving the artist power to prevent his work from appearing in distorted forms that would be dishonourable to him. In Britain the artist is left 'free' to sell his copyright for a mess of pottage in which the inducement of an urgently needed lump sum down is often combined with a publisher's refusal to publish or to commission the work at all unless the writer surrenders his copyright and, with it, his control over the use it is put to as well as his entitlement to any further sums it may earn. The weakness of British copyright law and the poverty of British writers are matters of international notoriety. In 1978 more than one United States firm was scouring the literary agencies of Britain seeking to buy up the copyrights of British writers to serve as plausible tax losses for New York business men. (Rumour had it, perhaps with merely poetic justice, that they were mostly dentists.)

So long as they were deceived into thinking themselves capitalists, British writers were liable to the disgruntled and individualistic bloody-mindedness that often overtakes a class of small-scale property owners when it finds that its supposed birthright is bringing in neither the income nor the prestige it expected—a mentality that made writers ripe for picking off by publishers one by one. In 1972, however, some writers organized themselves into a militant pressure group (WAG) in order to secure public lending right and secure it, moreover, in the form writers needed. (They achieved this with the passage of the Labour government's Public Lending Right Act in 1979, under which, if the present government sticks to schedule for the administrative preliminaries, payments will begin to trickle to the writers in 1982–83.) Not only was it vital that Public

Lending Right be financed from central public funds, because any alternative would have cost writers on the swings what they gained on the roundabouts, but it had to be made to benefit all writers whose books were lent from the libraries, not just the authors of new publications. Psychologically, it was the second stipulation that counted, because it was dictated by a determination to protect old writers who might not produce new works but whose earlier ones were still being borrowed by the public. It was a glimmer of *organized* solidarity in a profession that had previously run only, though profusely, to the generosity of la vie de bohème.

The next step was analytic. Writers discovered that they were not capitalists at all but workers—indeed, low-paid manual labour. What the English language romantically calls a freelance (I wonder whether the metaphor is chivalric or mercenary) is in economic reality an employee. However, because the freelance is technically classified as self-employed, his de facto employer, the publisher, escapes all the obligations that twentieth-century legislation has placed on employers for the protection of their employees, down to the employer's obligation to contribute to the employee's N.I. stamp. A writer can publish a book a year with the same firm for forty years and find his forty-first rejected without explanation let alone severance pay.

Perception of their real economic status led writers of books into the trade union movement. In 1975, at the initiative of WAG, writers of books, poems, and plays for the theatre were made eligible to join the Writers' Guild, a T.U.C. affiliated (but non-party-political) union of, until then, script-writers for television and films. Within a couple of years the Writers' Guild signed (with Hamish Hamilton) the first agreement in Britain between a union and a publisher to lay down minimum terms for book publication. Agreements followed with some other publishers, but on the whole the response of publishers to the unionization of writers is still a vehement hostility to an act they can't help showing they consider cheek. In consequence, now that the sudden intensification of the crisis has knocked publishers sideways, most have no alliance with the only social group that has a vital interest (that cannot be diversified elsewhere) in keeping publishers going, and have not even secured their supply lines to the source of their primary material. They have not consulted the writers about framing a strategy for the continuation of the British book trade, let alone of English Literature, and, having already lopped every advance and royalty rate they could get at, are now lopping mildly at their administrative staffs and wildly at their lists.

In Britain, writers, publishers, and booksellers are all victims of a unique national treasure, the public library service. Since the end of World War II, the network has grown to the point where it makes more loans—not merely proportionately to population but absolutely—than the libraries of any other western country, including the United States. Every book sold in Britain to an individual customer is sold against the competition of the fact that you can borrow the identical article for nothing from a library that can, into the bargain, offer you a wider choice than a bookshop and that is, in most parts of Britain, easier of access, as well as being less deterrent to the socially unassured.

The consequences for professional writers are summed up in a comparison with West Germany, which makes only a quarter to a third of the number of library loans made in Britain but has twice as many bookshops and publishes *more* new titles. It is writers of fiction who suffer most. The selling price of hardback fiction (and in consequence the writer's royalty on it) is kept down to about two-thirds of the average hardback price, in order to induce the public libraries to buy fiction; and at the same time fiction, far from being the outmoded and unwanted stuff that some ignorant critics suppose, is the most popular category with public library borrowers and accounts for seventy per cent of all loans to adults.

In these unique circumstances, British books have relied heavily, perhaps lop-sidedly, on the English-language export market—a legacy of empire that may not last much longer—and at home have wobbled along on narrow margins, shaken by every rumour of cuts in public library buying. Chronically under-capitalized, publishing has lived largely on hopes of best-seller jackpots, which it is not always equipped to exploit to the full when it hits them. Since no publisher's formula for costing a book has ever dreamed of incorporating a living wage for the writer or a return related to his work as distinct from his sales—which ought to be the publisher's work—British publishing has in reality operated on a series of subsidies, all of them dependent on lucky turns of chance. Much recent writing (my own included) has been invisibly subsidized by *husbands*. Specialist and scholarly non-fiction has been subsidized—and several publishers of it have led comfortable lives at upper-middle-class standard—through the employment of amateur writers, who, receiving regular salaries from universities or museums, feel no need to demand the going rate for the literary job or even to find out what that is.

Subsidized in these ways, the turnover of titles, necessary to keep a business in business and to increase the publisher's gambling chance of a jackpot, has—*just*—been kept turning. And this business has, in a sense, subsidized Literature. If life is a parasite on matter, Literature is a parasite on the book business. Deliberate buyers of works of literary art do not number enough to float a single title and would, moreover, never agree on a single title that *was* a work of art. The art of Literature will survive and continue to be made available to readers only if the host body, the ninety per cent of books that are manufactured readable articles, many of them perfectly honourably and entertainingly manufactured, continues to be large and healthy enough to carry the ten per cent of works that aspire to be Literature, of which perhaps three per cent truly *are*, although no one's taste being proveably infallible, no one can indisputably specify *which* three per cent.

Even so, this carrying trade has often failed, with the result that a good (to my judgment) writer has more than once had to be rescued by fluke. When I first read the name Vladimir Nabokov it was in a remainder tray. It was on a copy of his first novel in English, *The Real Life of Sebastian Knight*, in the Poetry London edition of 1945. From the author's point of view, that must have been a barely commercial proposition in the first place; and the fact that the book was being sold off within three or four years of publication, at a time when remaindering was not the independent industry it is now becoming, would normally have presaged the appearance of no more Nabokov novels in Britain. What intervened, in 1955, was *Lolita*—which did not, however, appear in Britain until 1959. The interval was occupied by praise (for the Paris edition) from Graham Greene, plus the hope of scandal and the threat of prosecution (both unrealized), a combination that turned Nabokov from a predestined refusé or remainder into a predestined best-seller.

Since then the law and the public have become more blasé about sexual subject matter, at least in books (arguably indicative less of tolerance than of disregard of books). We can't depend on a fluke of that sort to save a good writer again, and libertarians can't even wish we could. Egalitarians must feel the same about the yet more extreme fluke that belatedly made a wide public acquainted with Ronald Firbank, to my taste (which I have expressed elsewhere to the extent of 592 pages) one of the supreme masters of fiction. Between the middle of World War I and the middle of the twenties—a period sometimes presented now as a golden age of 'the Modern'—Firbank was unable to find what is normally meant by a publisher. He was the author of six mature, 'Modern' and (in all but length) major novels before he found—in the United States—a publisher who in 1924 issued his seventh (*Prancing Nigger*) as a commercial venture. Its commercial success was so small that, for his eighth and last (*Concerning the Eccentricities of Cardinal Pirelli*), Firbank had to revert to his previous practice of paying for 'publication' himself, besides leaving money in his will for the posthumous reissue of his whole mature *oeuvre*.

Complacency—whose motto is 'All's well that ends well' and whose logic argues that there can't have been anything amiss with that bridge since it didn't collapse until after we'd crossed—considers the Firbank case no cause for agitation. After all, the novels did get into print and into bindings (black ones during his perhaps mourning lifetime, and the 'rainbow' ones of the posthumous edition), with the satisfactory result that they were *there*, accessible not merely to after-the-event eulogists like me but to Duckworth, who in 1961 published them in the 'complete' omnibus volume, and to Penguin who in the same year canonized three of them in one paperback as 'modern classics'.

You might answer that readers ought not to be kept waiting so long, which invites the reply that until 1961 there was not a sufficiency of readers who wanted Firbank, which provokes the question how, given that he was unpublicized and not commercially available, readers could tell whether they wanted him or not. Better, you might point out that writers *can't* be kept waiting so long. By 1961 Firbank would have been 75. But such altercations only hide the fact where the crucial warning resides. Firbank's ability to support himself while he wrote the books, an intensive and full-time job, together with his ability to have them 'published' at his own expense and thus left lying about for posterity to take up at its own (or a commercial publisher's) good time, hung by the slenderest thread of the most random chance. It happened that Firbank's grandfather had qualities that transformed him from a miner into a railway magnate; his father lacked qualities that might have led him to spend the old man's fortune to the last drop; and so a small private income filtered down to the third generation.

Thus through pure accident was English Literature of the twentieth century subsidized by the railway boom of the 1840s to 1880s. Grandfather Joseph Firbank built, among many others, the Brighton Line—of blessed Wildean cadence. Perhaps one should make a point of reading Firbank on the Southern Region (arguably the most dilapidated section of the railway system that ASLEF describes as 'falling apart'), in order to reflect that, despite the internal contradictions of a socialism that never nationalizes anything until the capitalists have pounded all the profit out of it and it is tottering towards disintegration, some good from the railways has reached the community.

Instead of taking warning from the narrowness of the squeak and resolving that never again should English Literature have to depend on the improbable chance of literary genius and a private income falling to the lot of the same baby, Britain has still further reduced Literature's chances of survival by suffering the literary apparatus to begin to disintegrate on the same pattern as the railways. Every writer now knows that the better he writes, even if he is not capable of writing very well, the less likely is a publisher to see him as a potential jackpot hitter. A respectable chance of a respectable sale is no longer enough for good writers or indifferent writers to get by on. As the crisis gets worse, publishers pitch their jackpot fantasies higher and higher, and some are already hysterically deciding that they must aim at a towering inferno of a best-seller or nothing. This panic puts in doubt not only the continued existence of professional writing in Britain but that of professional publishing. If they are not careful, British publishers will panic themselves into becoming the mere offshore licensees of United States best-sellers, in which case the British will probably be under-sold and put out of business by dumped remainders of the United States editions.

Should the whole apparatus disintegrate, the very people who hissed the unionization of writers and warned off booksellers who stocked the work of successful authors when they published it under their own imprint (publishers didn't bother to fear competition from the unsuccessful), together with the people who gibbered at that remotest (in book-disrespectful Britain) of bogeys, political control of publishing, will shriek for the industry to be in some way nationalized, taken over either by the state or by co-operatives of writers. The writers, however, have no capital, communal or, for the most part, individual, having suffered years of impoverishment, some of it deliberately if not quite consciously inflicted by publishers as the best way of keeping them in their lowly place and of getting the next book out of them. As for the state, it might well balk at taking over yet another industry from which someone else has already extracted the profit; and, if the Great Depression II continues as it has begun, the state will have no capital anyway.

The internal crisis of books need not end thus. (For the external crisis no one can make any sort of prognosis.) There could still be a rapprochement, leading to realistic analysis and planning, between writers and publishers and the neglected (by both) third party, booksellers. The diminution of public library buying, already severe and likely to get worse, destroys the accepted, small-scale economics of British publishing, but it might yet be seen by a united industry as the opportunity to enlarge the scale of the thing and sell more books to individuals.

Neither need publishers fear a take over of their offices by rabid writers. They have a simple and efficient protection. A union of writers—or, indeed, any group of writers organized beyond the purposes of a dining club—has to practise impartiality between one member and another, eschewing even 'value judgments' on members' work in its discussions. It could never, and could never want to, take over the publisher's yea-and-nay function, which is in effect the employer's hire-and-fire function. Trade unions can work only in their own niche. They can't recruit among the unemployed, even though the unemployed may be in even greater need of their services than the employed. The Writers' Guild maintains the professional nature of its membership by making commercial publication its criterion of eligibility, thus adopting a standard it may not endorse and, probably, excluding good writers; but at least the standard is external and to that extent impartial, though it would not pass muster in an ideal world. Writers need publishers to be independent. But they could contibute to the policies, as they do to the profits, that keep them independent.

However, nothing will be done towards salvation so long as complacency presides over the near ruin of our literary apparatus. 'I doubt,' said one of the replies to Bill Buford in *The Bookseller* of 25 October 1980, 'whether there are too many embryo Conrads . . . unpublished.' Okay, it's 'coolly' expressed. But philistinism shows through the litotes. A single Conrad unpublished is too many—even if he's young, which I take to be the force of the 'embryo'. Was Rimbaud at 19, by which age he had completed his *oeuvre*, an embryo Rimbaud? What the reply calls, in a considerable understatement, 'difficult economic conditions' will, it goes on to concede, 'make publishers look even harder at what they publish and this,' it concludes in a last smug litotes, 'may be no bad thing for us all.' In reality, it is an appalling thing for us all. No publisher is looking 'harder' with a literary eye, which a few publishers actually possess though one might disagree with their taste as with anyone else's. Lists are being sifted by the sole criterion of estimated saleability—and saleability, moreover, solely through the existing and now thoroughly rickety mechanisms for distribution and publicity. If it looks unlikely to reach an ever-rising ground floor of sales, out it goes. Masterpiece, pretentious rubbish, worthy dullness: all get the chop alike. Any publisher who believed he had enough pocket money left for a personal gesture would spend it not on a masterpiece but on the book whose schema he wrote on an envelope and commissioned a professional to expand to his design. Few publishers are as ardent about creative writing as they are about 'creative publishing'. (This is not a dismissive litotes. There *are*, to be fair, a few, just as there are a few writers who care about other writers' books as well as their own.)

Worse yet was the central idea in the *Bookseller* reply: 'The historical evidence is that genius is heard.' No. The historical evidence is that major and minor (in the form, often, of changes in fashion) dark ages do descend and sweep away works of genius. John Nash's genius for town planning has not been fully 'heard' or audible since his Regent Street was pulled down in the twenties. The 'historical evidence' includes not a shred of evidence that the fourteen operas of

Monteverdi lost to us were works of smaller genius than the few we (in sometimes dubious form) have. The seven tragedies of Sophocles that survive constitute about one seventeenth of his *oeuvre* of 120 or so plays. The continued existence of English Literature has been, at least in patches, dicey for several decades. Now that it is wholly and visibly imperilled, how *dare* its guardians be complacent?

GRANTA

JOHN SUTHERLAND
THE END OF A
GENTLEMAN'S
PROFESSION

John Sutherland

I t is convenient to think of fiction threading through four frames on its way to existence. Least obtrusive is the legal frame established by copyright, libel, and obscenity laws. Second is the commercial frame: the considerations of production, patronage, and market-consumption. Less easy to define is the 'ideological' frame. In totalitarian regimes, fiction is frankly an instance of the state's propaganda; in liberal democracies, publishing houses may also, despite their supposed autonomy, connive 'gutlessly' with state aims (this was Orwell's conclusion after the near universal boycott of *Animal Farm*). Finally, there is a fourth frame which I can best call 'aesthetic competence'. Novelists, that is, cannot work far in advance of the narrative equipment bequeathed them by their predecessors or on loan from their most ambitious contemporaries. Put absurdly, Fielding—however innovative—could not have devised a stream of consciousness technique. Or in the familiar jargon of literary criticism, the individual talent has only a very restricted scope within the tradition.

Within the incongruities of these frames, the novelist strives to maximize the area of his freedom. In this note, I want to look at the space currently afforded by the commercial apparatus which delivers fiction to the Anglo-American market-place and its customers. I am making, of course, two large initial assumptions: first that fiction must necessarily be delivered by the machinery of commerce; second that one can—for various purposes of discussion—lump Britain and America together. Briefly, to justify these assumptions: the novel is, by virtue of its length, the most expensive of current literary forms. It requires inordinate investments of authorial time and publishers' capital, both laid out on a hazardous chance of success; of all forms, novel publishing is most akin to gambling (advertising and various play-safe strategies have only a limited capacity to lower odds). Hence the novel is closely tied to the progressive technology, commercial management, and dictatorship of the market. If it comes to the Blakean dilemma of making his own system or being enslaved by the other man's, the novelist usually has little alternative to slavery, mitigated by whatever Joycean resource of cunning he can muster. There is always, of course, the drastic resort to samizdat. Current practice suggests that this alternative supply system only flourishes where there is a coercive establishment whose censorious rigidity leaves no aperture for even moderately subversive literature. One of the interesting features of alternative publishing houses in the West—say the American Fiction Collective, the British Writers and Readers, or the feminist presses, Virago for instance—is that they either defy the conditions of the market-place and go under, or they survive and compromise principle. (Each of the forementioned, for example, have made accommodation with the 'straight' publishing world to get distribution and access to retail outlets.) Fiction, then, is less detachable from the dominant commercial system than poetry or drama, which have self-publishing and fringe facilities. Nor given the general trade publishing pattern, with its elaborate cross-subsidizations, is fiction entirely detachable from what is happening with other categories of book.

The question of present Anglo-American consolidation is slightly less clear cut. Historically, the American book trade has operated with a more *laissez-faire* ethos than the British. This is particularly the case after 1900, at which date the British book trade comes to be firmly controlled by a superstructure of professional trade bodies. The Booksellers Association was founded in 1894, the Society of Authors in 1883, and the Publishers Association in 1896; and in 1900, they combined to establish and subsequently enforce the momentous Net Book Agreement. This agreement, inhibiting retail competitiveness, fostered the growth of codes of professional gentility so characteristic of the book trade today (America, in contrast, retained discount selling, and, with fiercely competitive advertising has developed more of a dog-eat-dog book world).

Another factor tending to differentiate national styles was the establishment of the British public library system on a scale to drive out commercial competition--a process largely set in motion by the great nationalizing government of 1945 and confirmed by the Roberts Report of 1956. This, together with the inhibition on new sales through book clubs until the 1970s, and the stubborn survival of the Net Book Agreement, has created a formal 'institutional' structure in the British book trade and its dependent literary culture, which is remarkably unlike anything present in America (or, for that matter, any other country).

A third factor, and in economic terms the most important, is that the British book industry after 1947 enjoyed the near global hemisphere of the old British empire as a preserved sales territory. There is no doubt that the Traditional Market Agreement carved up the English speaking world grossly in Britain's favour until 1975, when at American insistence, it was dissolved. The Traditional Market Agreement, together with a chronically weak post-war pound and the status of English as a, if not *the*, world language (though the guarantor of this status, the superpower America, had until recently little interest in exporting books) made the export of British books an important component in British book production: in the last thirty years, between forty and fifty per cent has been sold abroad (contrasted with France whose percentage is barely in double figures).

The character of the British fiction industry, resting on this base in the 1960s, and prospering from the various surplus values, was roughly as follows. The production of 'quality' (the term is symptomatic) novels was customarily two tiered relying on two markets. A new hardback would appear, typically under the imprint of a middle-sized house with an otherwise mixed list. Typically, too, different strata of fiction might be represented within the broad 'quality' category—in the 1960s, for instance, Cape's list would carry both Fleming and Fowles. The book's inevitable high price would be justified by its being, fundamentally, a library edition. Institutional sale would underwrite most ventures 'certified' by a respectable imprint. After a sifting process (in which critical reception and reader response would play a part) the work might reappear in paperback—ideally under the Penguin imprint. Penguin at this time did not offer high sums to primary producers—nor at any stage in the process were large advances customary. In paperbacks even very best-sellers would sell modestly by today's standards. And printing costs, relative to America, were low.

There was, of course, a lower stratification of the British book world, in which various genre products (romance, thrillers, westerns, soft pornography, science fiction) might, circumventing the two-tier system, be directed at the one market of its readers. But, as regards books that 'mattered', this two-tiered system was left undisturbed by a trade that continued to be low pressured and civilized (there was little advertising or publicity in British bookselling at this period—a war hangover which lasted a surprisingly long time; and, notoriously, publicity was an undervalued department which recruited women:

men were editors). The machinery was smooth and regulated by custom and decency. Things were—as was often protested—on a 'human' scale. The 1962 defence of the Net Book Agreement on the grounds that 'Books are Different' confirmed the sense that publishing was licensed to operate in an idiosyncratic and anachronistic fashion. Other industries might be dragged kicking and screaming into the twentieth century, but not the book trade.

In the 1960s, the gap between British and American book trades was never larger. In contrast to British restraint and stasis, American publishers had flung headlong into change. Houses and imprints, swallowed up by mergers and corporate take-overs, were melting into the conglomerate mazes from which they have never since emerged. The trend, as Richard Snyder put it quite recently, was towards books assimilating with other lines of merchandise; ultimately there would be a complete rationalization in which, like the seven sisters of the oil trade, there would be seven giant, corporate-owned, American publishing houses (only semantic inertia, however, can justify calling Simon and Schuster, Doubleday, or Holt, Rinehart, and Winston 'houses'). The corporate mergers immediately preceded what might be called the second paperback revolution in America. In the 1970s fiction for the first time sold above the ten million threshold in paperback (*Jaws* did so in less than two years), indicative of an utterly unprecedented intensity of 'bestsellerism'. Since 1895, America had always had best-seller lists at the centre of its book trade; but in the period 1960 to 1980, 'hype' and 'all time record' advances for putative blockbusters reached new heights, culminating in the more than five million dollars which Judith Krantz earned for a novel which was not only unprinted, but as yet largely unwritten. Given the vertical interlocking of conglomerate American industry, new tie-in arrangements were logical: Judith Rossner's *Looking for Mr Goodbar* (1975), for example, came out from Simon and Schuster in hardback, Pocket Books in paperback, and as a film by Paramount. All three are owned by Gulf and Western. Such a versatile monopoly is still fairly rare, but there is clearly a significant trend towards it.

The differences between British and America—so pronounced in the early 1960s—are now, however, rapidly diminishing. The Traditional Market Agreement no longer preserves the large

Empire territories of British publishing (for which American expansionism is not entirely responsible: some of the most lucrative foreign markets, notably Nigeria, are increasingly intolerant of book colonialism). Ever since the Second World War, when enterprising publishers like Mark Goulden and Victor Gollancz went on shopping expeditions for rights, the two great English speaking markets have increasingly tended to concentrate around the same titles, especially where best-sellers are concerned. This concentration has inexorably led to an assimilation of book trade operations. Big fiction ventures—for instance *The Thornbirds* or *The Devil's Alternative*—are conceived by their makers as multi-national in appeal (Forsyth, for example, estimates that eighty per cent of his income comes from overseas; and for *The Thornbirds*, McCullough undertook successive promotional tours of America, Britain, and Australia).

British middle-sized 'human-scale' trade publishers, with a dominant figure-head proprietor, are losing ground. Just as a matter of generation, many of the older, individualistic proprietors are retiring or dead, replaced, if not with the dreaded representatives of 'slide rule publishing', by something more akin to the American 'editor': an operator interested less in literary patronage than processing typescript. The emergence of agents as a major presence on the literary market-place has further tended to separate the hardback house from its authors, disrupting the traditional 'primary relationship' of loyal novelist and loyal publisher, and introducing an aggressive friction into relations (a recent profile of Pat Kavanagh in *Tatler* positively celebrated her macho toughness in dealings with publishers). Agents, the least chauvinistic of British book people, look well beyond the first form of literary property (the book) to all possible exploitations of it (Ed Victor, responsible for the biggest coup in recent years, namely the advance subsidiary rights sales for Stephen Sheppard's *The Four Hundred*, is an American resident in England and was clearly more interested in Warner Brothers than any hardback firm). Agents are looking for the immediate return, naturally screwing up the advance money that they can get for a novel or even, as in the case of Carol Smith, the idea for a novel; and, while Britain still lags behind America (the record paperback advance here, for example, is £250,000 for a synopsis of *The Devil's Alternative*; in

America it stands at over three million dollars), we are certainly moving Americawards. And, frankly, there is little to keep us from going in that direction. Even public library patronage, while still important, is no longer able to support the book industry as it once could, and despite desperate attempts to keep retail prices below unofficial thresholds (hence £3.95, £4.95, £5.95, etc.), there is a distinct possibility that the British hardback will price itself out of the public library market. It is a mark of how close the British and American systems have come, that a serious need is now felt for a British best-seller list equivalent, say, to that of the *New York Times Book Review* (reportedly based on some 1,400 outlets for hardback and 40,000 for paperback; the *Sunday Times* list, in contrast, is based on 300 respondents, apparently). A best-seller list would have been seen as a barbarous cultural surrender in the 1960s.

Assimilation of the British and American booktrades could be seen as an evolutionary and even a progressive integration. These things change over a long period and with a long enough perspective fall into a healthy give-and-take pattern (from 1890 to 1910, for instance, America followed British initiatives, establishing trade and professional organizations on the same lines as those in London). But the recent changes appear to be different, originating less from internal evolutionary drives than an external economic crisis. No one is quite certain how recession affects the booktrade. There are those who, like Paul Hamlyn, declare books to be recession proof. Others maintain that since publishing has a longer pipeline than other businesses, bad things simply take that much longer to come through. Both parties can support their case from the perplexing fact that recent statistics show no decrease in title or volume-of-trade figures. Despite gloom, a boom of sorts is still with us.

None the less, the pound, held artificially high as a petro-currency, cannot but eventually damage a trade which expects to export half its product. High interest rates are similarly damaging to a business which (in the case of a novelist's advance, for instance) may have to wait five years for return on outlay. And during the last two years particularly, complaints have been voiced that British printing has made itself uneconomic (to the point that Tom Rosenthal, the Director of Secker and Warburg, now reckons that the standard price for British printed novels should be an entirely prohibitive ten pounds). There is, despite the 'gloom boom', more than enough evidence that these malign conditions are combining to hurt British publishers. Three leading firms—Collins, Penguin, and Hutchinson—have had unusually bad years, upsetting decades of progressive expansion and financial cheer (the case of Hutchinson—who have novelists of as varied quality but 'sure-fire' popularity as Forsyth, Burgess, and Amis—is especially ominous.

Predictions about the booktrade are notoriously hazardous, particularly for those not concerned directly with it. But there would seem to me to be one likely outcome of all this. The middle-sized houses are in danger, and it is unlikely that they—despite their long histories and remarkably catholic lists (Cape, Deutsch, Secker and Warburg, and Chatto and Windus would be representative cases)—will be in the vanguard of publishing fiction in the future. Such houses are now squeezed in all sorts of distorting ways—by the .problem of raising cash for huge advances and long term investments, the debilitation of public libraries, and the general movements in the trade which have given a greater importance to, for instance, paperback publishers. A rather different constellation may emerge. Bigger firms will continue producing bigger blockbusters. There will be bigger, better, and more paperback genre and tie-in products. As in America, book clubs (with their restricted choice, and powerful advertisement effort) will absorb a larger part of the British book market.

In the shadow of this commercialism, however, the responsibility of initiating or cultivating new and minority-taste fiction may well devolve more on ideologically committed houses—outfits like Pluto, Virago, and Writers and Readers. These differ from the traditional middle-sized houses (as I have called them) in a number of ways. They are frequently short-life, rather than dynastic in their outlook; consequently their attitude to 'risk' is different. They take a frankly engaged, often adversarial stand rather than being traditionally open-minded in their publishing decisions (one might, to change a label, call them 'specific' trade publishers). They subscribe less to the two-tier system, preferring a 'midway' form which they control rather than lease out and which encourages financial self-sufficiency. Finally, these publishing houses have succeeded in opening a more direct line of access to the elusive 'youth market' and various, book buying pressure groups.

GRANTA

DAVID CAUTE
SWEAT SHOP LABOUR

In 1906 Bernard Shaw addressed the annual dinner of the Society of Authors:

> What a heart-breaking job it is trying to combine authors for their own protection . . . .Those of you who, like myself, have studied 'sweating' as an industrial phenomenon, are aware that it occurs at its very worst in those trades where the employer, instead of having the work done in his own factory, gives it out to workers who do it in their own homes. You can get at the factory through the factory inspector and your Factory Acts, but you cannot get at the private home. Without union and collective action, we are helpless. When we begin working, we are so poor and so busy that we have neither the time nor the means to defend ourselves against the commercial organizations which exploit us. When we become famous, we become famous suddenly, passing at one bound . . . to a state in which our time is so valuable that it is not worth our while wasting any of it on lawsuits and bad debts. We all, eminent and obscure alike, need the Authors' Society. We all owe it a share of our time, our means, our influence.

Shaw was active on the Committee of Management of the Society of Authors for ten years, from 1905 to 1915, when—Victor Bonham-Carter tells us in his *Authors by Profession*—'he diplomatically withdrew seeking characteristically to avoid any dissension in the Society due to his unpopular opinions about the war.' Nevertheless, more than sixty years elapsed before the Society grasped the nettle of trade unionism. As Bonham-Carter puts it,

> the majority of members long resisted it: partly because they disliked the face of trade unionism as displayed in industrial action; partly because they considered it impracticable in that any attempt to enforce a closed shop (as the ultimate sanction) would fail, since a number of writers would always disregard the ban; but at heart because they felt that to regiment writers was tantamount to dictatorship over the mind, and would result in the

denial of a fundamental human right—that of freedom of expression.

This passage encapsulates the whole package of liberal myths still prevalent among genteel authors who recoil from the rough and vulgar style of working-class trade unionism. For 'freedom of expression' read 'smooth white hands' or 'gentlemanly agreements'. Among not only authors but also publishing house editors a depressingly high proportion feel it is demeaning to join a union chapel and risk the loss of dignity and status involved in industrial confrontation. 'I'm not a natural joiner' signals the speaker's pride in having a mind of his own; and, often, it betrays a total confusion about how our island-race achieved and defended its liberties. In practice the weakest defence of vital freedoms under threat comes from those middle-class individualists who equate independence with isolation and fastidiously refuse to join *n'importe quel* combination. But when the recession strikes and redundancies ravage the ranks of the genteel, then your non-union editors begin to wail and whine, hastily swallowing their 'principles' and filling in union application forms with anxious pleas that they should qualify for full union protection from the moment of signing.

Bonham-Carter refers to 'a closed shop', dictatorship, and regimentation as if authors regarded these dangers as the inevitable corollaries of trade unionism rather than evils which trade unionists are perfectly capable of avoiding. Let's begin by taking a look at a recent and fairly extreme example of 'regimentation'—and one without precedent in the history of British publishing—by the Writers' Guild of Great Britain, a union affiliated to the TUC. Announcing that it was in dispute with W. H. Allen and its paperback division, Star Books, the Guild instructed its members: (1) Not to enter into any new contract or agreement with W. H. Allen or Star Books as from 1 July 1980; and (2) not to enter into any contract or agreement assigning to W. H. Allen or Star Books the publication rights to any television or film screenplay, play, series, or serial.

And more as well. There can be no doubt that when the Guild thus instructs its members, compliance is obligatory; nor can it be denied that such an instruction temporarily restricts the member writer's economic freedom. This is a weapon to be used sparingly and only after the most painstaking research into the viability of the 'strike' and the degree of support and solidarity prevailing among the writers most directly involved. Orders and commands barked out *de haut en bas* cut no ice with those who script *Dr Who*. The happy result of this industrial action, a Minimum Terms Agreement between the Guild and W. H. Allen Star Books, is likely in the long run to improve generally the contractual terms obtainable from book publishers by the majority of writers—including those who despise trade unionism. The current situation is analogous to the case of the Public Lending Right, for which an active minority campaigned, year after depressing year: yet every author will benefit from the heroic labours of Brigid Brophy, Maureen Duffy, and their colleagues.

Of course fear of regimentation, dictatorship, and closed shops is not the only factor causing authors to recoil from active trade unionism. More prosaically, they hate paying a subscription to an organization which may not bring them an immediate and tangible benefit. Quite a few complete their subscription forms with genuine enthusiasm, only to baulk at the last hurdle, the signing of the cheque.

Nor should one leave out of account the rather drab image projected by do-gooders, proselytizers, and bores with single-track needles. Those 'writers' with time to sit on committees, attend general meetings, and visit the House of Commons surely have nothing better to do with their lives? Are they not second-rate artists or burnt-out cases, like the dons who escape in middle age from the real work of scholarship and writing into administration, faculty boards, deanships, and proctorial perambulations? These busybodies, forever hectoring their colleagues, are they not engaged in a surrogate drama, the only one available to writers no longer capable of writing good novels, poems, or plays?

One recognizes bores when the cause is not one's own—the moralists, vigilantes, and defenders of the subjunctive. Yet the writer who becomes an active, as distinct from a mere card-carrying trade unionist must become a bore by design, making himself a slave of repetition, of the drip-drip torture of his colleagues into agreement or, failing that, exhausted submission. So what, broadly, is the message which needs to be repeated *ad nauseam*?

What needs to be changed are the rules of the game. The aim is to coax the writer out of the isolation which keeps one end of the publishing industry comfortably in the nineteenth century, in Gissing's Grub Street, while publishers bend their twentieth century minds to the rigours of competition, production, marketing, and promotion. The clauses of a publisher's standard printed contract were drafted to benefit the publisher, not the writer. It is the publishers who have traditionally laid down the ground rules, maintained the psychological ascendency, and thus put themselves in the position of magnanimously granting 'concessions' when the writer growls indignantly or lifts his begging bowl in meek supplication. Enough of that!

We alter the rules of the game by laying them down ourselves, by drawing up Minimum Terms Agreements to protect our legitimate interests as primary producers and copyright holders. In this way—to recall Shaw's image—we bring the Factory Acts into our cottage industry. Book publishers, after all, are merely the last literary entrepreneurs to acknowledge the inevitability and justice of writers representing their own collective interests through trade unions. Every contract that a television dramatist signs with the BBC or the independent companies is protected by a Minimum Terms Agreement between the Writers' Guild and the Corporation or Company. These minimum terms provide a floor only; the ceiling for successful writers remains open to negotiation and their agents thrive on the system. As for tangible results, take the case of BBC television drama rates of payment. As I write, the 'going rate' for an established playwright for a sixty minute television play is £2,450. In 1975 it was only £1,150. When the Guild signed its first radio drama agreement, in collaboration with the Society of Authors, six years ago, the going rate for an original play was £5.50 per minute; as a result of annual negotiations it is now £13 to £15 per minute. Four years ago an established playwright signed a contract with the National Theatre and was rewarded with an advance against royalties of £150. That was before the National Theatre entered into a Minimum Terms Agreement with the Guild and the Theatre Writers' Union. Today that playwright would be guaranteed £2,000 for the finished work.

For all of which we must light candles to the deity of collective bargaining. Last year I published a comparative survey of sixty British publishers' printed contracts, examined them clause by clause, and demonstrated that publishers are offering terms anarchically divergent and cruelly exploitative because there is as yet no effective network of Minimum Terms Agreement to protect authors of books ('Publish and be damned', *New Statesman*, June 13, 1980). The current publishing crisis naturally provides an ideal alibi for offering deteriorating terms. As an example, one could cite a new series of critical studies to be launched by Methuen: the advance will be paid half on acceptance of the finished typescript, and half on publication. In my experience it's unheard of for a publisher to commission a book without offering any money on signature of the contract to fuel the writer's labour. It's damned cheek, too. And what happens if the editors of the series judge the manuscript to be unacceptable?

But wait: what need hath our writer of a union if blessed with a bright and burning agent? This question is often posed, not least by agents. To begin with, the majority of writers neither do nor can engage an agent to represent them; agents, no less than publishers, have a nose for success. Thirty to forty thousand original titles are published every year, yet London's literary agents are reckoned to represent only five to six thousand clients. Of a sample cross-section of writers who belong either to the Society of Authors or the Writers' Guild, less than forty per cent reported that they were represented by an agent. Secondly, a contract contains a wide variety of non-financial clauses which literary agents have customarily accepted uncritically but which are of acute concern to any writer anxious to guard the artistic integrity of his work. Thirdly, a Minimum Terms Agreement can provide a kind of protection which the writer or his agent simply cannot achieve in isolation. Take, for example, the most vital moment in any writer's working life, the acceptance or rejection of his manuscript.

The only manuscript for which the typical publisher or editor feels unalloyed enthusiasm is the one as yet unwritten—the future project. That's the lobster and winter strawberries phase. During the two or three years that elapse from that time of euphoria to the chill moment of delivering the finished product, one or all of the following disasters will almost inevitably occur:

—your publisher is bought by a conglomerate determined to

'rationalize' his list;
—your enthusiastic commissioning editor departs under a cloud—or just departs;
—market trends are said to indicate that you have written the wrong book for the wrong audience at the wrong time.

All of which adds up to a note of rejection very possibly accompanied by a brash demand for the return of the advance payment. The money, of course, has gone: your children ate it. This is the worst thing that can happen to a writer and it happens all the time. In fact the publisher may have quietly prepared the terrain by inserting in the contract an apparently innocuous 'satisfactory' clause, entitling him to reject the finished work on the ground that in his opinion, and in his opinion alone, it is 'not satisfactory'—and no argument. Not only does this monstrous clause enable the publisher to withhold the portions of the advance payable to the writer on 'acceptance' and 'publication', it may even enable him to demand *repayment* of the money that he advanced on signature of the contract two or three years previously. As the American Authors' Guild has wisely pointed out in the September-October issue of its *Bulletin*, when this happens the publisher in effect: (1) transforms the advance into a repayable loan; (2) deprives the author of his or her investment of time, labour, and money; (3) provides the publisher with a free, exclusive option on the work-in-progress.

In a recent court case, *Random House versus Herbert Gold*, the United States District Court ruled that 'the requirement that the manuscript be satisfactory to the publisher gives it [i.e. the publisher] the right to reject a work if it acts in good faith.' The fact that other publishers may subsequently bid for and publish the same manuscript makes no difference at all—a point I can illustrate by quoting from a letter written to me on April 8, 1976 by the Editor-in-Chief at McGraw-Hill, the wonderful Frederic W. Hills. 'McGraw-Hill,' he announced, 'has rejected your manuscript as unpublishable.' (Mr Hills, needless to add, had not been the commissioning editor four years previously: *that* one had passed on or, possibly, away.) Therefore, continued Fred, 'It is entirely correct of McGraw-Hill to seek the return of their money if the book is placed elsewhere.' But now we come to the nicest cut of all: *'Every other book publisher in existence could be eager to publish your book and it would have absolutely no legal bearing on our editorial judgment'* (my italics). Such was Hills's 'editorial judgment' that shortly thereafter he joined the publishing house which took the book after he'd rejected it. Like they say, life is worse than fiction.

How does one avoid such traumas? By insuring contractually that the second part of the advance, payable on 'acceptance', must be handed over unless the publisher can demonstrate *to arbitrators* that the finished work does not meet the technical requirements of the contract. But only a *collective agreement* can provide for rapid, effective, and inexpensive arbitration.

We are now one long step nearer getting one. This results from a significant shift of attitude on the part of the Society of Authors, which has not only registered as a trade union but, more recently, come round to full acceptance of the necessity of minimum terms agreements to cover book contracts. For the past year the Guild and the Society have collaborated in drawing up a new and more comprehensive Minimum Terms Agreement which, it is hoped, will be jointly administered by the two unions. The proposed formula for dealing with that odious 'satisfactory' clause is as follows:

Clause 1: Delivery and Acceptance of the Typescript

(a) The Author shall deliver not later than . . . [date] one legible copy of the typescript of the work which shall consist of . . . [insert fullest possible details of subject, length, number, and type of illustrations, index, etc.]. The Author shall deliver a script which, in style and content, is professionally competent and fit for publication.

(b) The Publishers shall notify the Author of any changes required in the script within thirty days. Should the Publishers reject the script on the ground that it fails to meet the specifications in (a) above, they shall within thirty days provide the Author with a written notice of not less than 250 words in which the grounds for rejecting the script shall be set out in such a manner as to facilitate arbitration . . . .

(c) The Publishers shall not reject the script for any reason other than its failure to meet the specifications above.

Legalese is always off-putting; but there is real value in this formula. It greatly reduces the risk of the commissioned writer receiving a curt or cryptic note of rejection: 'We regret to inform you that we find your book disappointing/lacking in conviction/not up to your usual standard/unlikely to achieve a remunerative sale in the present climate . . .'. What is more, the arbitration clause of the Agreement requires the publisher to convince an arbitration panel that his adverse verdict, his outright rejection of the text, is justified—the panel to consist of two representatives of the unions and two appointed by the publishers 'but not connected with their company'. Failing unanimous agreement, the dispute goes to a single arbitrator, and only if the contending parties cannot agree on the choice of the arbitrator is the case referred to the more time-consuming and costly London Court of Arbitration. Private arbitration—rapid, cheap, and fair—is a service which only the union can offer to the writer. So slow and expensive is normal litigation that in practice the writer has virtually no redress against the publisher who dishonours his obligations under the contract.

So there you have it: a new deal, no less. Of course the beneficiaries will be the members of the two unions, the Guild and the Society; those writers who wish to preserve their independence, constitutional liberties, and civil rights by rejecting the stifling conformism of trade unionism will remain perfectly free to be taken to the cleaners whenever they put pen to paper.

Further information can be obtained by writing to the Writers' Guild of Great Britain, 430 Edgware Road, London W2 1EH, or the Society of Authors, 84 Drayton Gardens, London SW10 9SD

GRANTA

BLAKE MORRISON
POETRY AND
THE POETRY BUSINESS

Blake Morrison

I f there is one image that has dominated our notion of English poetry since 1945 it is that of restraint. Though many different kinds of poetry have been written here during that period, and many different kinds of critical terminology have been developed to talk about them, this common language remains: restraint, restriction, limitation, moderation, diminution, containment—with these words or others like them we know where we are. The terms are as indispensable to our discussion of contemporary poetry as are notions of 'The Death of the English Novel' or 'The End of Realism' in our discussion of fiction and of 'The Revival of the English Stage after 1956' in our discussion of drama. Though one can take issue as well as agree, of course, these are the terms of the argument.

To trace the evolution of this image of restraint would be an arduous process; to provide instances of it is less so. A fairly typical example can be found in Donald Davie's *Thomas Hardy and British Poetry* (1973), where Davie finds himself trying to explain 'the features of later British poetry which have baffled and offended readers, especially in America—I have in mind an apparent meanness of spirit, a painful modesty of intention, extremely limited objectives.' Perversely, Davie wants to suggest that British poets may be 'right in curtailing for themselves the liberties that other poets continue to take,' but the metaphor still dominates his procedure: modesty as against ambition, limits as against freedom, meanness as against profusion. And indeed images of restraint seem naturally to cluster round our poetry: we speak of small presses, slim volumes, little magazines.

Of course the main point is that this image passes judgement, pejoratively suggesting that poetry since 1945 has been largely undistinguished. But the image also serves other purposes. It divides English poets from American ones: they are the risk-takers and expansionists, the confessionals and Beats; our poets, it is felt, are small beer. The image indicates too that after the big, bold advances of Modernism our poets have in some way held themselves back. And finally it concedes that our poets are very far from being prolific: we have as our unofficial Poet Laureate a writer, Philip Larkin, whose output from the mid-1950s to the mid-1970s was about three poems a year. Since 1977 he has published nothing at all.

Explanations as to why English poetry has been thus restrained have not been lacking. From time to time a racial theory is put forward, with talk of the English 'stiff upper lip' and of a fatal tendency towards gentility and decorum. And there is also the geographical theory—the smallness of the island and the insularity it encourages. But the most widely propagated theory has been the socio-economic one: a link is thought to exist between the state of poetry and the state of the nation. We have lost our Empire and world influence and also, it is suggested, our poets of international standing; our pound has shrunk and so have our literary ambitions; our productivity is down, poetic as well as economic. According to this interpretation, our poets are very largely exonerated: their limitations are merely a reflection of a larger national distress.

Though there has been no reluctance to make these rather grandiose connections between English poetry and the English economy, the economics of poetry itself—the publishing, distribution, reviewing, buying, and reading of it—have gone virtually ignored. This might seem surprising: any investigation of the state of our poetry should touch on sales figures, publishing trends, audiences, and so on; certainly no comprehensive study of the English novel or theatre would ignore these matters. There are, however, a number of reasons for this neglect. Poetry, clearly a much smaller enterprise than fiction or drama, is as such far less attractive to the cultural historian. *Fiction and the Fiction Industry* was the title of John Sutherland's recent book about the publishing of contemporary novels; to get the equivalent scale we'd have to talk of 'Poetry and the Poetry Business', a matter of the small-time entrepreneurs, minuscule sales, and (at best) miniature profit margins of published verse—an altogether less enticing topic than the wheeling-and-dealing of fiction and drama. But the reasons for the inattention to the poetry business lie deeper: in the place granted to poetry since nineteenth century Romanticism and before. If one looks at the history of poetry over the last two hundred years one regularly finds examples of poets declaring their indifference to how much they earn, to whom (if anyone) reads them, and to what reviewers say about their books. Keats in his fragment 'Ode to May' dreams of dying 'unheard/Save of the quiet Primrose, and the span/Of heaven and few ears'. Shelley in his *Defence of Poetry* describes the poet as 'a nightingale who sits in darkness and sings to cheer its own solitude'. Yeats claims that he will have 'nothing to do with the great public'. Poetry is granted a privileged status, elevated above common concerns, becoming what Wordsworth called 'the breath and spirit of finer knowledge'. And in the special rarefied atmosphere that poets breathe, matters such as publishing and sales seem inherently vulgarizing. Such attitudes continue to this day: in a 1972 published symposium in the *Review*, Patricia Beer remarked that she was 'glad there is no money in poetry', the suggestion being that money would sully the purity of the art. And these attitudes inevitably influence critics as well as poets, deterring certain kinds of critical apparatus from being brought to bear on poetry. Critics don't want to sully poetry either, don't want to speak of the unspoken. Instead they enjoy the stories of T. S. Eliot in his bank and Wallace Stevens in his insurance business trying to conceal their poetic activities from work colleagues ('Wally? A poet?'); such stories reassure us that the worlds of money and poetry are by their nature entirely separate, and should remain that way.

It need hardly be said that poets have generally been more used to hard-nosed business negotiation, and rather less indifferent to income and sales, than all this would suggest. Pope made over £5,000 through subscriptions to the *Iliad*; Byron earned nearly £3,000 for the copyright of *Childe Harold*, then asked for and got from John Murray £3,000 for one Canto of *Don Juan*; Tennyson's reaction on being offered what was then the largest fee for a poetry book was to say: 'My dear! We are much richer than we thought we were. Mr Smith has just offered me 5,000 guineas for a book the size of the Idylls. And if Mr Smith offers 5,000, of course the book is worth ten.' Later Tennyson is said to have been offered £20,000 for a lecture tour in America.

But the myths die hard, not just because of Romantic notions of the poet starving in his garret, but because of the place of poetry even further back, in the Renaissance and Restoration, when the custom was to write for a patron and for the amusement of a few friends, and when poetry consisted of manuscripts to be handed round privately, not of a commercial transaction between writer, publisher, and reader. This, if you like, is the amateur tradition, poetry as accomplishment, as a mark of civility; and its persistence caused the squeamishness that affected Prior when he published his *Poems* in 1716: the book earned him over £4,000 through a subscription system, but Prior in his postscript seems uneasy about the fact of publishing at all: 'I published

my Poems formerly, as Monsieur Jourdain sold his silk: He would not
be thought a Tradesman; but ordered some Pieces to be measured out
to his particular Friends. Now I give up my shop, and dispose of all my
Poetical Goods at once.'

These are some of the factors that lie behind our long-standing
reluctance to consider poetry as a material fact, a worldly activity, a
matter involving not just individual authors but printers, publishers,
patrons, editors, reviewers, and readers. Yet one doesn't have to
subscribe to a Marxist view of literature to see that the question of the
production, distribution, and consumption is of paramount
importance in assessing the general state of poetry. As the French
sociologist Robert Escarpit writes in his *Sociology of Literature*:

> If we wish to understand writers in our time, we cannot
> forget that writing is a profession—or at least a lucrative
> activity—practised within the framework of economic
> systems which exert undeniable influences on creativity.
> We cannot forget, if we wish to understand literature, that
> a book is a manufactured product, commercially
> distributed, and thus subject to the laws of supply and
> demand.

What I want to do here is to approach poetry in this way, to look at
poetry and the poetry business, and to suggest that the restraint and
limitation to which contemporary poetry is widely believed to be
subject may be attributed in part to certain specific factors within that
business; to suggest, that is, that the production, distribution, and
consumption of English poetry today is such as to favour certain
poetic forms and modes and to disadvantage others.

Looking in the early 1950s through the annual *Bookseller* list of
the various categories of books published in the preceding year,
J. W. Saunders was disturbed to find that poetry (then
bracketed with drama) had fallen from sixth place in 1935 to ninth
place in 1949. He'd certainly be disturbed to see the *Bookseller* of
January 3, 1981, which shows that poetry now occupies twenty-first
place: in 1980 there were less poetry books published than there were

bibliographies, or indeed books about commerce, engineering, and mathematics. Publishing generally has been badly hit, of course, and poetry, on the periphery of most publishers' lists, is an obvious target for trimming. Many firms—among them Collins, Weidenfeld, and Hamish Hamilton—published no poetry at all last year, and indeed have not had a poetry list for some time. A number of others—including Allen Lane, Macmillan, and Eyre Methuen—published only anthologies, the one kind of poetry book which can normally be relied on to achieve reasonably good sales and which has also some possibility of a deal with a book club. A number of other firms have reduced their lists to the point where they rely almost exclusively on a single poet: André Deutsch on Geoffrey Hill (who has published four collections in twenty-five years) and RKP on Jon Silkin. Cape, meanwhile, has backed the popular and fashionable: last year it published collections by Adrian Henri ('Liverpool poet' and live performer) and Herman Hesse: this year Cape have brought out the latest of Clive James's satires, which, thanks to his TV following and the calculated topicality of his new subject (Prince Charles), can be relied on to be a best-seller. In fact only three major publishers—Faber, OUP, and Secker—have anything that could be called a poetry list. Even Penguin—with its famous 'Penguin Modern Poets' series, so successful in the 1960s, but which foundered and then finally sunk without trace in the 1970s—now publishes anthologies and little else. For the rest, poetry is left almost entirely to the small presses like Carcanet, Anvil, Bloodaxe, and Peterloo, all of which depend on Arts Council support for their survival; or indeed to smaller presses than these, private operations run by enthusiastic individuals in back-rooms and garden sheds.

Secker and Warburg, neither a large university press like OUP, nor having the special tradition in poetry publishing enjoyed by Faber, provides the most instructive and most approximately representative example of what having a decent-sized poetry list means to a major publisher. Its list is comparatively recent: until about 1970 there was no consistent policy towards poetry, but then on the initiative of Anthony Thwaite, who continues to act as the chief selector, a proper list was set up. Now eight books of poetry are published a year (two every quarter) and the list has a judicious mix of the well-established (John Fuller and Alan Brownjohn, for example) and the young and new. The current printing and sales figures at Secker make fairly chastening reading. The average print run for a poetry book is 500 (it used to be 800); these are in hardback only, an earlier experiment in simultaneously issuing hard and paperback copies having failed; and the bulk of sales are to libraries. Efforts to get bookshops to stock poetry are particularly unrewarding. The traditional way, through the advance hawking of dust-jackets, has left Secker in the absurd position of producing perhaps 1,000 dust-jackets when it can hope at best to sell 500 books. Not surprisingly Secker falls well short of recouping the £25,000 a year it spends on poetry—the return is about £15,000—and there is no prospect, as there can be with fiction, of some later lucrative deal. In fiction, with far larger hardback print runs (2 to 4,000), there is some chance of subsequent paperback publication by another firm.

On the face of it, the case of Secker does much to support the view that poetry is published largely out of charity. C. Day Lewis remarked in 1950 that 'for the last 150 years the publishers themselves have been the chief patrons of poetry. Good publishers have been willing to lose money on a writer they believed in.' Most publishers would take the same line today: if they publish poetry at all, it is, they say, because they think it deserves to be kept alive not because there are any benefits to be had from it. The case, however, is rather more complex. To begin with, having a poetry list invariably lends some kind of prestige: it can help the look of a firm to have the 'highbrow' or 'quality' element which poetry represents; poetry is a good insurance policy, a useful thing to have, if only to attract especially talented authors (a John Updike or a Graham Greene, for instance). Again, the Arts Council Literature Panel, which grew after all out of what was at first a Poetry Panel, is inclined to look favourably on publishers with a poetry list: it has regularly shown itself willing to fund poetry and other loss-making enterprises.

Besides the indirect material benefits of a poetry list there are, for all the talk of the folly of magnanimity of publishing poetry, some very *direct* ones as well. The Arts Council-subsidized Poetry Book Society scheme, over twenty-five years old, offers one of these: in return for an outlay which is currently twelve pounds a year, members of this book club receive a selected volume of contemporary poetry each quarter; and since there are approximately 1,000 members of the club, publishers fortunate enough to have one of their books chosen can increase their print run by 1,000 and be sure of making a profit. A few Poetry Book Society choices can make all the difference to poetry lists, as indeed can picking up new poets and reviving neglected ones, both of which have been factors in the comparative success of the OUP and Carcanet lists in recent years. The OUP poetry list is traditionally a part of the firm not expected to pay its way: but lately—with poets like Peter Porter, D. J. Enright, and Craig Raine proving very successful in their sales—poetry has more than broken even. Carcanet, set up twelve years ago as a small press, now publishes eighteen to twenty poetry titles a year; it still relies on the Arts Council for about twenty per cent of its income, but is now sufficiently stable to be planning further significant additions—including a fiction list—to its rapidly expanding programme.

Indeed there is evidence that a properly managed poetry list, run with flair and initiative, stands a much better chance of success today than before the Second World War, in spite of the supposed current crisis. To compare the sales figures of Auden and MacNeice in the 1930s and 1940s with those of Ted Hughes and Seamus Heaney in the 1960s is to be brought up against a very important change in the market for poetry. With the development of a large school and university reading public, and with the changes in syllabuses which have led to the inclusion of contemporary poets as set texts, there is now a potentially large market for poetry in cheap paperback editions. Faber, for example, was very astute bringing out a joint paperback selection of Ted Hughes and Thom Gunn. Publishing two contemporaries together in one book is historically almost without precedent, but made tremendous economic sense because Hughes and Gunn are so widely taught together on school and university syllabuses: the book's success was guaranteed; or, put another way, the market has determined the book. That Hughes/Gunn paperback selection has now sold well over 100,000 copies.

If there has been this 'growth area', why is it that poetry publishing generally should nevertheless be in a critical state? Why is it that publishers are doing comparatively less poetry, not more? The answer lies partly in the fact that the syllabus boom in contemporary poetry hasn't brought about the general interest one might have anticipated; attention remains firmly fixed on the chosen few rather than filtering out to include peers and confederates; and though students read 'set poets', they don't voluntarily read or buy contemporary poetry in books or magazines (the point is rather devastatingly borne out in a 1978 survey by the magazine *New Poetry*, which revealed that a mere two per cent of its subscribers were aged twenty or under). Rising prices are also offered as an explanation as to why poetry is such a poor proposition: the typical hardback has gone up from 10/6 in 1962 to £1.50 in 1972 to £3 and even £3.95 in 1981. And to that might be added poor standards of poetry book design: the typical poetry book is about as attractive as (and indeed often resembles) a plain brown envelope: there is none of the thought and imagination going into it that is lavished on fiction covers. Those 'striped toothpaste' covers that are standard with Secker are representative.

But all this only scratches the surface: what needs radical examination is the whole notion of the 'slim volume of contemporary verse' to which our publishers, whether they risk bringing out such volumes or not, seem irrevocably wedded. The slim volume of poetry seems, even when new, to be covered in a fine layer of dust. It isn't so much that the slim volume offends ideas of 'getting one's money's worth' (though such attitudes can't be wholly discounted) but that it has acquired, it seems, deadening associations—snobbery, for example (one can imagine Orwell using it as the identifying feature of one of his effete upper class young men), and nostalgia (when Jimmy Porter tries to evoke the spirit of Edwardian England in *Look Back in Anger* he speaks of 'high summer, the long days in the sun, slim volumes of verse'). The associations are archaic or antiquarian: the slim volume of contemporary poetry preserves the spectre of the privately circulated manuscript, the courteous gift to one's courtly friends. And though that spectre might be thought to have no place in the realities of publishing today, it continues to determine the expectations of young poets. To say that slim volumes encourage slim ambitions is perhaps putting it too strongly. But certainly most poets in their twenties hoping for a collection from a leading publisher will know how unvaried the format is. Thirty or so poems, most of them less than a page long, to be published in a small hardback edition with an advance of perhaps £50 or £100. And of course such volumes will be bought by only a tiny fraction of the reading public. Indeed even the poetry reading public fails to buy them: the *New Poetry* survey also revealed that of its subscribers (all of whom were interested in poetry, of course, and 81% of whom were regular users of libraries), very few regularly bought poetry books.

Where, then, if not in slim volumes, do people read poetry? Apart from anthologies, the most important source is magazines; and not little magazines, with their necessarily limited number of subscribers, but the so-called 'quality' magazines, the weekly, fortnightly, and monthly periodicals which give over a substantial amount of their space to book-reviewing: the *New Statesman, Listener, Spectator, TLS, London Review of Books, Encounter, Quarto,* and *London Magazine.* For every one person prepared to buy a book of poems, there are, it would seem, one hundred prepared to take a weekly magazine; for where the total sale of a book of poems is often around the 400, the weekly sales of, for example, the *Listener, TLS* and *New Statesman* are each around 40,000. And most of these periodicals do include poems, some of them (particularly the monthlies like *Quarto* or *Encounter*) averaging as many as six or eight an issue. Not everyone taking these periodicals will bother to read the poems, of course, but they at least have the opportunity to do so; here, undeniably, is the major source for the publishing of contemporary poetry.

There is nothing especially new about this. Nineteenth-century periodicals like the *Fortnightly, Blackwoods,* and the *Cornhill Magazine* published poetry too, some anonymous, some initialled, and some by named authors. Still, there does seem to have been a significant increase in the amount of poetry published in periodicals. The *Listener,* for example, began in 1930 by publishing about a dozen poems annually as 'previews': that is, poems to be read over the air the week subsequent to publication. By 1940 the *Listener's* poems were no longer linked to broadcasts, and about thirty-five were published annually. By 1950 this figure had risen to 100, and by 1960 to 115. Today the *Listener* publishes rather less poetry (like all magazines it is subject to editorial fluctuations), but still a respectable amount. Another example is the *TLS,* which published no poetry at all until 1950: it broke the tradition in that year with a poem by Roy Fuller, and has gone on steadily increasing the amount ever since. Fuller's poem was entitled, appropriately, 'The Fifties', and the 1950s do seem to have been the beginning of a great increase in the printing of poems, from scholarly publications like *Essays in Criticism* to any number of periodicals that have appeared since the little magazine 'boom' in the 60s.

Magazines, particularly the established ones, play a crucial role for poets: it is through them that the process of graduating towards a book is conducted. In a typical career, a poet will publish work first in very small magazines (perhaps locally or university-based), then in the better-known little magazines (*Outposts, New Poetry, Samphire* and so on), then break into the weeklies (it's here that he or she is likely to get for the first time a fee of over £10—though it won't be more than £25), gradually accumulate enough poems to have a pamphlet come out with a small publisher or perhaps a selection with one of the big publishers (Faber, Gollancz, Chatto, Carcanet) who sometimes issue poetry samplers or 'introductions', and then finally reach the position of having a first full-length collection. It is perfectly natural for publishers to look to magazines as a testing ground, but the system sometimes operates with depressing rigidity: there are few opportunities for poets to 'come from nowhere', even if they've a mature collection waiting, for publishers seem to want the imprimatur which magazine appearances provide. The acknowledgements which preface poetry collections are more than traditional politeness to the magazines which first printed particular poems: they are a display of credentials, a certificate to show that the poet has come through his or her apprenticeship.

Editors of magazines, no less than publishers, affect to serve poetry in a magnanimous and disinterested way: but of course poetry has its use for them, too, and this use has a bearing on poetic forms. Like illustrations and advertisements, poems can make a magazine look visually attractive, and are useful in breaking up the solid acres of print: they are natural breaks, intermissions between one article and the next. In the *New Statesman* they are usually tucked away in a corner, set across a single column so that any line of slightly more than medium length is made to turn awkwardly. Other magazines avoid this problem by setting their poems across two or three columns, but they inevitably relegate their poems to the bottom of the page. The end result suggests that poetry is—almost literally—a marginal activity.

The poems appear as the visual equivalents of a crossword or a publisher's advertisement or lonely hearts' column: the odds and sods that fill out the paper, not uninteresting perhaps but taking place away from the centre.

It is not just a question of the status of poems in magazines, nor simply of the reading habits which that status encourages: there is also the crucial matter of space. Most literary editors of magazines are very pressed for space, so that to take a poem of more than average length becomes a major decision: such a poem deprives an editor of room he might want for up-to-the-minute articles and reviews. Short poems, on the other hand, present no such problem: on the contrary, they can be very useful in filling out a page, or in avoiding an awkward cut or 'turn' or in saving someone in the editorial office from having to write a filler. Many poets who submit work to magazines realize only too well that short poems get used up more quickly and more regularly than do long ones. The conditions under which weekly magazines are produced, then, and under which poems are printed in them, do have a very direct bearing on poetic forms, favouring certain kinds (sonnets, villanelles and haikus, for instance; I met one literary editor who expressed his glee at getting some haikus from a leading poet: 'I took them all—perfect fillers'), and discouraging others (anything over thirty lines becomes problematic). One can see now, I think, something other than a literary-historical significance in the popularity during the 1960s and early 1970s of the minimalist lyrics of Ian Hamilton and his confederates at the *Review*, lyrics that had no more than six lines. And only last year Peter Conrad, in making the *New Statesman's* Prudence Farmer award to Craig Raine and Christopher Reid, suggested a connection between the poems printed in that paper and the cramped conditions in which they appear:

> Poems in these columns, where there's a weekly scramble
> for available space, are squeezed on all sides . . . . Most
> often the form has segmented the images. Denied room in
> which to expand or extrapolate, the poem recoils into itself
> and resorts to a desperate shorthand: objects are displaced
> by imagistic riddles.

As Conrad suggests lack of space isn't wholly damaging, but there is no doubt that magazine publication exerts a certain kind of pressure on poetry, encouraging what might be called 'Movement' or mainstream poems: easy to assimilate, unambitious, conventional in appearance, able like the articles around them to offer some readily accessible moral insight. And if it is objected that poems after all are also published in books, where they're less subject to these constrictions, then the question must be asked 'Yes, but where do publishers find their poets?'.

Magazines have a further important relationship with poetry: they not only print it, but review it. Here, on the face of it, there is less cause for misgiving. The editors of our magazines, and indeed of our daily and weekly newspapers, still, it seems, take poetry seriously enough to give it reviewing space and to employ some of our best poets and academics to write the reviews. Again poetry is still taken seriously enough for at least some collections—in the last year or so the new Heaney, the Collected Ewart, the posthumous Lowell—to be thought worthy of long, often leading, articles. And some magazines—*Quarto* is the striking example—indeed give over a very large part of their content to poetry reviewing.

Closer attention to poetry reviewing presents a rather less encouraging picture, however. In English departments poetry is still, so far as I can tell, accorded a significance equivalent to that of fiction and drama. But in the world of newspapers and magazines, poetry is the poor cousin, something that gets reviewed not weekly but at intervals of about six or eight weeks. This has various implications: to begin with it means that poetry reviewing is invariably done selectively and in batches. Drama and fiction are often subjected to batch treatment too, of course: but whereas the better-than-average play or novel will certainly get separate treatment—not just the Goldings and Pinters but the Penelope Livelys and Alan Ayckbourns—that kind of treatment is rarely meted out to the above-average poet. Only an élite of three or four can look forward to separate attention: the rest can hope for perhaps 400 to 500 words in a review of 1,000 words taking in three other collections. Here things do seem to have deteriorated. Derek Roper's recent study *Reviewing Before the Edinburgh* reveals that the *Lyrical Ballads* were given an average of 6–8 pages coverage in the reviewing weeklies of the day: no contemporary poet would be so lucky. And these space limitations inevitably encourage a certain kind of reviewing: it's brief, impressionistic, and able at best to fit in the odd quote, the odd jibe, and the odd *bon mot*: there's none of that sustained coming to terms with a book that the single review quite literally allows room for.

The other implication of the occasional nature of poetry reviewing is that the strange but not inconceivable creature—the professional poetry reviewer—simply does not exist. Most weekly magazines and papers have their drama critics on a full-time salary; and though this is less the case with novel reviewers, regular novel reviewers can—with fees, additional work, and the sale of review copies—eke out some sort of living. The poetry critic can't survive in this way: he isn't used regularly enough, he is paid less, and second hand-booksellers don't want his review copies. The last poetry critic to have made a living in this country was G. S. Fraser in the late 1940s and early 1950s; today the most highly paid reviewers could earn at best £500 to £1,000 a year. It might be argued that there isn't enough poetry published to justify the reviewing of poetry on a weekly basis. But with small presses, little magazines, readings, performances, competitions, and simply news, a weekly column of some sort would not necessarily be an extravagant gesture.

There are other difficulties. In Britain, a small country with a closely concentrated literary establishment, the reviewing of poetry exacerbates the already incestuous quality of the poetry world. Few plays are reviewed by playwrights, and few novels by novelists who are friends of the author; but I would estimate that of every ten books of poetry sent to reviewers in our leading journals, six will be by poets personally known to them. For poetry in England, as everyone admits, is a small world, one in which a few public readings, an event at the Poetry Society, and a publisher's party or two, will bring one across a significant percentage of those involved in it; and one in which, for example, someone like Anthony Thwaite can be adviser to the Secker poetry list, send out poetry books for review as literary editor of *Encounter*, review himself in the *TLS* or on Critics' Forum, sit on the Arts Council Literature Panel deciding which poetry magazines deserve subsidy, and help the Society of Authors to decide which young poets should get Gregory Awards. It isn't so much a matter of organized conspiracies, but of a narrow world in which the few influential positions go to those who can be bothered to take an interest. And though young poets may start out reviewing with enthusiasm and high critical standards, the point will come very soon when they'll be asked to review a book of poems by a friend. Such reviews need not be wholly illegitimate perhaps, but they do place reviewers in a difficult and dubious position. It's little wonder that some very good poetry reviewers quickly come to see the attractions of withdrawal and silence; and that those who don't contribute to the tendency of English poetry to be a mutual admiration society.

One further serious problem in the reviewing of poetry today is that it invariably seems to carry with it a language of restraint: poets are almost inevitably commended for their understatement and discipline or reprimanded for their exuberance and excess. Perhaps this has something to do with the incestuous world I have been describing: for the language is that of existing club members assessing the claims of each new applicant: how well can he or she abide by the rules? Its roots, though, are in the tradition of reviewing poetry that grew up out of late eighteenth, and early nineteenth century periodicals like the *Edinburgh Review*. The fact that so many of the early reviewers of poetry in these journals were lawyers by profession seems not entirely beside the point here, for notions of law, order, rule, and restraint figure very prominently in their reviewing. It is revealing to survey these early reviews, even if only casually: 'Mr Coleridge's blemishes are such as are incident to young men of luxuriant imaginations'; 'The Author's first piece, The Rime of the Ancyent Mariner . . . is the strangest story of a cock and a bull that we ever saw on paper . . . a rhapsody of unintelligible wildness and incoherence'; 'Poor Smart, careless, hasty and needy, was never solicitous, nor at leisure, to polish'; Landor should 'give to his pieces that effect which can only be produced by a steady adherence to a judicious and well-digested plan'; Thomas Moore has 'a lively though not sufficiently regulated imagination . . . . If he learns to restrain that imagination within due bounds . . . few poets of the present day will equal him'. A clear line through to a current language of restraint is hard to mistake.

There is a final aspect to the poetry business which, a mere three years ago, it would not have been necessary to mention at all, but which now looms very large: poetry competitions. On a small scale such competitions have existed for some time, but over the last few years there has been an enormous boom: the winter of 1980–81, for instance, saw two competitions hotly competing with each other, the Poetry Society's £1,000 first prize being trumped by the Arvon Foundation's £5,000. The format of these and other competitions tends to be similar: an entry fee of £1 or £1.50 per poem, a panel of big name judges, plus awards ceremonies linked to television or radio. And they have attracted enormous entries: the Poetry Society's 1979 competition had 27,000 and this year's Arvon over 35,000; even a competition organized by the local borough of Wandsworth, modestly advertized in local libraries, had a staggering 11,000 entries. The names of some of the winners of competitions in recent years—Tony Harrison, Charles Tomlinson, Hugo Williams, Craig Raine—make it clear that established poets as well as amateur ones find the competitions worth going in for.

These competitions have demonstrated that though few people in the country seem to read poetry, vast numbers are writing it: poetry, it appears, is much more of a participator sport than fiction. But the competitions have aroused some controversy—not surprisingly, since the question of how far they serve the interests of poetry is indeed a vexed one. A typically hostile view was that expressed by Geoffrey Grigson in the *TLS* in January 1981 when he wrote that competitions are a vulgarization of the art, that good poets can 'smell each other out' naturally without these bazaars, and that none of the great poets of the past would ever have gone in for them. This last speculation seems doubtful: a spirit of rivalry has affected poets from the Restoration wits down to the present day when, for example, Andrew Motion and Craig Raine competed with each other to write a poem about Ulster. And many poets would argue that if you have some poems written, it's no more demeaning to submit them to a competition than to a magazine, and the former has considerably more financial inducement. Moreover, there can be no doubt that these competitions do stimulate interest in poetry: since 1978 the year of its first competition, membership of the Poetry Society in Earls Court Square has more than trebled, its readings and events are much better attended, and the Society has found itself with an extra £20,000 a year income from competition entry fees. It is, in short, possible to claim, not wholly whimsically, that competitions are the great new patron of poetry, and that, at a time when the Arts Council has abandoned its grants to individual writers, competitions provide a privileged few with a new form of subsidy.

For all that, it is possible to feel strong reservations about these competitions. The problem is that they concentrate attention on the single poem: what is judged is not a book or even a small group of poems but *one* poem. Moreover, prize-winning poems occupy a peculiar status: they exist not to be read so much as acclaimed, deprecated, or placed alongside one's real or imaginary entry and judged accordingly. Their relation to the rest of a poet's work or to that of predecessors is not at issue. Though ostensibly objects of attention, competition poems are, like many of the poems in weekly magazines, isolated and marginalized, removed from the cultural mainstream.

It's easy, of course, to end up sounding unduly pious: aren't poetry competitions, it might reasonably be asked, a harmless and passing fad? I'd like to be able to take this view. But it seems to me that, on the contrary, poetry competitions are here to stay because they dovetail so neatly with other established characteristics of the poetry business. We come back again here to the question of the short poem. Publishers, I suggested, have become attached to the idea of the slim volume of poetry with its thirty or so slim poems. Magazines favour short poems because they are convenient as space fillers. Now poetry competitions have added their weight to this, for many of them lay down restrictions on the length of poems that may be entered; and one can see that even in those that don't, the judges, having waded through vast numbers of entries, are not likely to be well-disposed towards long narratives or epics.

It may be said that the real business of poetry, as opposed to the poetry business, goes on elsewhere. And it may be thought that our educational system tolerates and preserves a diversity of poetic modes. I am not, however, convinced by this. For short poems also form a central part of the school and university curriculum. In the typical class—somewhere between forty minutes and an hour—discussion of one such poem or comparison of two is an ideal way of practising close textual criticism; and it's felt to be much more satisfying to teach one

111

of Blake's *Songs of Experience* than an extract from *Paradise Lost*. Indeed the short poem is fundamental to the whole notion of the practical criticism to which I. A. Richard's book of 1929 gave its name: Richards, it will be remembered, tested the critical responses of his students with thirteen anonymous poems: the longest of those poems was in fact thirty-two lines, coincidentally the length limit of several poetry competitions today.

I don't wish to seem to be idealizing the long poem. The view that there is no work of literature which couldn't be improved by being shorter is one with which I have some sympathy; and clearly the lyric which condenses and crystallizes experience, the poem which is an intellectual and emotional complex in an instant of time, will always be one of the primary poetic modes. But we need to worry if sustained intellectual and emotional endeavour of an epic or narrative kind is being discouraged. Keats was certainly worried about this in his day: 'A long poem,' he wrote to Bailey in October 1817, complaining of short poetry to be got over with 'before breakfast', 'is a test of invention, which I take to be the polar star of poetry, as fancy is the sail and imagination the rudder. Did our great poets ever write short pieces? I mean in the shape of tales. This same invention seems indeed of late years to have been forgotten as a poetical excellence.'

The long poem as a test of invention: would any poet starting out today be foolhardy enough to embark on such an undertaking? I doubt it, for poets, publishers, reviewers, and readers have become so accustomed to the quick consumption 'before breakfast' that they would not (unless perhaps the poem was satiric light verse by Clive James) be disposed to give it the time of day. That seems to me to be not only a pity but one of the reasons why the restraints and limitations that have been felt to mar contemporary English poetry have a very important connection with the economics of publishing: why, that is, the business of poetry is being very largely regulated by the poetry business.

GRANTA

PER GEDIN
A HAND MADE ART

Per Gedin

John Sutherland's new book, *The Bestsellers**, is important for the subject it addresses. It is, however, disappointing for its insistent failure to complete the task it has taken on. It is curious, for instance, that by the end of Sutherland's examination we do not really have a clear idea of what he was examining: we cannot even be sure of what Sutherland believes constitutes the 'best-seller', a confusion aggravated by the various definitions offered at different points in his discussion, even though each is ultimately dismissed ('It is clearly unwise to be artificially precise'). A vague distinction is made between the literary novel and the best-selling one, but, after that, no further distinctions are developed—or from another point of view—*nothing but distinctions are developed*, making up an endless catalogue of nearly every blockbuster (mostly American) of the last ten years: the new westerns, the escapist fantasies, the holocausts fictions, the women novels, and, most dominant, the frighteners.

Sutherland's book is, really, an extended descriptive bibliography, and while I admire his perseverance—the number of books he has volunteered to read is truly staggering—I cannot take his 'study' seriously. His book, however, *is* important, but not actually for what it accomplishes, which is negligible, but for its occasion. The subject, the phenomenon of the best-seller, is indeed worthy of examination.

As early as 1700 Daniel Defoe had sold 80,000 copies of his verse pamphlet in support of William of Orange, and throughout the nineteenth century to be an established author—Dickens, Scott, Dumas, Eugéne Sue—meant to be a best-selling one: that is, with sales of around 50,000 for each novel published. The term *best-seller* first surfaced at the end of the nineteenth century, however, in the American trade journal *Publisher's Weekly* (a New York bookseller having asked a newsagent for his 'best-selling books'). It is appropriate, of course, that the *best-seller*, as a trade phrase, should originate in the United States, just as it is also appropriate that the best-seller list should originate there as well, the first one appearing in

---

*John Sutherland's *Bestsellers* (£8.95 ISBN 07100-0750-7) is published by Routledge and Kegan Paul.

the *Bookman* in 1885 and in *Publisher's Weekly* twenty-three years later: publishing has always been more aggressive and market-orientated in the United States than in either England or Europe.

The best-seller, I am suggesting, is as old as publishing, and, in fact, there is much about the way hardback fiction is sold that has changed very little in its history. Two features, for instance, have emerged as fairly constant characteristics. First, the very big selling novels are invariably international successes. If a British best-seller list had existed—and as yet there is still no reliable one—it would have included most of the titles on the American list, and the same would have been the case in France or Germany of Scandinavia. Second, the actual number of sales of hardback fiction has, throughout the entire history of publishing, changed very little, despite changes in education, technology, and marketing. Sienkiewicz's *Quo Vadis* sold, in 1897, 300,000 copies, and twenty years later, H. G. Wells's *Mr Britling* sold only 50,000 more. Analogously, in 1959, the two international big successes—Pasternak's *Doctor Zhivago* and Leon Uris's *Exodus*—both sold 400,000.

Since 1959, however, hardcover fiction has encountered nothing but trouble. What has changed is not so much the novel as the marketplace in which it must establish its identity. Hardcover fiction is threatened by a number of factors, the first of which is simply overproduction—specifically the overproduction of non-fiction books in numbers so vast and subjects so diversified as to crowd fiction virtually out of the bookshops. The sheer output of books over the course of the last two decades has expanded enormously. Curtis Benjamin, in 'The Weaving of a Tangled Economic Web' (*Publisher's Weekly*, April 24, 1981), points out that the output of what he describes as the 'practical and professional books' has exploded, quadrupling in the last twenty years, while the literary books—novels, biographies, memoirs—unquestionably the dominant category before the war, has not even doubled during the same period. Literary books, at one time the books that sold best, now occupy a distinctly secondary position: statistically, non-fiction has emerged as the commercially more reliable venture, sustaining a longer shelf life than fiction (of the twenty-one books to have sold more than three million, only three are novels; and, among the non-fiction titles, seven are cookbooks), and often selling many times more (Elia Kazan's *The Arrangement*, for instance, which, with 200,000 copies sold or what is roughly average for best-selling fiction, was the most successful novel in 1967, but compares badly with William Manchester's book of the same year, *Death of a President*, one of the first big non-fiction sellers, with an unprecedented half-million sales). 'The day of the big best-selling hardcover novel,' Alice Payne-Heckett argues in *Eighty Years of Best-Sellers*, 'seems to be waning. The hardcover book that attains bestsellerdom today is one that requires a hard cover for practical purposes—a cook book, a juvenile or a reference book.'

The new importance of the non-fiction book coincides with a more important development in publishing, the determination to produce, and be sustained by, the *blockbuster*. Today, the best-selling book takes up more of a publisher's budget than at any other time in publishing history—not only in fees to authors, but, more importantly, in its marketing and promotion. The restructuring of the publisher's budget has predictable and self-perpetuating results: minor writers or serious-but-not-especially-well-selling authors are promoted less or not at all or—far worse but increasingly more common—not published in the first place. The pressure to produce the best-seller calls for a greater concentration around fewer and fewer books. 'Our top ten selling titles,' French publisher Robert Laffont wrote recently in the *Bookseller*, 'used to account for only a small percentage of our turnover, but the percentage is rising rapidly, while other titles are selling less and less well. This concentration is very dangerous for the future of the book trade' (March 7, 1981).

This new kind of 'planned' best-seller invariably influences every other form of book production, most notably that of the book selling. Booksellers, having to deal with the problems of space, profitability, and, most recently, the restraints resulting from recession, are attracted to the commercial successes, but—with more 'big' books pushed more aggressively than ever before—most booksellers have ended up neglecting the majority of books produced. This new merchandising of the book is evident in the FNAC chain in France or in W. H. Smith in Britain, but especially among the retailers, chains, and book clubs of the United States. The most illustrative instance is in the American B. Dalton bookseller, which, having begun with one shop in 1966 in a suburban shopping centre in a midwestern town, now dominates American bookselling with over five hundred shops across the country, and plan to establish eight hundred by 1983. The Dalton chain buys books in large quantities, arranges them prominently, strategically (at awkward, impassable angles in shop entrances, for instance), and consistently, to insure maximum exposure and maximum possible sales. The Dalton chain also compiles its own best-sellers list, unique not as a list of the books that are selling, but as a list of those which the management has decided *should* sell. Sales are tallied through computer cash-registers which, concurrent with recording the total of the purchase, also reorder more copies of the more popular books to be positioned, once again, in their sale-winning shop space. Thomas Whiteside, writing of current publishing in the United States for the *New Yorker* last year, noted the importance the big chains have assumed, exercising an influence over not merely what gets sold but what actually gets published: 'The B. Dalton organization, in particular,' Whiteside observes, 'seems to represent a certain initiating force in the big-book business as well as an effective selling force. What the B. Dalton people indicate that they think about a book at the proof-bound stage, prior to publication, or even earlier than that, can have a considerable effect on its fortunes after publication, and their opinions are eagerly sought after within the publishing industry. A pale-green printed memorandum called the B. Dalton Merchandise Bulletin, which is prepared by Kay Sexton, a B. Dalton vice-president, and sent out weekly at all B. Dalton stores, and also to most publishers, is closely studied at trade-publishing houses, hardcover or paperback, and has become one of the most influential publications in the entire book-publishing business.' It is, of course, not particularly surprising that literary merit plays little, if any, part in what books are selected for promotion. 'We're not going to make George Gissing fans out of people,' one bookshop executive mentioned. 'We're massmerchandising the product' (September 29, 1980).[1]

Amid these developments, the hardback publisher still sustains an interest in fiction, but the interest has changed in important ways.

---

[1]Peter Whiteside's articles have been collected into a book, *The Blockbuster Complex*, to be published this autumn by Wesleyan University Press.

Publishers seem more and more to be moving away from the reading public, for which books are (presumably) written, to other publishers—who, through the purchase of reprint rights, represent a more immediate, and a more lucrative, source of income than the actual individual purchasers of novels. Until recently, the original hardback publisher got fifty percent of an author's income through subsidiary rights, and, while publishers get significantly less today, this income nevertheless constistutes the main means of survival for the publisher of general and literary books. Again, Whiteside observes that the erosion of the control traditionally held by hardcover houses, and the correspondingly increased dominance of the paperback publisher, has tended to make the hardback houses more dependent than ever on revenues from rights: 'Winthrop Knowlton, the chairman and chief executive officer of Harper & Row, which is the tenth largest book publisher in the country, said that in 1977 Harper & Row's trade-book department had earned six hundred thousand dollars, after taxes, from hardcover sales and eight hundred thousand dollars from subsidiary rights. Knowlton's statement conveyed the clear implication that if the subsidiary rights income of Harper and Row's trade-book department had fallen off substantially that year, the company's trade-book business as a whole would have been operating at a loss. And Roger W. Straus, Jr., the president of Farrar, Straus & Giroux, and the most vocal spokesman concerning the independent publisher's situation, has declared that his company "would be destitute without subsidiary rights income."'

Paperback publishers are, predictably, not entirely happy with the current economic arrangement. Since 1935, when Allen Lane was established in Britain, and 1939, when Pocket Books was established in the United States, paperback publishing has unquestionably dominated publishing. In 1979, for instance, sixty-eight percent of the total volume of books sold in the United States were paperbacks (although, significantly, they constituted only thirty-four percent of the sales value). Nevertheless, paperback publishing has relied, for its titles, upon what the hardback houses publish, a financial relationship that is proving to be, as Oscar Dystel recently pointed out in *Publisher's Weekly* ('Mass Market Publishing: More Observations, Speculations, and Provocations', December 12, 1980), a tremendous strain on an industry notoriously plagued with problems of over-production and over-payment. The relationship cannot endure forever: 'We have bankrolled hardcover publishing too long, and I believe the trip is about over,' a sentiment, while expressed by only one mass market publisher, is certainly representative of most. The prognostication makes a great deal of sense—why should mass paperback publishing 'bankroll' hardback houses?—until you realize its implications. Mass market paperback publishers have, more than any other agency, orchestrated the current obsession with the best-seller, concentrating fewer and fewer titles to sell in increasingly larger editions. Among the ten best-selling fiction titles of the last eighty years, *seven* were published in the seventies alone—surely the decade to be remembered for the major developments in the mass marketing and mass merchandising of fiction—led in sales by the *Godfather* (twelve million copies) and in a paid advance by *Princess Daisy* (earning Judith Krantz 3.2 million dollars before her book was completed). (Big money advances, big money promotion, and big money books also threaten to become big money losses: in the case of Judith Krantz, who will get twenty-five cents on every copy of her book sold, her publisher will have to sell thirteen million copies in order to retrieve his advance.)

As much of this discussion assumes, the most important questions of publishing today are questions of economic control. Best-seller publishing— as the *Godfather* and *Princess Daisy* adequately illustrate—presupposes financial strength and access to the mass media. Best-seller publishing, that is, cannot be sustained by the small houses, and it is noteworthy that the major changes in the shape of the publishing industry over the course of the last two decades have occurred at the level of management. In the United States, Britain, France, Germany, and Sweden as well, most of the medium-sized and small publishing houses have been purchased by large corporations. The old family firms have disappeared, merging with conglomerates, or, more disconcerting, have sunk without trace, into the City, Wall Street, and the big business of the big media of television and film.

Part of these management changes results directly from the pressure to produce a best-seller, requiring—for an author's advance and book production and promotion—far more capital than most independent publishing firms possess. The changes are, however,

119

again, self-perpetuating: the returns of best-sellers must be utilized for investment in future best-sellers, a very different principle from what has traditionally characterized publishing, in which the returns from best-sellers were used to support and cultivate young talent. Publishing, now dominated by accountants and economists, is run on a set of values very different from those at any other point in its history.

The most extraordinary expression of this shift was in the recent revival of James Bond, where an author was pressed by the corporation into shaping a corporation 'product'. As John Gardner, the new 'author', said recently in the *Sunday Times* 'The Board of Glidrose Limited, the subsidiary of Booker McDonnell which owns the literary copyright of the character of James Bond . . . imposed definite guidelines. They wanted Bond lifted, from where Ian Fleming had so untimely left him in the sixties, straight into the eighties—age not having wearied him nor the years condemned' (May 17, 1981). Gardner, unashamed, goes on to outline the changes that were deemed appropriate, providing us with a Bond who drives a Saab Turbo instead of the Bentley; who has replaced his Turkish cigarettes with a low tar variety; who abstains from dry Martinis, but indulges in the occasional champagne; who spends money with more care, aware of the problems of inflation; and who, sensitive to the injunctions against sexism, aspires to be nothing more than a 'gentleman'. There is, of course, historical precedent for this reversal of the traditional relationship between an author's work and the marketplace. An analogous pressure occasioned the return of Sherlock Holmes. And as one contemporary observed of Walter Scott: 'In his stories the public got the upper hand of the novelist and it has kept its advantage, with a few setbacks, ever since' (cited in Royal A. Getmann's *A Victorian Publisher: A Study of the Bentley Papers*). And we could make similar observations of Richardson or Dickens or even Henry James. What has changed, however, is not an author's vulnerability to being influenced, but the source from which those influences originate: not among his readers, but his bankers.

The most alarming aspect of this shift is evident in the relationship between the book and the media. Now the deals transpire before publication, before composition, and, often, before complete conception, excluding not merely the reading public but also—for much of the discussion—the author as well. Whiteside, for whom one Californian executive described the new style of multimedia deal as 'the spontaneous generation of a literary property', was outlined a fairly representative transaction by George Diskant, a partner in the literary agency of Ziegler, Diskant. The deal involved Diskant; George Englund, an independent producer; Paul Erdman, an author; a film director; the hardcover house Simon & Schuster; and the paperback house Pocket books. The outline deserves to be quoted in full:

> George Englund approached us with an idea. Englund is very close to Clifford Perlman, the chairman of Caesars World [in Las Vegas]. Englund saw him as a great background source for a motion picture about the gambling phenomenon in this country ... Englund wanted to discuss with us the possibility of developing a motion picture on this subject. Englund had no beginning, no middle, and no end for the movie, and he had no characters. He had an idea, and he figured that his relationship with Cliff Perlman would provide him with top-level access to the gambling scene all around the country. We thought the idea had great possibilities. A few days later, taking things a step farther, we put Englund in touch with Paul Erdman as a possible writer—after we had explained to Erdman what it was all about. Erdman loved the idea .... Then, early in 1978, I called up Dick Snyder of Simon & Schuster, who's Erdman's publisher .... I said 'We've got the producer; I want to get an important director involved, and an important writer. I want this to start with a book. I want to have it published even before the screenplay might be completed. I want the book to be a publishing event on its own. I've got the author to agree to consult with the screenwriter while the book is being written .... After a few months, on the basis of conversations between Dick and me, and Erdman's outlines, Dick agreed to publish the book under our terms. In June of 1978, Simon & Schuster agreed to seven-figure advance—a *hard* seven figure advance.
>
> (*New Yorker*, October 6, 1980)

Thus: *Atlantic City*, available all over the world, as a hardback, a paperback, and, most recently, a film.

The position the book occupies in today's society necessarily represents the values of that society. And the society in which literature must now fight for its way is a consumer society, dominated by an enveloping mass media organized to dictate our tastes and our purchasing habits. It is impossible to separate literature from the industry producing it, and the industry producing it today has very little room to accommodate literature.

The traditional book trade is changing in important ways. Instead of a uniform sale to a relatively limited class of book buyers with a steady demand for many books—as characterized the nineteenth and early twentieth century trade, for instance—we now are witnessing the mass media influenced demand for *one* book. It does not require a restricted number of widely spread, well-stocked bookshops to fulfill this need, but rather a vast number of sales outlets stocked with just this book. The traditional, middle-class trade bookshop—with its expensively maintained sevices, trade knowledge, and stockholding, protected by fixed book prices and the limitations on establishing new shops—is now in declining need. The purchase of books over a broad spectrum of subjects is no longer the pattern of a specific social class but merely the requirement of a few enthusiasts, much the same as modelling hobbies or stamp collecting. In the future, we can also count on booksellers having similar types of shops—specialist shops for poetry or drama or Eastern European literature or simply serious fiction—which will replace bookshops that carry a wide assortment of books. It seems unlikely there will be many; in a mass market system they will represent a greatly reduced demand.

In the nineteenth century, the literary critic was an arbitrator of taste, a guide, radical or conservative, a George Brandes or a Sainte-Beuve, exercising a measureable influence upon a homogeneous book-buying public. It was not without reason that Sainte-Beuve was called 'The Emperor'. The critic today, whose influence has contracted to the extent that it is impossible to measure what influence, *if any*, he exercises upon any public—seems only to address his peers: his colleagues of writers and fellow critics. The real audience of today is a mass audience, accessible only through the mass media.

The true critics of today are not individual writers but various and assorted boards of managers and directors. National television, movies, the daily newspapers, the book-clubs: they determine what we have the opportunity to read. And they are in the position of doing so by concentrating on a few books—in the current vocabulary, on the books that *move*—with the result that fewer and fewer books are bought by increasingly more people. Thus, the polarization characteristic of the book trade in virtually every country of the world: there are the big best-sellers—and they are very big—and there are the *others*, that rarely even earn back the money put forward to pay for their production.

Fiction no longer occupies the central position in our culture that it once did. Nevertheless, it is an irreplaceable part of it. But the novel can only survive and flourish with a reasonably broad offering, if it is to reach its public in a natural way. To keep it from being isolated it must be given powerful support by society. From my vantage place, I see the battle of the eighties as one fought between artificial products—super-promoted by the conglomerate publishers—and the old fashioned well-written story. I know what side needs support and what side I will be fighting on.

There is not one literary novel among the top ten best-sellers of the last decade. Nevertheless, there have been a number of extremely good selling *good* literary books. They are being written; they are engaging; they are well-crafted; and they are the most important things around. The wise publisher who wants to save his big money should look out for real literary talent as the best, serious investment for the future.

GRANTA

ERIC BURNS
PUBLISHING IN AMERICA:
AN INTERVIEW WITH
DAVID GODINE

David R. Godine is a respected, adventurous, out-spoken publisher and a *soi-disant* cultural elitist. On a staff of ten, he runs his small and surprisingly successful, young house—David R. Godine Press—from the basement of a shabby genteel, back-bay Boston mansion, organized, as he puts it, as a 'participatory dictatorship'. Since Godine set up shop ten years ago on family capital, the annual list has grown to forty titles—or what one journalist recently described as .0001 per cent of America's annually published books. But what sets the Godine fraction apart from most others is his unflinching commitment to the highest standards, with respect to content *and* production.

In a publishing era plagued by conglomerate financing, increasing bureaucratic specialization, high-rolling agents, pre-fabricated best-sellers, seven-figure advances, the media 'blitz', and paperbacks that fall apart in one reading, the Godine Press is something of an anomaly. Godine's house is independent and small—in size though not in scope—and essentially intends to stay that way. Hating agents and avoiding big money promotion, Godine relies instead on the intrinsic quality of his books, good and prominent reviews, word-of-mouth advertising, and a healthy relationship with a range of bookshops that regularly stand by him. His books, some of the few in the country to carry a colophon, reveal a meticulous attention to the quality of paper (invariably acid-free), bindings (always sewn, even on the paperbacks), type-face, type-setting and design. The care taken with production shows too in the judiciously selected and deliberately eclectic range of books he publishes—art, photography, chap-books, history, fiction, and inexpensive, hardbound editions of poetry. How he has managed this hat-trick—quality content, quality production, *and* increasing market acceptability during a recession—is something of a mystery. With the mannered cultivation of the theatrically iconoclastic, Godine offers his own explanation: 'I'll tell you a well-kept secret in publishing. If you publish good books and keep your expectations within the bounds of reality and run a fairly tight ship, you're going to make money—there's no way not to. But if you build a house of trash, some day it will burn.'

This kind of go-ahead prescription doesn't account for how Godine has succeeded so much as it simply reiterates the fact that he has done so. But the aggressiveness and bluntness reveal more than they say. Godine is a master of the re-tooled cliché, the pithy and promotional aphorism, which shows in his glib—and sometimes meretricious—desire to surprise. Taking aim at one of his *bêtes noires*—technology and its deleterious effects on the aesthetics of publishing—Godine will say: 'One of the prime rules of life is that as technology improves, aesthetics deteriorates. Speed substitutes for quality. Invention is the mother of problems.' Part of the secret of Godine's success is his straight-forward self-promotion and disarming conceit.

But part of it too is his anachronistic commitment to the nuts and bolts of his trade. Godine studied typography at Dartmouth, bibliography at Oxford, and print-making with the artist Leonard Baskin, and since his teens has been a devoted collector of fine books, passionate about the refinements in production and design. This background and an almost renaissance affection for the art of printing (indeed Godine believes that 'the most glorious books ever produced were produced in France between 1520 and 1550' in monotype) show as much in the books Godine publishes as in their peerless quality. The current list includes two works on calligraphy *and* the classical alphabets alone, and the writers and artists to whom Godine is typically attracted demonstrate the same cultivated attitude toward their craft as Godine himself, whether it be William Gass's conscientious love of words or Jill Krementz's rigorous respect for the photographic image. Put these two together—the arrogant pushiness of Madison Avenue and the old world commitment to quality—and you have something of the secret of Godine's success.

Nevertheless, Godine's bullish iconoclasm shatters even the conventional image of the iconoclast. Talking with him the other day overlooking Grand Central Station from the potted-palm lounge of the New York City Yale Club, it was clear that if the Godine Press offers any kind of alternative to the commercial quagmire of most publishing today, it's still no simple question of David versus Goliath.

Eric Burns

Granta: In the American book business, the David Godine Press has a reputation as a serious, quality publisher providing an alternative to a trade characterized by a variety of ills. Nevertheless, looking over your list, it's difficult to see what makes Godine special. You publish little fiction, for instance, and fiction, especially the literary novel, is in more trouble than any other kind of book today. If the Godine Press is doing so few novels, how can anyone claim that it is satisfying any of the current needs in publishing?

Godine: We don't pretend to be and we never claimed that we were. We satisfy other needs. For serious criticism, where we publish Sullivan, Gass, and Nemerov. For serious books of photography, art, and history. For serious books for children. Children's publishing, for example, has traditionally aimed at the lowest common denominator; we try for the highest (a child is not going to read Dylan Thomas for fun; but you might read it to your children for fun because it's more fun for you to read Thomas than googa). Also we satisfy a need for serious books from other countries: we do a great many translations. In the current spring list, we have a six hundred page novel by Ernesto Sabato that cost $8,000 just to translate. I think it's terrific and hope it gets a front page review. But that's a risk: the kind of risk you take with a serious, eclectic list; not the kind of risk you take with a list consisting of books about duck decoys and Martha's Vineyard.

Your question, though, puts an intellectual premium on people who write novels as opposed to people who paint or take pictures or write non-fiction, criticism, or poetry. There are always creators. That a novelist may or may not be getting hurt in the squeeze speaks more for the condition of the culture and what book buyers are willing to pay for than it does for a lack or principles within the publishing trade. It's like blaming the thermometer for the temperature.

As for fiction, Aharon Appelfeld (*Badenheim 1939*) is our

boy along with Benedict Kiely and William Gass. But we don't publish much fiction.

Granta: **Why?**

Godine: Because you have to pay too much for fiction. Because it's risky. Because it's the last thing a small publisher should get into. And it's the last thing a small publisher should get into mainly because of the agent. What distinguishes publishing today from what it was thirty, forty, or fifty years ago is the presence of the agent. We deal with agents but only because of the interest we might already have in an author who happens to have an agent and basically says, 'Listen, I want to do this book with Godine, make the best deal you can.' That is not the same as saying, 'I have to have $10,000 or no deal.'

Large publishers today have no control. They have no control over their main asset—their authors— because their authors don't belong to them. They belong to agents. If the publishing house does a book poorly, the asset leaves. If it does the job well, the asset triples the asking price. The average trade publisher is rewarded only for mediocrity, not so bad the author's agent tells the author to leave, not so good they've created a star. God help anyone who relies on agents.

Granta: **What do you think, then, of the argument that fiction is suffering because of the overall state of the publishing industry?**

Godine: I think that's horseshit. The kind of anxious questions being batted around the publishing world about the 'state of fiction' are really non-questions. Good fiction like bad fiction will continue to be published. If a Joseph Conrad or a William Faulkner or a Norman Mailer were out there he'd be published by a respectable press. There's no dearth of good writing, and publishers are neither so venal nor so stupid nor so short-sighted that they're not going to snap up the next John Irving. We're a small house and we must get in 90 manuscripts a week, of which maybe 89.7 are absolutely worthless. I mean, one weeps for the trees, they're that bad.

Granta: **Sure, good fiction is getting published. But as only one, relatively constant item in lists which increase year after year, isn't there more than enough evidence of its neglect?**

Godine: It's possible that an argument can be made that fewer first novels are published. But maybe that's because there are more second and third novels published. On the other hand, look at Knopf publishing 17 new novels, and that, while not typical, is a staggering number.

What is changing is the profile of the industry: the powerhouses are disappearing. Godine is not pre-eminent in its commitment to the novel, but we publish more good novels than Scribners. And that is absolutely amazing: thirty or forty years ago, Scribners was publishing every fiction writer of any consequence in the country. The house was without a rival, and could get anyone it wanted. Now, its influence is negligible.

Unfortunately, Scribners is not an exception. There are a great many publishers who, from the position of doing good fiction with good design and good editors, now publish so poorly and so diffidently that they print books in numbers of 2,500 after which they disappear. We're not so good, *really*; it's only that everyone else is so bad. We stand out not by virtue of our excellence but because there are fewer and fewer houses publishing well than there were twenty or thirty years ago.

Granta: **What did you have in mind when you said recently that 'emotionally and financially small houses struggle, but our existence is essential to readers'?**

Godine: I suppose our existence could be seen as essential to readers because it is essential to writers. It's different for an author to work with a house like Godine from even a good house like Random House.

Granta: How?

Godine: It's more human. I'm personally involved with every book we produce. I can tell you the paper it's printed on and the type it's set in. I've read the text. I've edited a good deal of them. And the same is true of everyone in this house. That's not true of large houses. Robert Bernstein has not read every book that Random House publishes, let alone its subsidiaries Knopf and Pantheon. He's an administrator—a good one, I'm sure—but not someone who feels a compulsion to be personally involved in everything that goes out under his name—at least in the way that Alfred Knopf did or that Roger Straus does today.

We have the philosophy that good books make money and bad books don't. If you publish good books, realistically contain your expectations, and run a fairly tight ship, you're going to make money; there's no way not to.

And you can't subsidize good books with bad books. If you publish schlock, you inevitably produce it like schlock, and consequently it comes out looking like schlock. You can't look at a Doubleday list—even if you don't know anything about literature—and really take those books seriously, even though some of them are probably serious books: they look so terrible.

Granta: Being involved at every level of the production of a book, would you describe yourself as an autocratic publisher? Do you initiate most of the titles?

Godine: No. Bill Goodman, an editor from Harvard University Press and Harcourt, Brace, Jovanovich, originates a lot of the books. The two front page reviews we got last year in the *New York Times* were Bill Goodman books. I had nothing to do with them, except design. A lot of the children's books are done by someone else. Our publicity manager has a book. Our receptionist has a book. I think that everybody in the company, except the people in sales, should have a book that they're responsible for. I also think it's important that people here have a feeling they have a share in the operation—that's the only way to attract good people in the first place, with the escalating demands of publishing today, although I'd like to be able to pay the people who work here more. Ultimately, I want to make the company employee-owned, like Norton.

Granta: **Do you envision the Godine Press developing into a big house?**

Godine: No. The maximum number of people should be twenty or twenty-five. And then perhaps fifty to sixty really exciting books a year. Original books, not reprints. I'd be very happy with that.

Granta: **How are you reaching your market as, apart from what you set aside for direct mailing shots, you obviously don't have a massive advertising budget? Are your sales largely from reviews and word-of-mouth recommendations?**

Godine: Very much. And bookstores: they're great allies and sell our books very aggressively.

I remember one of our early annual Halloween parties in 1973. I went over to a neighbouring silo to make sure that people weren't smoking too much. It was where we stored our unsold books. That turned out to be a moment of epiphany. We were printing beautiful books and not selling them. I resolved from that moment on that I would have to find out how to be a publisher, to put it all together—editorial, sales, marketing, all the rest of it. Until then I had just been a privasher not a publisher.

To think we're out of the woods now or will be in the next five or ten years, however, is not true. Any publisher at any time can slip up. We're certainly more vulnerable than most because we have a shorter backlist; we're only less vulnerable because we employ fewer people and because our overhead is commensurately less.

But we're not stupid and we're aggressive. When you're small you have to be. You have got to go out after the Stanley Elkins of the world; they're not going to come to you. There's hardly a book in the catalogue that we didn't go out ourselves and get. And we didn't pay very much money for them because we went out and found them.

Granta: **You have an interesting 'out there' mentality towards publishing. If the market is 'out there', people will buy the book; if the talent is 'out there', you can find it. Is that the way you understand it? I sense that you don't see the Godine Press creating any particular tendency in writing or buying, or stimulating the development of a specific market, but rather just picking up the possibilities for sales that already exist 'out there'.**

Godine: I hope that as we get richer we will experiment more with our list and the way we produce it. I would like to publish a few really unusual books every year, books that test and push against the conventionally accepted limitations of the form.

I do believe, however, that we are creating, if not a particular tendency in writing or buying, a particular way of producing books. The point we are trying to make again and again is this: quality books do not necessarily cost more money to make. The extra expense is not significant and will generate, we believe, extra sales. If we have a mission, it's to make people ask for truth in labelling. When a consumer buys a book, he has nowhere near the protection he has when he buys almost everything else. Buy marmalade and it says on the jar what's in it. Buy a suit and a label says what the material is. But buy a book and you won't have a clue about the way it's made or the quality of the paper or the nature of the binding.

Granta: **There seems to a quaint, old world diletantism about producing quality books under today's economic conditions.**

Godine: No, I don't think so. I think there is a hunger for quality in books. When a book cost $2.95 or $3.95, which they did until recently, I don't think people thought too much about it. Today a big novel costs $15 or $17.50. People are thinking how many socks or groceries $17.50 would buy. At that price, they want a book to be around for their children to read. I think that if you publish Gass, for instance, you want to produce a book that will be read for twenty-five or forty or a hundred years.

Granta: **From what you say, it appears that you are not creating a market, but that a market will always exist for a quality book, in respect to its content and its production. Why, then, aren't there more houses like the Godine Press? Are you in a position significantly better than most because you are in Boston.**

Godine: We couldn't survive in New York. The overhead would be too big, and we couldn't afford the editors or the production people or the talent. I think we'd get caught up in certain Manhatten publishing trade practices that would destroy a small press like our own. On a more basic level, my energies would be diluted managing the company and our minimal resources drained lunching and dining in New York. Also, it's easier to stay away from the professional sharks in Boston, though I don't think we'd ever be dumb enough to be prey to sharks in the first place or we wouldn't be in business. There are, moreover, a number of advantages to Boston. We have direct access to a sophisticated intellectual community, with both Harvard and MIT across the river.

Granta: **Is this representative of a more general decentralization in American publishing? A trend away from New York?**

Godine: There are advantages to being away from New York. Nevertheless, it would be difficult to be a trade publisher without regular access to New York. One of us is down here virtually every day.

Most people think of us as a speciality publisher, but we probably have more books in book clubs per list than any publisher. We do a lot of first serial rights, sub-rights; we are out to squeeze seven cents out of every nickel, marketing the copyright as an asset. We couldn't survive without New York because we do all this business here. If we were in Chicago or Des Moines we would be that much further from the source of an enormous amount of our profit.

Granta: **In the past, you've expressed irritation at the suggestion that your own money keeps your press in business.**

Godine: I am not irritated by it; it is just not true. I am irritated by the suggestion that I'm not under the same necessity to make a profit as the big publishers. My personal investment in the Press is actually very modest, and the financing is arranged in such a way that I have to make up personally anything we lose, and believe me I can't afford for that to be too much. There's been no new capital investment in the company in the past two years, and the claim that we must subsidize our books to price them so low is completely unfounded: it's hogwash.

It is true, though, that I was fortunate to have had enough capital or enough access to capital to start a press at a time when one needed only a reasonable outlay.

Granta: **It would be harder today?**

Godine: I think it's very tough today. We've built up a backlist—not comparable to that of New Directions, Pantheon, or Knopf—but a respectable backlist of a hundred titles that sell fairly reasonably. To establish that kind of list today you'd have to publish for three very expensive and difficult years doing—if you could afford it—thirty books a year. And that assumes every book's a hit, and God knows they won't be.

Granta: **Are the economic conditions today preventing the emergence of new publishers?**

Godine: It's going to be very tough to enter New York trade publishing without big dollars and big backers. There are a lot of books around for people who hustle and look for them. There are good authors around with terrific projects. But you need an organization—that is, you need to carry an overhead—that can run your company while you're out sniffing around for those books. That's the real problem for the small publisher today. The small press publisher is everything: cook, bottle washer, editor, production manager, sales manager: you get so bogged down in the details that you can't see the forest for the trees.

Granta: **I'm wondering if the situation is any different in London. What do you think about the publishing situation in England?**

Godine: It's a real mess. Again we tend to blame the industry for incompetence or overexpansion. But to me the real problem in England is that people don't read. The British market—the number of people that can be relied on to buy a book—is a lot smaller than ours. Worse, the whole Commonwealth market is falling to pieces. Australia has been taken away, New Zealand has been taken away, and Canada is on its way. British publishers used to have an export market which accounted for maybe sixty per cent of an edition: now it accounts for maybe twenty: that's got to be tough.

Then there's the British typographic unions: those guys are making more money than the chief executive at Simon and Schuster. It's outrageous what they're making. And, on top of that, British publishers insist on remaining loyal enough to their 'reading public' and their country to continue printing in England, and consequently they must sell books at a price that isn't competitive on an open market. The American edition of any British book is always going to be twenty to thirty per cent cheaper. Nobody's going to buy the U.K. edition, and that's got to hurt.

We're very lucky in the U.S. right now. Our dollar buys more. Our printing, paper, and binding industries are very competitive. And we've got the raw materials: it's awesome, especially compared to England, what we can choose from in raw materials.

Granta: **Do you have many connections with British publishing?**

Godine: Yeah, too many.

Granta: **How so?**

Godine: Because they always come across being so meek and mild, and whenever we make a deal with them we always get killed. Either the pound goes up or the dollar goes down or something terrible happens. It's just not a happy situation.

Granta: **It seems, even as you talk about the problems facing British publishers, that if you have an adversary, it's technology.**

Godine: I suppose. As a cultural elitist you have mass culture as an adversary. Conglomerates dominate book publishing—just as they have dominated radio and television—and the pressure for profit they impose tends to homogenize everything: not just the effort of production but what is produced. The truly excellent is regarded with a certain amount of hostility or suspicion just by virtue of its excellence or its difference.

The recent publicity about publishing has proved, if nothing else, that anybody with a reasonable amount of intelligence and perhaps a smidgen of talent can anticipate what the market wants and will pay for. But I don't think that most writers, successful or unsuccessful, really write for the market. I can't imagine Norman Mailer changing his style because he thought it would sell more copies of his book.

But, you're right, the more basic problem is simply technology. The most glorious books ever produced were produced in France between 1520 and 1550. In no other period have books been so exquisitely illustrated and made in terms of the typography, the quality of the paper, and the inventiveness of the binding. The art of printing was perfected in the 1500s and has gone steadily downhill since. Computer typesetting, for example, is no step forward over the linotype, and the linotype is no step forward over the monotype, and the monotype was basically a fast way to do hand setting. I don't believe in old techniques just for the sake of their being old, but the fact is that you look at a typeface set in linotype and compare it to the same face set in a computer system there is a world of difference in the character of the letters, the shape of the letters, the quality of the letters, and all the niceties that make for decent typography.

You can witness in Harper and Row and so many other houses like it a terrific deterioration of standards. It's not necessarily because less money per book is spent or that the cost of the material as it relates to the price of the book has increased. It's merely that what is available to a publisher today is so much more inferior to what was available twenty and thirty years ago, in respect to the reproducing technology and the people using it. One of the prime rules of our life is that as technology improves, aesthetics deteriorate.

Personally I'd love to go back to monotype if it were feasible. I'd love to. It was the best system of manufacturing, fitting, and designing letters—ever.

Granta: **What kind of future do you foresee for publishing?**

Godine: The number of people who care about books, who care about words, is declining. Publishers are professional optimists. They work in a shrinking market and it has been shrinking for five years. It's a problem of education. I think the education in this country is at the point of breaking down, or at least not fulfilling the kind of rational expectation placed upon it in the past. The home and the society no longer regard basic literary values as important. They were very important during the immigrant waves of the 1890s through the 1920s when every Jew and Italian and Irish kid learned to read and write because it was like a gift. Today, becoming educated is looked on as a chore.

Granta: **What kind of future do you foresee for the Godine Press? Can you imagine your list changing significantly?**

Godine: Each list is so different it's hard to say. We publish many illustrated and expensive books so I hope the economy holds up. I think things in this country are going to get worse and then they're going to get better. I think they're going to get better in late 1982, both the economy and publishing, and Reagan will have something to do with that.

As for our future, I'm really excited about a book we're doing now on architecture by William Eisman for which William Gass has written the text. It's going to be dynamite. It's an adventurous book designed like a house and is

139

virtually unreadable: it's printed in modules of 13, with a reflecting milar centre-piece, and has to be tipped over just to get to the text. It's going to be a very difficult book to bring off, and I hope to keep the price down to $15 or $20. We'll do it by printing 10,000, and floating it initially on the reputation of Gass, and on the fact that it will really be an interesting object as a book.

GRANTA

WALTER ABISH
BUT WHY WRITE?
THE WRITER-TO-BE

Walter Abish

For Uri Felix Rosenheim with gratitude

That very curious enterprise: writing. How does one explain that desire to write? How does one explain that sudden intrusion in one's life of that singular resolve to become a writer, someone who passes his or her days in a self-imposed isolation concocting a fictitious world peopled by fictitious characters. Albeit, a fiction that continuously forces its lifelikeness and verisimilitude upon the reader, regardless of the fact that these fictitious accounts and characters may or may not have been based on actual events and people.

Why write?

How to explain this resolve to write, this firm unwavering intent to become a writer on the part of someone who may not even really care for books or, for that matter, read many books, or buy books, or collect books.

The term 'writer', a by now all encompassing, frequently maligned, frequently misused, frequently misapplied term that also denotes a profession, a person, male or female, who earns or at the very least attempts to earn his or her living as a writer, stands as an enticing objective for the writer-to-be. For the time being the word 'writer' remains just outside his or her reach since it represents, at the very least, a level of achievement; perhaps, because it remains out of reach, the term is invested with a richness, an authority, and a mystique to which countless poets and writers have—intentionally or not—added layers of meaning, often false, often misleading. It's all there in the diaries, the journals, the self-portraits, the candid and less than candid confessions, the biographies, the letters, the essays, even down to the accounts of the specialists of the psyche, the undertakers of the trade: the psychiatrists and psychologists.

From the start does the writer-to-be understand that his enterprise is in the nature of a quest, really a romantic quest for a number of interrelated things: (1) his text-to-be; (2) the idea as well as the material for the text; (3) his resolve to emulate and follow in the footsteps of the legendary heroes of writing: Hemingway, Miller, Thomas Wolfe,

Mailer, Kerouac, etc.; (4) and finally the quest for meaning. I mean by that the ontological search for an answer to the question: Why am I *I*, here, writing, thinking? This idealized vision of a quest is closely related to that pursuit of knowledge described in such *minute* detail in Somerset Maugham's novel *The Razor's Edge* in which the protagonist Larry Darrell, a former WWI fighter pilot, loses (or sacrifices?) the woman he loves in his determined quest, this mythic search for the truth. Evidently for Maugham, as for the credulous reader, Larry's studies at the Sorbonne in the many libraries (we are presented with an impressive list of books Larry has been reading), and finally his spiritual 'immersion' in India, the place to where so many quests lead, and where Larry stayed in the company of a Guru, is taken to designate the logical stages (or steps?) in this search for knowledge, for understanding, for self-fulfillment, and for—in Larry's words—inner purity. Upon returning from his pilgrimage in India, Larry resolves to settle in New York City where he, quixotically, intends to become a cab driver (perhaps one of the more democratic aspects of this ontological quest for self-hood) and spend his free time at the 42nd Street Public Library. While still in France, just prior to his return to America, Larry had published a book of essays on Goethe, Rubens, Lord Chesterfield, the dictator Sulla, and the Mogul conqueror Akbar: all men, to quote Maugham, who made a 'supreme success of life'. Although the self-publication of this book may entitle Larry to be considered a writer or, at the very least, a writer-to-be, he is in fact neither: he is and remains a prototype, a romantic paradigm for the writer-to-be. Albeit, in Maugham's novel Larry is made to resemble a rather saintly shepherd in search of a flock; is he not also, in embracing the world of books in his quest for meaning and self-fulfillment, confirming the priorities of the writer-to-be for whom the book-to-be is both a text as well as a prescription for the journey of self-discovery?

How rational is this decision to write? How applicable to the task set for himself by the writer-to-be is the Guru's dictum: 'One knows, perceives, understands that by which everything is known, perceived, and understood'?

When did I first think of becoming a writer?

143

For the writer the parade of words—initially a triumphant parade—represents a kind of welcome unburdening or emptying of the brain's images. What is the writer-to-be looking for when he examines and re-examines his own work—at least what there is of it? Does he optimistically scrutinize the text for evidence of his ability to write? Does he view it as a first step to a self-attainment, a self-fulfillment, a task that must also take into consideration the possibility of a 'heroic' risk of failure, a risk that is after all part of the undertaking? But can there be any doubt that there is also a certain undeniable satisfaction to be derived from simply covering page after page with words. Just that in itself is an achievement, a triumph. For doesn't it indicate the initial unfolding of what promises to become the new experience, the new understanding.

Is there an intrinsic process or procedure to writing poetry or fiction?

There are moments in the life of the writer-to-be when what he has written seems to call for a special attention because it bears what appears to him to be the overwhelming promise of truth and originality. Dare he believe it that no one before him has had the perception to make his observations? What catches his eye may be nothing more than the following: 'The headlights of the oncoming black Pontiac were ablaze like a challenge in the bright afternoon sun of that hot sultry summer's day as he stood on the sidewalk hypnotically staring at the bright twin lights, as the car abruptly pulled up in front of the building and four men wearing identical black hats stepped out.' Is it possible that the writer-to-be, identifying himself with the nameless narrator, the familiar 'he' of fiction, clings to the sinister promise of the word 'blazing'? But what next? Should the writer-to-be introduce the protesting burnt rubber squeal of the front tire as it was squeezed in an unwelcome union against the hard cement edge of the pavement?

In a sense, the text is the writer's skin—the outermost delineation of his sensibility, his way of expressing, remembering, and furiously rendering what he believes to be the exactitude of his feelings. As the pages pile up they are numbered and renumbered, typed and retyped, they are inserted in folders, placed in binders, set on desk tops, placed in desk drawers and carried around in plastic briefcases and mailed in manila envelopes. These pages are an extension of the writer's nervous system, and his fingerprints on the pages testify to this nervous proximity, this incestuous intimacy to the text or, to be more precise, to the text-to-be.

But why write?

The writer-to-be lives under the impression that everything, literally everything he experiences can be accurately transferred onto paper (the allusion to photography is intentional) and, what is more, elucidated and enriched. He still believes that for everything under the sun there is a corresponding sign or word, and that the intensity of his ardour, his passion for life, will impress upon the pages the determination of his new commitment. If for the present the words with which he attempts to depict the preciseness of his vision continue to elude him, can he not expect that with time, with a certain practice, this will be rectified.

Is what I write really true?

The writer-to-be lives in a dream-like state, and remains content as long as this buoyant state of expectation is not directly threatened, thwarted, or shattered; in essence, though he need not be aware of it, the writer-to-be is establishing a zone of vulnerability: a kind of defensive perimeter for his new persona.

Impelled or driven by an anthropocentric concern, the writer-to-be entertains the expectation that in time the text-to-be will yield an explanation, and will spell out that as yet elusive equation for his own existence. Consequently, is it far-fetched to maintain that for the writer-to-be the inescapable assumption of: 'I write therefore I am' has as much, if not more, veracity as the Cartesian claim 'I think therefore I am'?

For the writer-to-be the rituals of writing, the concern for his text-to-be, is largely free of the always menacing and oppressive conditions of the reality principle. For the time being the ego-deflating encounters

145

with the publishing world can still be postponed. Is it possible that, initially, the writer-to-be does not feel the necessity to struggle over his text as much as he sees a need to accommodate himself to the reality of his persona and the obligations that are a result of this new critical and censorious self?

That very curious enterprise: writing. Isn't it an almost unreal, chimerical, and evanescent enterprise?

The writer-to-be experiences a desire, a craving to write. Why? Does this desire presuppose the absence of some vital element in the writer's life? Does writing become a surrogate for what would otherwise remain out of reach for the writer? A substitute for something unattainable?

But, in so far as this intent to write is serious, what makes the writer so certain that he or she is cut out for this monastic existence? Is it, as the bookjacket of Maugham's popular novel *The Razor's Edge* announces: a search for a faith? A peripatetic search inflamed by a vivid imagination, a refined sensibility, and a passionate love for literature? Yet, the decision to become a writer—hardly a rational decision—is not predicated on one's aptitude as a writer. Just the intense earnest desire to become a writer is sufficient reason to convince the writer-to-be—inasmuch as he needs to be convinced—of the veracity of his undertaking. But how does this desire differ, for instance, from someone's longing to become an actor? Or does the solitary nature of the writer's occupation permit and even encourage a quantitatively greater self-delusion? For the writer-to-be can forever postpone the test of publication and, as a result, forever cling to his identity as a writer. I've met unpublished writers who, in late middle age, continue to hold on with an obdurate determination to the mystique of the writer and inhabit, or so it seems, that state of youthful timelessness, so peculiar to the writer-to-be. Do they also retain that euphoric naïveté, that optimism of the young writer? For *it* may still happen as *it* has happened to others. Recognition, acceptance, fame may arrive belatedly. One can never tell. In most instances, I think, the elderly writer might gladly give up the burden of his expectation, might gladly give up writing, if this did not also entail the surrender of an integral part of the self.

Years ago, while vacationing in the Carribean, I met an ex-New Yorker who with his family had settled there in the fifties; a middle aged man, he diligently wrote for several hours each day and then in the evening, according to one of his friends, burned what he had written. I assume by continuing to write he kept a certain meaning alive and by destroying his text he was rebelliously, whether consciously or not, affirming a self-destructive affinity with Rimbaud, who had ceased to write at nineteen, and with Kafka, who in his conversations with Janouch, stated: 'Personal proofs of my human weaknesses are printed, and even sold, because my friends, with Max Brod at their head, have conceived the idea of making literature of them, and because I have not the strength to destroy this evidence of solitude.'[1] Kafka's request that after his death Max Brod was to destroy his three unpublished novels is a matter of record. That this request was not intended to be taken at face value is another matter. The man I met in the Carribean lived with his wife and children in a beautiful house he had designed. But when I visited it, the Edenic setting upon which he had exercised so much care and attention had begun to show serious signs of age and neglect. It was the 'tropical' paradise occupied by a man who could have stepped out of a novel by Conrad or Evelyn Waugh, the exile, the man who could not drive himself past a few pages; the man who continued with great perspicacity to cling to his role as a writer, and for whom the ritual of writing had become irreversably linked to the ritual of destruction, a self-purging. But is it possible that I am misreading his resolve to write? Is it Conrad or Waugh who obscure my understanding of his actions?

But why write?

> Every transformative or creative process comprises stages of possession. To be moved, captivated, spellbound, signify to be possessed by something; and without such a fascination and emotional tension connected with it, no concentration, no lasting interest, no creative process, are possible.[2]

Proclaiming that one intends to become a writer was once a way of informing others that one intended to undertake a long and most arduous journey, a solitary, self-consuming journey of 'self-discovery' in which no one else could participate.

How easily the writer-to-be develops an exaggerated sense of his mission as he, convinced of his capabilities (I hesitate to use the word *talent*), sets out to realize them. To what extent is the decision to write also a rebellion against prevailing societal values, and to what extent does it (writing a novel, for instance) imply a submission to the standards by which the novel as a form of entertainment is judged and evaluated.

How rational is this decision to write?

The writer-to-be, engaging in a frenzied parody of writing, produces a page here and there; he has yet to be infected (if one can regard writing as an ailment) by the need to write. For it would seem that in order to establish or acquire a need to write one first would have to exercise this need fully—something the writer-to-be has had little practice in doing. Still, I expect, one can always develop this need upon recognizing it to be a necessary stimulant. But might not the result be the development of a need that as yet cannot be fulfilled? Whatever the case, in order to habituate himself to his need, this prerequisite of writing, the writer-to-be nourishes and stimulates it in order to keep it alive, in order to absorb it better, in order to familiarize himself with its characteristics. Perhaps he is aware that within this need is located the origin of his desires, and that now in response to the omnipresent question 'Why write?' his answer will be 'Because I need to.'

When did I first think of becoming a writer?

I am attempting to depict a stage in the writer's life that precedes publication: a stage that precedes any but the vaguest awareness of what getting one's work into print might entail; a stage that precedes the first rejections. It is a condition dominated by a curious and unsettling longing. With some exceptions it is a short lived state of innocence, a kind of state that does not yet attempt to question or negate the popular données with respect to the persona of the 'literary' writer: these assumptions and fantasies have greatly contributed to a myth in which the 'idealized' author, becoming inextricably identified with the more 'dynamic' or 'tragic' or 'picaresque' characters of his or her books, could only be evaluated on a 'heroic' level. To be sure, the reader's awareness of Hemingway's toughness, tests of courage, and finally the 'manly' shotgun suicide, or Mailer's belligerent accusatory self-advertisements, unprovoked fights, and constant challenges to others to compete, provides a further stimulating insight into the writer as a heroic oddity, and a somewhat misleading picture of that curious enterprise, writing, since the writer-to-be is left with the impression that these all too well documented acts of physical courage are essential to the production of a text. Indeed, Mailer feels it is necessary to state how silly *A Farewell to Arms* or *Death in the Afternoon* would have been had they been written by a man who was five-four, had acne, wore glasses, spoke in a shrill voice, and was a physical coward. How does one then view that self-denigrating masterpiece of writing, *Manhood*, by Michel Leiris? Does it or does it not take a certain courage to write: 'Above all, I wanted to free myself of that hideous sense of impotence—as much genital as intellectual—from which I still suffer today.'[3]

How soon does the writer-to-be establish the priorities of his new function in life and, based in part on his ability to identify with a role model, form an understanding of this role, absorbing, and emblematizing it in daily life? And is this role frequently not more tangible than anything he may as yet have produced on paper. As he dispassionately observes himself, in his capacity as documenter, can the writer-to-be fail to seize upon the pronoun *I* as a suitable subject, the ideal subject for the first text. It is a self-absorbed beginning that feeds on its dissatisfactions, its self-deprivation, on anything that will generate the text.

Why write?

Is everything coloured by one's desire to write?

If one were to attempt to place the writer-to-be in a historical as well as literary context, would this phenomena be linked to the advent of printing or, rather, to the 'modern' or 'bourgeois' novel written in the eighteenth century? For as far as the seventeenth century audience was concerned, the act of reading, for instance, Madame de Lafayette's *La Princess de Cleve*, could hardly be distinguished from the social prerequisites that circumscribed and defined the courtly world of Louis XIV.[4] It seems unlikely that any writer of that period could remove himself sufficiently from the society of which he was an integral part. Accordingly, the role of the writer and his identity was not defined by his wish or need to write, but by his precise position in the social hierarchy. Writing was something a gentleman or a lady may also have done. The writer-to-be, with his single-minded intent, could only emerge when class within the strongly class structured and class conscious society had ceased—as far as the writer was concerned—to be a major impediment, and the popular enthusiasm and demand for the printed text conferred upon him the dreams, the desire, and ambition which we now recognize as the attributes of the writer-to-be. It should be kept in mind that for the gentleman writer—Swift, for instance, refused payment for his writings—writing was a calling not a profession.

To what extent was my entire stay in Tel Aviv, where I began to write, coloured by my desire to write?

In confiding to others his intentions to write, the writer-to-be is made aware of the tenuousness of his position. Everything his friends have to say to him, encouraging or otherwise, arouses his innate misgivings; what rings false in his ears is not the general goodwill of their platitudinous response, but the excessive childishness of his voiced intentions. While there is nothing wrong with wishing to become a writer, everything is wrong in exuberantly expressing that wish, perhaps, because it is an all too familiar and popular desire.

In the 1979 PEN American Center survey on the income of writers, mailed to all the members of PEN, the final and to me most intriguing question was: 'Which of the following influenced you to become a writer (mark those which are applicable, numbering the most important influences with a '1' and the secondary with a '2'):

___a teacher   ___financial opportunities   ___a strong able model

___accidental   ___the need to write   ___not wanting to work from 9–5

___fame   ___a desire to instruct   ___literature: reading a particular body of work

___wanting to be part of the literary community   ___other (please specify)'

By the age of twelve or thirteen I belonged to three lending libraries in Shanghai, where I grew up. It signaled that excess of feeling I have always had with respect to books. Yet, despite this love, I remained for a long time a somewhat reckless and indiscriminate reader. Until years later in Tel Aviv it never occurred to me to write: to make that all too plausible transition from one who loves to read to someone who entertains the idea of becoming a writer. While in school in Shanghai I entered a short story competition and, much to my astonishment, walked off with the first prize. It was my first short story. The writing was excruciatingly bad, but I won on the strength of the rather ingenious plot—it had caught my attention since it too dealt with a short story competition—which I promptly and appropriately, so it seemed to me at the time, lifted from a collection of short stories I had borrowed from the library. Recently, on re-reading Sartre's *Words*, I discovered with a certain satisfaction that all his early writings, albeit at the age of eight or nine, were plagiarized—something I had missed in my earlier reading of the book. I also overlooked the evident delight Sartre took in this *performance*. 'Now and then, I used to stop writing and pretend to hesitate so that I could feel I was, with my furrowed brow and far-away look, a *writer*.'[5] Unlike Sartre, I took no pleasure in writing my first text. I still remember the tediousness and arduousness of writing it. Having lifted the plot and seeing in my mind all its details, all the necessities that would make it work, I felt, as I wrote, a resistance, something that wished to prevent me from carrying out my objective. I did not feel that I was a writer. I wrote with an anger and impatience at being tied to this text instead of free to do something

151

else.

Why write?

In enlarging the topography of his new existence, the writer-to-be feeds on a literary past, his new history, in which Stendhal becomes identified with Julien Sorel, Kafka and Joseph K., Camus with Merrseult, Sartre with Roquentin, Hemingway with Jake, Joyce with Stephen Dedalus: but what possibly can be wrong with that, other than the deceptive ranking or elevation of the author to the level of the fictitious character?

Why write?

> The whole of *A la recherche du temps perdu* is a preparation for the writing career which, it has not escaped some critics, Marcel by the end of the novel is unlikely ever really to begin.[6]
>
> The beginning of a career is the moment when the writer looks to his text as any man looks to his future, so all inclusive are the exigencies of his work.[7]
>
> Marcel's meditations on his future text indicate, as I said above, the exaggerated value attached by the writer to his career. They reflect Proust's own case, if not in every detail than in the fact of the detail, as well as in the temporal hyperbole by which thoughts of or about a text yet to be produced seem to engulf even the practical, everyday acts of writing without which no text can be produced. Walter Benjamin rightly says that 'since the Spiritual Exercises of Loyola there has hardly been a more radical attempt at self-absorption.'[8]

My first room, a furnished room, was located in Madame Rothschild's large ground floor apartment on Rehov Hess in Tel Aviv. I remember her as being small, sharp-tongued, and spiteful; I found her presence unnerving, and stayed out of her path as much as possible. Somewhere in the distant past a French cavalry officer, Captain Rothschild, her husband long deceased, in giving her his name had provided her with the only link she still had to the Rothschilds.

The long and extremely narrow room was dominated by a large ancient bed, a massive chest with three drawers and a streaked mirror, and the wood shutters on the tall window that faced the courtyard. Hot water was available three times a week. I expressed my detestation of Madame Rothschild by using her toothbrush to remove the grey hair that clogged the bathtub drain. The narrow table on which I heaped my books and on which I occasionally wrote was set against the window ledge; there was just enough space for the single chair between the foot of the bed and the table. To the left of the chest was a rust stained wash basin. The room's location, however, was ideal. I was only a block away from the American Library where I was working at the time (it was then located in a small attractive villa on Rehov Bialik), and a three minute walk from the Cafe Niza and Felix Rosenheim's antiquarian bookstore on Rehov Allenby across from the Niza.

On the walls of the rather bleak room hung several cheap Skira and Abrams reproductions. One was *The View of Toledo*, another a painting by Ingres. I had just discovered El Greco and the music of Mahler, the poetry of Lorca and Prevert:

> Terrible
> is the soft sound of a hardboiled egg
> cracking on a zinc counter
> and terrible is that sound
> when it moves in the memory
> of a man who is hungry.[9]

Why write?

Does the writer-to-be attach to everything he or she does a literary significance? For instance, can a writer-to-be view love anything but a text-to-be, something that evokes the work of Benjamin Constant, or Raymond Radiguet, or Theodor Fontane, or Ford Madox Ford? For love offers a clearly definable almost superbly self-contained development in which all moves and responses of the lovers conform to an almost recognizable pattern—an almost classic pattern. There is a beginning, a middle, and the inevitable ending of the romantic attachment. As a lover, the writer-to-be also participates as the solicitously inquiring and absorbed reader of his affair; falling in love is analogous to reviewing the text. Are the demands the writer makes as the reviewer of his affair also the demands he will place on the future text? Ultimately, does the writer-to-be take the same pride in his love affair that he would in a successful text based on it? Is that what Benjamin concluded when he wrote that Breton was closer to the things Nadja was close to than to her?

I must admit that as a writer-to-be I could not have fabricated a more 'perfect' affair. A beginning of evasion and an ending only made conclusive by my departure. The affair encapsulated the sublime, the tragic: the ideal text.

The beginning: we met in the home of a mutual friend, a musician. There may have been two dozen people, mostly musicians, crowded in the small penthouse apartment from the terrace of which one had an excellent view of Independence Park and the Mediterranean. We were about to leave together when I heard, coming from another room where Klaus kept his record player, the opening bars of Smetana's *The Bartered Bride*. I find it difficult not to attach a significance to the title. Was it for the sake of the future text that I found myself compelled to listen to the first side of the record and then, finding that she had left although she had promised to wait, to the second? But had I really expected her to wait compliantly for me? Had I succeeded in delaying the beginning? In postponing it?

The beginning: weeks later I ran into her at the Tachanat Merkazit, the main bus terminal in Tel Aviv. She was on her way to spend the weekend with her parents in the country. When we met the second time at the bus terminal I vaguely proposed that we get together; whereupon she invited me to have dinner with her the following week. Is the writer-to-be incapable of writing about an affair unless he has had one? Does the writer-to-be fall in love because he wishes to introduce his newly formed persona to the methodology of passion?

Am I spinning cobwebs? Am I making this up? Am I permitting past events to run away with me? Am I distorting something for the sake of the text?

Does the emotional insecurity of the writer-to-be always make him retreat to the text?

The new interior: her apartment. Located on the third floor of a new apartment building in Tel Aviv. The raw looking unpainted cement exterior of the building was a yet unmarked by the weather. She occupied the corner apartment which unlike the other apartments on that floor had two balconies, one facing East the other facing the two or three identical looking apartment buildings at the rear. I recall being surprised by the large aquarium near the window and by the emptiness of the large apartment. The white walled interior: bare, cool, remote, almost verging on the impersonal. The two or three framed reproductions on the wall provided a certain colour and were an attestation of an interest rather than evidence of any strong attachment. The apartment was an exercise in control, or perhaps I should say order. I remember a small watercolour reproduction by Dürer and a painting by Van Gogh near the entrance in the hallway. I'm fond of Van Gogh she said, and then—I no longer remember why—stated that if he were alive she would not care to meet him. This announcement made quite seriously was intended, I believe, to convey her position in the face of my somewhat *disorderly* life. This position, by the way, was entirely consistent with her reluctance to acknowledge my stated intention of becoming a writer.

Almost two years later, after we had been living apart for more than six months, we were married. It was a marriage of convenience, her convenience, since as a married woman she would not have to serve in the army and postpone her intention to study law. In many respects, it was a perfectly reasonable and plausible arrangement for a writer-to-be who is intent on complicating as well as delaying the inevitable ending. Beside us, only three or four people knew of our 'secret' marriage. The awareness of what I had done intensified and

155

heightened my 'impression of living'. I chose to interpret my impulsive act as a poetic gesture. Arrabal defined a poet as someone who doesn't necessarily write poetry, but was a terrorist or provocateur. I had accomplished something. In misrepresenting my own role as groom at the wedding, I had—so to speak—nullified the ceremony and what it represented. After our wedding I avoided her. Was this part of my intention, a condition I set? Since I had rented a furnished room (she happened to have found for me) in the vicinity of her apartment I would occasionally see her from my window. Why did I continue to avoid her? Sometimes we'd meet at the Niza. Did we ever refer to our marriage? Am I being unfair to her? Am I permitting the theory that a love affair represents the ideal first text-to-be to distort what actually took place?

I have omitted a certain resentment, anger, petulance, and the wish to punish someone I had loved. The unforgiving writer-to-be returns to the text to re-experience his losses.

At one time I used to breakfast at the Niza and at another cafe on Ben Yehuda, the name of which now slips my mind. At the Niza I preferred the bright and cheerful back room; at the other cafe I always headed for the corner table next to the window. Breakfast: soft boiled eggs, a fresh roll, butter, jam, and coffee. I came prepared to write. My affairs were going badly. My text-to-be was virtually non-existent. My spiral notebook and my Pelikan fountain pen on display on the round marble-topped table, as I read the *Jerusalem Post* and watched people passing on the street; in spite of my desire or need to write, I had to fight a distinct disinclination to lift the pen up and write. How to explain this lethargy, this distaste, this boredom? My persistence, for I did not relinquish the hope of becoming a writer, was based on a determination that seemed to defy understanding. I was infatuated with the idea of writing.

Her apartment: for reasons that are no longer clear to me, a few weeks after that first evening in her apartment, we moved the convertible couch from the North wall of the living room to the West wall. After we parted, but before we were married, the furniture was moved once again, as if to erase my former presence. I can understand the movement of the furniture as well and as passionately as I understand Schubert's sonatas. The aquarium with its dozen guppies was by now long gone. After we were married but living apart, she once again moved the couch. I often wonder if I avoided sleeping with her after we were married for the sake of the text-to-be? I believe that she had not read *The Sun Also Rises* but her parting words seemed straight out of that all too familiar last exchange in the novel. Am I reading into her parting gift, Malraux's *The Voice of Silence*, a meaning that wasn't there?

Why write?

I was crossing the parade ground in Ramle during my second year in the Tank Corps when quite suddenly the idea of becoming a writer flashed through my mind. A moment of pure exhilaration.

On November 28, 1905 André Gide made the following entry in his journal:

> I have come to hate this apartment, this furniture, this house. No concentration is possible here; I am defenceless against anything, against anyone; the least noise from the street or from within the house reaches me. It is years since my head has been warm; I think of that happy fever which, all the time I was writing Paludes, kept my book awake. The reading of Rimbaud and of the Sixth Chant de Maldoror has made me ashamed of my works and disgusted with everything that is merely the result of culture. It seems to me that I was born for something different. But perhaps there is still time ... perhaps in Auteuil ... Oh! how I long ....[10]

The Eternal Hope: Uri Felix Rosenheim kept a journal since his arrival in Jaffa in 1936 when he was twenty-four. In essence, it was and remained the journal of the foreigner, someone who resisted the mental and physical demands the Mediterranean climate, the people, the stark architecture, the extraordinary biblical landscape made on him. In his journal, the carefully chiselled German prose, the classical

German of Goethe and Schiller, conferred upon the text the cool, ironic, and detached substance of an *orderly* existence that was at one and the same time so withdrawn, so minute in its exposure to the dynamics of change in the Israeli society, and yet so formidable in its discerning response to the classics and the past. The journal was the means by which the present was relived and scrutinized, dissected, and immobilized, and the recent past slowly committed or wed to the more distant past, a time in which Arabs still pastured their camels within sight of the ancient harbour of Jaffa. To every move, to every face, to every remark in the journal was affixed the resignation, the lethargy of the aging writer, the eternal European, the man of letters, the writer without any readers who yet expected any day now (so the heart claimed) to be surprised, to be overwhelmed by a recognition, a sign long overdue.

It was the journal of a man who had quietly, somberly selected his spot on Allenby Street and in his room, the bust of Goethe, the hand-wound gramophone, the ancient Bach records, and the exactitude of his imprisonment—I am referring to a physical confinement—as he daily in an unvarying routine walked from his room to his bookstore located in the entrance to an alley, and then in the evening retraced his steps. His conversation was punctuated by an occasional ironic laugh. A laugh designed to draw attention to the essential humour of injustice. I imagine when Kafka's mother returned to Kafka the forty-page accusatory letter he had written to his father, the letter his father never received, Kafka must have expressed his feelings with a similar laugh. At that time, so preoccupied was I with my own affairs, that I did not comprehend when Rosenheim described his father's recent arrival in Israel; his father, President of one of the religious parties, as well as the author of numerous books and pamphlets on theology and education, was greeted at Lydda airport by thousands of his followers who were celebrating his arrival by ecstatically dancing in front of the terminal, exuberant that he had finally come to live in Israel; and Uri Rosenheim who had gone to the airport to welcome his father could not fight his way through the throng of admirers surrounding him. Was it because he didn't try hard enough? It is immaterial.

Rosenheim and I used the formal German 'Sie' in addressing each other. How could I possibly understand his gloom. I have a number of letters in my possession. In one he mentions having lost his briefcase containing a large part of his journal; after weeks of despondency he pulled himself together and feverishly attempted to reconstruct as much as possible of the lost sections. In another letter he referred to a certain reluctance on his part to continue our correspondence, for as he put it, he felt disinclined to shoot arrows into the air without a more specific target. Probably he was, as he had frequently been in the past, irritated by my apparent lack of seriousness. I think he also was distressed by what he took to be my frivolous attachment to matters and books that were not worth the consideration I paid them. It may seem ironic that although Rosenheim had once read from his work at a gathering in the apartment of Max Brod, with whom he was acquainted, Brod, the great supporter and friend of Kafka, could not discern in Rosenheim the common anguished topography he shared with Kafka. Admittedly, Rosenheim's outward diffidence, and his stated unresponsiveness to Kafka's work, may have made Brod's task a difficult one.

Some time ago I came across a listing of Jewish authors writing in the German language and there, under Uri Felix Rosenheim's name, was listed his first book, *Verbannung*, a collection of prose and poetry.[11] I have written to the publisher Gafni Verlag, Tel Aviv, ordering the book and requesting Rosenheim's present address. I am still waiting for a reply from Gafni. In the meantime I have found a copy of the book at the Leo Baeck Institute. Below from the German is the last line of *Die Einsame Palme* a poem that is, I think, an appropriate ending for this meditation, since Felix Uri Rosenheim introduced into his published text the self-absorbed expectations and intense longings of his prolonged insular existence as a writer-to-be.

> Finally he stood, a palm tree amidst deserts. No one
> to watch him grow, or enjoy his fruit.
> Unconcerned, with slender fronds, he raged upwards.
> Nothing further to hope for or to fear.
> Uri Rosenheim

Notes

1. Gustav Janouch, *Conversations with Kafka*, trans. Goronwy Ress (New York, 1971).

2. Erich Neumann, *Art and the Creative Unconscious*, trans. Ralph Manheim (New York, 1959), p. 177.

3. Michel Leiris, *Manhood: A Journey from Childhood into the Fierce Order of Virility*, trans. Richard Howard (New York, 1963), p. 138.

4. David I. Grossvogel, *Limits of the Novel: Evolution of a Form from Chaucer to Robbe-Grillet* (Ithaca, 1971), p. 257.

5. Jean-Paul Sartre, *Words*, trans. Irene Claphane (London, 1964), p. 99.

6. Edward W. Said, *Beginnings: Intention and Method* (New York, 1975), p. 243.

7. *Ibid.*, p. 249.

8. *Ibid.*, p. 249.

9. Jacques Prévert, 'Late Rising', trans. Selden Rodman, from *One Hundred Modern Poems* selected by Selden Rodman (New York, 1952), p. 54.

10. André Gide, *The Journals of André Gide*, Vol. 1 1889—1913, trans. Justin O'Brien (New York, 1950), p. 158.

11. Desider Stern, *Werke Jüdischer Autoren Deutscher Sprache*, Sonderausgabe der 3, Auflage 1970 für B'nai B'rith Loge, Wien (Desider Stern, Wien, Wollzeile 20, Druck: Frühmorgen and Holzmann, München), p. 309. The first edition of this extensive listing of Jewish authors writing in the German language was compiled by Desider Stern for the B'nai B'rith Book Fair in the Künstlerhaus in Vienna, Austria, 5 to 14 May 1967.

GRANTA

LISA ZEIDNER
LUCY

Lisa Zeidner

Mozart spiced up a house that always smelled like cedar. I needed to sit on two dictionaries to reach the piano, which was respectable, black, and dimly European. On Thursdays, Lucy washed it with lemon to soak up the sun that coasted, at three o'clock, from my school to the high old window.

I was pigeon-toed and skinny, with flakes of dry skin at my elbows, wrists, and knees. I thought that eczema was a pet name for my special relationship with the sun. The sun, I thought, could be owned, like goldfish, and I owned it. Wherever I went, the sun was directly overhead, more stubborn than a shadow.

My father, who could fit his hand around my elbow, didn't challenge this misconception. He thought it was endearing in the Santa Claus sense. Like most fathers, Jeremy Spell was a huge man. He was far too big to call Jerry, so I forfeited the nickname Jenny at an early age, to be fair.

My father and I had the same initials—J.S., as in Bach. We also looked alike. Jeremy Spell had, the reviewers liked to say, a 'spacious heart'. The reviews of his violin-playing were taped to the side of the refrigerator. I learned to read from them. Sometimes I was allowed to draw faces on the reviews in crayon, adding mustaches and long gaudy tongues.

Lucy Werner Spell was my mother. She was something brought back, at great cost, in a suitcase. She always had a suntan; she wore colourful high-heeled shoes and an ankle-bracelet. When she put on bright lipstick, there was nothing else in the world but her mouth. For all my talents, I hadn't mastered pronouncing *L*'s and *W*'s. As these stubborn sounds were my mother's nimbus—a written recrimination on some of her handkerchiefs and on her pocketbook—I was often made to recite, with my father:

> Let's lay a week in Lucy's lap,
> That bicycle built for two,
> And as a celebrational nightcap
> Let's sing the Honolulu Blues.

Blues came out *booze*, which made my mother laugh, then cry, because laughing hurt. While Lucy didn't play an instrument, her laugh was as foreign as a mandora or a carillon, rare instruments I'd

162

marked with red ink in my World Book. She never looked right in pictures. In the one my father still has on his dresser, she's on a horse in Massachusetts, her face lit from underneath—majestic, diabolical.

I do remember the zoo. I went on my father's shoulders, the week before the family fell apart.

'Say a sentence,' I said, looking down on my mother's careful hair.

'Mind over matter,' Jeremy said.

'That's not a sentence. Say a sentence, Lucy.'

'The blue moon ate a rarity,' Lucy said.

'That's stupid. Say a paradox.'

'Nothing's either good or bad; 'tis thinking makes it so,' Jeremy said.

'Is that a paradox?'

'I don't know. Ask your mother.'

'Is that a paradox, Lucy?'

'It depends,' Lucy said.

Lucy was a master of equivocation.

Walking to the car wasn't pleasant. The pavement was strange after the pink, disfigured shine of an orang-utan's ass. Lucy cried in the car. During the drive, the sun hid behind a tree nastily. When I sat down to practise, my mother cried more.

This was not unusual. There was something wrong with my mother's brain. It wasn't going to kill her, but it would always hurt. One time, as an eloquent demonstration of chronic pain, she'd brushed my hair so hard that it came out in dramatic clumps. But then she'd scooped up my face in her hands and told me about nerve endings. Hers were disintegrating. I looked the word up in my dictionary.

'If the nerves are being destroyed,' I asked, 'then who is destroying them?'

'I wish I knew,' Lucy said. 'When you find out, will you let me know?'

I promised I would. Her hands, thanking me, were cold. The fingers were long, bluish, and knotty. All the pictures are like that too—blue and cold, like ice about to melt.

The night of the zoo, I'd insisted on kissing my fish good-night, despite the time. It was late, and my goldfish ritual was as protracted as the balcony scene in *Romeo and Juliet*, which we'd been reading out loud, curled up on a couch.

'Absolutely not,' Lucy said. 'You're too attached.'

I was not used to argument. I was a lucky person who owned the sun, five goldfish, and a happy childhood. All were gifts, I sensed, from my parents. Each dinner was Christmas. Each book was an intricate wind-up toy that my parents set in motion. So I cried. This was odd in a child who could use the word *incalcitrant* wrong, but with great aplomb, in a sentence, so my mother relented.

Four fish were dead.

They floated on the top of the bowl, on their backs, innocuous as seaweed.

Lucy took the fish out and rested them in her palm. She held them out to me.

She tickled one fish with a long fingernail. With Lucy's arm bent at the elbow, she brought the fish right under my nose. They didn't smell.

'You see?' she said. 'Death isn't so bad.'

I felt green. I wanted to run from the bathroom, but Jeremy framed the doorway, impassive.

'Careful,' he said, over my head.

'You see the big fish?' Lucy said. 'She's pregnant. That's why her belly is so translucent. Do you know why mother fish eat baby fish? Because there are lots of fish, and it's no great loss.'

Jeremy said, 'Your mother means to say that nothing's indispensable.'

I didn't know what *indispensable* meant. The word filled the room, medicinal as air freshener. My parents, too, seemed clean, clean and big.

Lucy was cross. 'I meant to tell you just what I said, Jennifer. Put it this way: never eat a whole box of chocolates looking for the one with the cherry centre when all you have to do is poke the bottoms.'

She still had the fish in her hand.

'Easy,' Jeremy warned.

I clung to his leg. Lucy glared at both of us and briskly flushed the fish down the toilet. I threw myself on the bathroom floor and started banging my fists on my mother's toes.

'These are fish,' Lucy said. 'Even people aren't worth this.'

There were new fish the next day. Lucy brought them in the

cardboard boxes used for take-out Chinese food. She had a bright scarf on and she was humming, but her eyes were red, and I could tell that she'd cried most of the night. We cleaned the bowl and inaugurated the new fish.

'You see, you can't tell the difference,' Lucy said, without much conviction.

I could tell that she thought I thought she killed my fish, and she was right, but there was something worse. The night before, I'd known my fish would be dead. I felt it in the lining of my stomach—a kind of low grade dread. But if a kiss had no curative powers, what good did it do to know things ahead of time? I watched my new fish tour their plastic shipwreck and worried.

I didn't worry for long, though, because I had to practise. My first recital was on Bach's birthday, the first day of spring. I woke up that morning with the stomach-feeling.

'Nerves,' Lucy said. 'You'll always have that before you play, even when you're famous. Your father still does.'

I was in the doorway of my parents' bedroom. Lucy was cross-legged on the floor, sorting through a heap of clothes. She still hadn't dressed.

'Are you going somewhere?' I asked.

'No, dear. Just spring-cleaning.'

Lucy was a bad liar. I knew she wouldn't be at my recital, and she wasn't.

I spent the morning at the library, as I did every Saturday, and then walked directly to my piano teacher's house. Neither of my parents was there, but Jeremy turned up, breathless, right before the recital started.

The seat next to his was empty. He looked small, grey, and hung over. I don't remember what I played. My hands just reached an octave. I had a Band-Aid on one knee.

Jeremy told me Lucy was gone when we got in the car.

'To Aunt Mara's?' I asked.

'No. She's dead.'

'When?'

'This morning.'

'Her head hurt.'

'Yes.'

We were driving badly. We passed the church with the huge mosaic of Jesus Christ which I hated. The Spells did not believe in God. We didn't like melodrama. We were, from what I could gather, more Behaviourists than anything else.

'You were at work,' I said.

'Yes.'

'Well, if you were at work, and I was at the library, then neither of us killed her.'

'Jennifer!'

'Then she must have killed herself.'

He admitted I was right. His eyes were big and hollow as a cartoon's. He even told me how she did it. She lined her stomach with toothpaste, so it couldn't be pumped, then took some drugs.

'You are six years old,' Jeremy said, as if that were news.

'Yes,' I said, 'but that won't last long.'

I didn't want to remember my mother in a Roadrunner cartoon, going off a cliff or slitting her wrists. Still, it didn't mean much. It wasn't dead goldfish; it wasn't a frantic bee trapped between the window and the screen. '*Suicide*' was like '*eczema*'. It could have meant hot chocolate spilled, or someone dented the car while shopping. *Your mother is dead* was a sentence like any other sentence. It could have meant 'Wear the green dress' or 'She's in the shower'.

By the time we got home, it was raining a bit. I excused myself to practise. Jeremy sat on the porch while I played. After I finished, I came out with two bowls of bananas and cream. Neither of us was very hungry. We ate slowly, listening to moths knock into the streetlamps and the spoons click against our teeth, until it got entirely dark.

Jeremy put his arm around me. I think he was crying. I know *I* was.

'You'll miss your mother,' he said.

'Yes.'

'Me too.'

Jeremy sat on the edge of my bed that night for longer than he had to. I could tell that he wanted to talk.

'Your mother wasn't crazy,' he said.

'I know,' I said. I smiled a bit and feigned sleep.

I could tell that Jeremy didn't want to go into their bedroom. He didn't want to hang up his clothes in the closet with her rows and rows of delicate dresses; he didn't want to shave next to the windowsill with her bottles of perfume and her one azalea blossom, hot pink, floating in a long-stemmed glass. From my bed I leaned over and watched him open his bedroom door. He opened it wide enough so I could see their bed. It was made. The pillows were against the wall, and the spread slightly rumpled—before she died, Lucy had sat there doing crossword puzzles.

Jeremy closed the door and began to do push-ups in the hall, right outside my door.

I couldn't tell whether he wanted me awake or asleep.

Both of us, I think, were angry with Lucy. I've learned a lot about Lucy over the years from my father's sister Mara, who was around fairly often to keep my father from becoming an alcoholic. Mara is about the only person who would talk to me about my mother. She is the only person who totally forgives Lucy. She says that none of us could even have begun to deal with pain as gracefully as Lucy did. It seems to me, though, that my mother's suicide was inept and desperate, like any suicide.

What we know about the suicide is that Lucy took pills and left a note taped to the bedroom door: *Don't open the door. I'm dead in here. Don't be angry, and by all means think of a decent way to tell Jennifer!* I've seen the note. Jeremy still has it in his bottom desk drawer. Mara thinks it's vulgar of him to have kept it, and so do I.

The door was locked from the inside. My father called Mara, who promised to get on a plane from Boston; then he called the police. He'd never seen a dead body, even in the war, and he wouldn't see one now. They brought Lucy out covered by a sheet. Jeremy waited for the ambulance to leave and then got sick.

I can barely imagine how he went through all that and then managed to sit through my recital, his hands folded in his lap. He probably worried the whole time about the trace of vomit on his breath. The whole time he stared slightly to the left of me, where my piano teacher sat. She had a finger missing, the middle finger on her right hand. Jeremy had never noticed it before and I'd never had the heart to tell him how repulsive it was, watching her play with the stump. Throughout the recital, Jeremy puzzled a look of radical disgust.

Lucy had a last fit of bad taste, which we didn't notice until later.

First she left a vase of fresh roses on the piano, like it was Mother's Day. Worse than that, the next day we found a casserole in the refrigerator with a note tucked into the tinfoil: *350° for 50 min. P.S. I love you.* It was her handwriting, large and childish. Jeremy carried the dish outside to the trash and threw it away. Glassware and all.

My father is the kind of person who actually remembers to have the newspaper delivery stopped when he goes on vacation. I don't think he had a response for a suicide. I suppose Lucy left the notes to make us feel better, but it didn't work. We wished she'd gone on a vacation, mailed us an ordinary loving postcard, and made the suicide look like an accident. She could have fallen off the roof at a dark party. She could have floated, blissfully, too far off at sea. Her note was an affront. It was too light, almost incidental. This was hard on me, but it was even harder, I imagine, for my father, who had loved Lucy right from the start, from across the lobby of a Cape Cod hotel.

Mara says my father rubbed lotion in Lucy's back as she sunbathed in a slatted chair; he watched her hold a hat on with one downy arm, her pelvis knocking the pier. If you listen to Mara, Lucy was clear and pink as a Forties script-girl. I find this hard to believe—my mother was over forty at that time, and already had her disease. She told him about her brain then, but it hadn't seemed credible, with Lucy so appealing, a book in her lap as he practised the violin. He proposed quickly because he figured he'd waited long enough; and Lucy thought she didn't have long to wait.

My grandparents were still alive then. Lucy and Jeremy were married at my grandparents' house in Wellesley. My grandparents never took to Lucy, who was to move to Baltimore, where my father would continue to play in the orchestra, and where Johns Hopkins might be able to say something about Lucy's disease.

The way Mara tells it, there was a generalized happiness that didn't last long. I got born in five minutes during a luscious remission, but then my mother's condition got worse and worse, and Mara would approach the suicide—at which point my father would come home, or Mara would get nervous and tell me to go do my homework.

I don't think about my mother when I think about the day of the suicide now. I think about my father in the hall, doing push-ups. I think about how gingerly and slowly he opened the bedroom door the second time and how, after a moment, I heard him say '*Shit*' and start flinging open drawers. Soon he was running violently all over the house, throwing open cabinets and cursing. He was in the linen closet right outside my door, shoving sheets and towels onto the carpet. Then he was in the guest room, where my mother kept her wedding gown in a plastic bag and her hooded sewing machine. He was screaming, '*I'm going to kill her.*'

I heard the front door slam. From my bedroom window I could see Jeremy walk down the steps separating our lawn from the median strip. It was still drizzling. He stood against our neighbour's car parked in front of the house. The car was new, shiny as a paper cut-out of a car. Then he started banging his head rhythmically against the glass of the car window, gripping the car with both hands. I didn't know what to do.

A taxi threaded down the street. I was relieved for a moment when I saw Aunt Mara get out of the car, but I couldn't hear anything and what I saw was awful. Mara put her suitcase down and tried to hug my father. He pushed her down. As she was getting up, he just fell over backwards, until he was flat against the pavement.

I crawled under my bed, dragging my blanket after me.

They came in the front door. I could hear them hanging up their coats. 'She wouldn't do that,' Mara was saying. She spoke slow and loud, like a nurse. 'You can't see anything in the dark anyway, and you're going to wake Jennifer. Wait until the morning.'

They moved into the kitchen, which was directly below my bedroom. I couldn't make out their talk over the ice hitting the sides of their glasses and the drone of the refrigerator.

I couldn't seem to get the room dark enough.

Then I heard my mother's voice, tiny at first as a key in a lock but soon wide and lucid in the dark room.

We were going somewhere in the old mint-green Rambler. There was honeysuckle out and the smell of freshly cut grass. We pulled up in front of a house. It became clear that I was going to a birthday party, and that the present in my lap—a box cleverly tied with licorice rather than string—was for a friend. It also became clear that neither of us was in any great hurry. We just sat there with the windows rolled down, taking the air.

Lucy had sunglasses on and was drumming the steering wheel with her nails, her head resting on the palm of the other hand. Her

Lisa Zeidner

scalp seemed soft; her hair was blue-black, the bruised colour of hair in comic books. In fact, her whole face looked puffy, the way it sometimes did when she came back from the hospital. She didn't seem in a good mood. I heard a lawn-mower and the bell on an ice cream truck. I began to sing, and what I sang, clear as day, was this:

> Miss Spell
> Won't go to Hell
> And stay there ever after.
> Her mother is dead;
> She was sick in the head.
> This is no laughing matter.

Then I flinched, because I thought Lucy was going to hit me, but she didn't. In fact, she smiled.

'Look at yourself in the mirror,' she commanded.

I craned my neck to centre myself in the rear-view mirror.

In the mirror *I* was *her*.

This is hard to explain. It wasn't as if I, six years old, was suddenly 57, married, unmusical, and dying of a brain disease. It seemed something very simple, like something in Latin written on a coin—something to notice and not to do anything about.

I was *her*.

No wonder I've been feeling so strange, I thought. I'm *her*.

'I suppose I should go in now,' I said in *her* voice.

Lucy bunched her knees up under her chin and asked me winsomely, in *my* voice, if there was anything she could do for me.

'Nobody can do anything for anyone else,' I said. I said it to be flip, but somehow I felt as if it were the truest thing I'd ever said. The present felt minuscule and false in my lap.

Lucy reached into her purse and handed me a pen and a piece of paper. Then she gave me a large key, maybe a skate key. I tried to look in the mirror to see if I was still her, but she held me down.

'I want you to remember what you just said,' she told me. 'I want you to write it down, sign it, and date it.'

'I don't know how to write yet,' I reminded her.

'Don't be ridiculous. If you can read music you can write a declarative sentence.'

170

She was right. Not only could I spell all the words correctly, but I wrote them in cursive—*her* cursive. I expected her to praise me for this, but she took the paper from my hand, folded it, and pressed the fist in which I still held the key.

'Put this piece of paper in the storage cabinet behind the linen closet,' she said. 'I want you to have this so you remember, so you don't blame me. But don't *ever* tell anyone you said that when you were six, because they're not going to believe you. They're going to think you made it up. Promise you'll never tell a soul what you said.'

'I promise,' I said.

'You promised,' she said. 'Now go inside.'

The next thing I knew, Jeremy was lifting me back into my bed. Mara was standing behind him.

'I was cold. I fell asleep.'

'Turn the air-conditioner down, Mara,' Jeremy said.

Both of them seemed fairly satisfied with my explanation. Jeremy tucked me in and Mara gave me a kiss on my forehead.

'Do you think you can sleep now?' Jeremy asked.

'Yes,' I said cautiously, 'but there's one thing. Are you looking for Lucy's things? Because I saw her pack some stuff this morning. Did you check the storage cabinet behind the linen closet?'

Jeremy almost knocked us both over to get to it. In the cabinet were neatly wrapped boxes. Lucy had even labeled them.

'Of course,' Jeremy said. 'I just wasn't thinking straight.'

Mara was staring at me, arms crossed, trying to read my mind.

'How much do you know,' she asked, 'about what happened this morning?'

'Here's everything,' Jeremy said. 'I just wasn't thinking. I should have thought of it myself.'

One of the boxes, smaller than the rest, said: *For Jennifer.*

'How much do you know?' Mara repeated.

'I know that my mother killed herself,' I said, 'because her head hurt.'

'You're awful cold-blooded about it.'

Jeremy said, 'Leave her alone.' He jogged into his bedroom and came back with a pair of nail clippers. He turned one of the boxes onto its side and started to undo it.

There it was: a little room with everything belonging to my

171

mother, behind the linen closet, right against my bed.

'What on earth are you doing that for?' Mara asked.

'I just want to make sure everything's here.'

I was in what is called a double bind. If the note my mother had asked me to write was in the box addressed to me, then Mara and Jeremy would see it and I would have betrayed my mother. If the note weren't in the box, then I'd have to disbelieve my mother, or think I was crazy.

'Please,' I said. 'I don't want to open my box.'

'It's probably jewellery,' Jeremy said. 'There's no point in leaving it here.'

I began to cry.

'Please,' I said, 'please let me open my box myself when I'm old enough. I'm not ready now, I'm sleepy. Please, Daddy, please please don't open it now.'

I'd called him Daddy. Even he had to listen to that.

It seemed like a long time before Jeremy finally repacked the boxes and closed the cabinet. We stood there even longer while Jeremy leaned against the wall, looking tired, with Mara still staring at me like I was a cripple on a bus.

'I think you should go to bed,' she said.

Jeremy snapped out of it. 'You sure should. I'll tuck you in again.'

'Jeremy?' I said. 'You don't think Lucy could be back, do you?'

They assured me she couldn't. As they tucked me in, even Mara's face was gentle and solicitous.

'Maybe she'll be back,' I said. 'If she's not back, then I'll get to see her in Heaven, right?'

I didn't believe in Heaven, of course. But they seemed to like me best as a child, and I didn't want to displease them.

GRANTA

NICOLE WARD JOUVE
THE DRAWER

A husband was a leech. Sucked, sucked your substance, and no feedback ever, and where were you to refuel? All the batteries, the cardiac muscles pumping in the red blood, the blood from the arteries, rich in oxygen, were all for him to plug in to. You, run-down you, were on the circuit of the veins. Seven   alarm rings children get up   Mummy Mummy let me in I'm in a hurry hammering at the door (not even time to shit in peace)   where has the hairbrush disappeared to   you pig you took it   Mummy did you get my blouse ironed   where are my trainers have you seen my swimming trunks   we need fifty pence for the hoop teacher ordered for us   no she wants change   she *did* say she wouldn't accept notes   and   and you're not going to school on an empty stomach come on have a bite not hungry (hope to goodness he's not about to fall ill   got exams to invigilate no way of getting out of that) who's taken the matches again   no milk left   shit   bet Daddy drank it during the night   hurry up   you're going to be late again   and the little swine have made a mess of their bedroom again   here we go   tidy up sweep up dust up   and my God where have I put my BM 545 cards   I bet the porter has thrown away those essays   now I'm in for it   and into the tube racing along the overheated corridors   those draughts of dust eternally stewed and stewed again and into another train among other barely visible ghosts the colour of dust stewed like the air   and up staircases smeared with graffiti and into a class-room where the chairs screech and someone has written on the wall facing your desk Prof=SS   and the infuriating whispers and giggles of that gang of idiots at the back of the class-room and the passionate quests and requests of the lost dogs begging for a little attention   who would gobble you up bones and all if you gave them the chance which you do but too often   and the ugliness and the queuing and the lavatories where you take care not to sit on the cold enamel the seats having been torn away long ago to prove something   what you're not sure   and stare at the scrawls prick and cunt and I like them like that and many-talented y.m. seeks y.m. to give him a good suck   and back home   tube again and again sagging under the weight of your brief-case then later on of the fruit and veg butter *et al.*   you should count yourself lucky   and queuing at the butcher's where you get propositioned by the local drunk   and don't say I've lost my keys again   and washing and ironing and aren't I fed up to the back teeth with nice economical little dishes which you have

to stew and stew again like dust to hell with family fare and good
housekeeping and the doctor your son is six pounds overweight here is
a leaflet to explain to you how to balance your meals (you old bugger,
who's asking for advice?) thank you doctor how kind. If I lived alone I
would be a vegetarian boiled vegetables boiled rice and long reveries in
front of a window through which would drift the scent of a lilac. And
all seasons would be equally sweet to me. Instead of which, the smell of
car fumes and my beautiful golden soul no one ever cleans unlike the
public monuments my soul all tarred tarnished choked with grime
(how do the plane trees manage to keep green beneath their coating of
city-dirt?), and his lordship gets up jaw set with bad temper or is it
hangover nerves on edge care-ridden his right to be isn't he the head of
the family of his section not for him your little dirty hanger-on junior
jobs, he, is seated on his Olympus his senior job (like this bastard Voles
who gave it to me just to get it off his chest, out of the blue, sprung it on
me, 'nine out of twenty only and this candidate is a native speaker let
me have a look at this essay where are the mistakes in grammar I'm
asking you to point out to me the mistakes in grammar, these
assistants are all bloody useless' and all the others there, all female, all
lower down the hierarchical scale than Voles the Vole senior Voles his
lordship Voles all the others licking his arse in respectful silence not
one of them to raise her voice in my defence and me for nights and
nights shouting out what I think of him bastard pulling me to pieces
when he had not read the essay which was stupid and badly written,
giving me hell out of the blue for fun or because he had heartburn or
his wife had a lover because I happen to be the nearest door-mat,
because he is a man and holds a senior post and I am a piece of cake
gentle and meek and I haven't told him to his face and it's choking me
it's vomit gulped back carbon it can't get out). And his lordship
holding court every day in his office   life padded for him by tiptoeing
females. You you sing your little happy days you get your laughs where
you can the gossip you overhear at the hairdresser's, 'my poor Bassie
it's very hard for her you know   they helped the basset hound climb on
to a stool and they held her and even like that he didn't make it   well of
course you've got to mate with dogs of the same race   everyone knows
that what's race for I ask you, well in the end it was a mongrel who had
her at the bottom of the garden.' But you can't stay too long under the
drier you've got to go and fetch your youngest from school to take her
to the dentist all those essays to make and the evening pie to concoct

175

lovingly damn and blast I've forgotten the fresh cream isn't it lucky, Annie, could you run down to the grocer's the one round the corner your favourite TV show well you'll miss your favourite TV show since you're a female you might as well get used to not counting on your pleasures. I only care about your brothers, do I   how do you have the gall when I spent every night of last week finishing your dress. And dinner over have to listen to his lordship's tale of woes credit's difficult to get governmental incompetence heavy administrative machinery grotesque in this day and age while the dirty dishes stare you in the face heaps of broken walnut-shells and orange peel littering the tablecloth offensive to your sight   but his lordship likes it that way he likes to look at the left-overs of a meal   it's festive he says he who never tidies up it's comfortable so you leave it you listen   has he no inside no silence no space into which he could pour it all rather than into your wasted blasted breast your blue blood. 'Good lord ten already I think I'll call on Philip urgent matters to discuss you don't mind darling do you your pie was simply superb you're a cordon blue cook does this tie go with my new shirt do you think you could just brush the collar of my jacket oh while I remember there is a button to be sewn on to my raincoat I'm going to need it tomorrow how noisy those kids are night after night don't know how you stand it are you sure you're not spoiling them do you mean to say you've helped Derek with his homework again you ought to let him do it by himself when I was his age don't wait for me darling you look a little tired you ought to watch it you know eat more I know you like going to bed early so goodnight then.' Kisskiss.

The winds have blown into her sails for so long that they are all in shreds now; and her body is nothing but broken rigging. Her bones ache. She has lost so much weight, so much calcium, having children. Eight pounds lost over the first when she was supposed to put on weight, twelve pounds over the second and third. They too, even before being born, proved to be leeches. They sucked everything from her, especially her calcium. Were born without fontanelles, to the amazement of the gynaecologist, born firm and hard with the calcium greedily sucked from their mother. She, torn open by the too solid skulls, sewn up three times. You'd better not have any more, the gynaecologist told her, her spine threatening as it did to collapse. She suffers from sciatica now, it paralyzes her as soon as the autumn rains swathe the sky. She remains in bed one day, two days, then drugged to the eyeballs with aspirin, valiantly gets going again, an old lugger battered by the oceans.

But every year she springs a few more leaks in her spine, where the calcium padding has gone.

Have I told you that she is called Nadia? And her husband Vassili. He is descended from Russian immigrant parents.

As the seasons revolve her head too springs leaks.

For Monday Tuesday Thursday Friday Saturday with the small variation of Wednesdays when she never teaches because the children are off-school and have to be taken out clothes to be bought medical check-ups cinema on festive occasions or a walk in the forest where all that space does not prevent them from fighting over ownership of a tree-stump or a stick, and from moaning that they are bored. Like the holidays which for her mean nothing but cases endlessly to be packed and unpacked parcels all over the option picnic bags anoraks wellingtons swimming-trunks what have I forgotten this time and in which you are subjected to ceaseless arguments shrieks blows the youngest daily attempting to commit suicide fall out of trees choke on his snorkel get sunstroke convulsions set fire to his clothes fall off rocks. And at every meal time her husband blowing his top.

But this summer beats them all. She has had the bright idea of renting part of a farmhouse in the mountains to get back to the good life. It has never stopped raining. The wood will no longer catch fire in the cast iron stove which is their only means of keeping warm, on which they're meant to cook, too, and the children moan and groan that they miss TV and obstinately refuse to collect plants or go mushroom-picking. They endlessly natter to each other, fight round the kitchen table. It's a condensed version of the usual purgatory.

She feels frantic when she thinks about her life. Just being alive makes her feel sour. The universal door-mat the one you can always blame for everything the drain pipe into which you spew the blue blood the one whose red blood calcium oxygen marrow even are being sucked off by the male and his offspring suck gobble down the oyster pearl and flesh at once the vomit-bag for your convenience the vagina into which you eject the rodent sperm the handler of the shit of babies the thrower away of vegetable peelings but above all the ear down which you pour rancour troubles cries cries arguments and erotic fantasies when she no longer knows what taste eros might have why not bra-less and pant-less and why not into your arse all normally constituted women dream of it. After all, not so many years left got to take advantage of what you have left of youth.

Until . . . her soul so overflows with unspeakable resentment that she strains towards . . . a preposition which in the world of Being does not exist, can only repeat itself again and again, the tap-tap of the cardiac pump, the tic-tac of the alarm clock that's about to ring, Christmas that will soon be round yet again, forty-three presents to buy if her list is complete, and oh, the abominable bustle of the main stores, the reving cars that save their fumes for the lungs of housewives and their cushions for the behinds of gentlemen-on-their-way-to-the-office, the howlings of sharp teeth, vamporizing children whose blossoming flesh signals the withering of your own.

The beats get fainter and fainter, until un-til un-t-il you suddenly say to yourself: a rose's life is but a day it blooms at morn it fades at night where are the snows of yesteryear sans eyes sans teeth sans hair sans everything. Then, supposing you're still capable of saying then, you say, I've been bitched. Let me now make myself like the dead weight of things to get them in their turn, they mustn't get away scot-free. Let us become the millstone of family property. Of family propriety. Let us spur our husbands into the rat-race, if yours gets his behind on a professional chair, mine will become divisional manager. Let us become, 'a holiday in Iran less banal than in Spain, architecture breathtaking truly not to be missed.' Let us become the embodiment of duty, the dead weight of things since our soul died of asphyxia long ago and we are nothing now but a drain pipe a bag full of not even a vomit bag a bag no longer capable of enticing sperm. All hail, Nadia said to the image of this exquisite creature-to-be she took herself for in the window which night made reflexive, all hail unkempt unwept beauty, exhausted seam, deserted mine-shaft in which the wheels screech, you should treasure the tatters of youth which still encourage forage bills to peck you.

The little forage bills were in bed, digesting their daily share of the maternal fuel: the great male bill was renewing his vacational energies with alternate supplies of *pastis* and local chatter in some village café, down in the valley. Or was testing his virility in some local vagina. He has always been a great basher of open doors.

Then she turned her back on the darkened window. On her

darkened being. For at this precise moment, with a sleep-walker's automatism, she was about to make herself a cup of hot chocolate: she put her hand in the drawer to take out a coffee spoon.

It was a revelation.

The rising of a dawn she thought she no longer believed in.

The cutlery had been tidied up. The old peasant woman, no doubt, from whom they rented the farm, and who did a little housework for them. In the soft shadow of the drawer, protected by four, oh so symmetrical partitions, over oil-cloth that was scrupulously clean, the knives and forks and spoons, lay. Lay in state, she felt, so august was their arrangement. It made you think of them as of sleeping emperors, of swords in their scabbards. From the forks, their four curved halberds in military line-up, and from the spoons, protectively laid against them, there rose a quiet sense of rigour. Tin-plate they were, and the knives had steel blades you rubbed clean with earth, and black wooden handles: so that the value which shone out of them was wholly spiritual. Rest, earned daily with the sweat of one's brow. Objects handled with thrift and precision, all matters carefully considered as important, as essential, a whole life, was manifested in this arrangement. Nadia put her hand on the cutlery without stirring any of it, so as to become imbued with its virtue. Eyes closed, lips apart: like those Italian women, a mantilla over their heads, who go and touch the foot of St Peter's statue in Rome. The air had begun to exist, and it spoke of silence. From the depths of her, words were rising, deep-water swimmers slowly waving their webbed feet, rising, rising through the luminous depths slantwise like the tower of Pisa, rising, rising, with weed-like hair, towards the recesses of her palate. While the crazy clock in the hall chimed seventeen times for eleven o'clock. The saucepans hanging from a wooden board in an order calculated for use and not for prettiness, the painted sideboard, the wooden floor that must not be swept crosswise, a large green marrow straddling the vegetable bowl, were all . . . real, filled with a no-nonsense actuality which had something noble about it, and words were being uttered somehow by all these things, whole, hale, holy (holy lord god of hosts?). And being alive here was so different from everything Nadia knew, she felt transported to another world, the floor of deep seas where movement was ease. Where the mineral world swarmed with mosses, breedings, caresses. Where her flesh, poor shellfish that she was, shorn bit by bit of its armour, could at last relax and feel.

Nadia waited, while a sweet whiteness warmed her face, for milk in the saucepan suddenly to rustle up frothing. Elbows on the table, palms fitting the burning curve of the bowl of the cup, letting go, clasping it again, she stared at the night beyond the window. The strong presence of the farm and everything in it, that was something to be earned. It took on the gestures and relationships of a lifetime. She was there, she felt everything there was to feel about it, yet generations partitioned her from these objects, evicted her from this drawer, to the edge of which she clung, if only they'd let her lie alongside the forks and spoons and rest, a living mummy, inside the shelter of this square sarcophagus. She would gladly have exchanged what she had left of youth for that fine peasant old age, for hands which would consecrate, knead, grow things instead of mishandling them in a routine nightmare of speed and frustration. She would have traded her still smooth flesh for a rough, wrinkled, sun-beaten one, expressing an essential, a peaceful relationship to the ground she trod, the air which penetrated her lungs, the food which became her substance. But she did not have the simple words, let alone the simple heart, which would have permitted even the rudiments of such an exchange. She had no soul to sell, no red blood with which to counter-sign such a contract: she was nothing but a skein of recriminations and absences. Speaking of her 'late husband' the peasant woman said 'my poor husband'. The words spoke of lifelong habit and accceptance: an affection so deep and so normal, so careless of itself, that no word from the vocabulary of love could describe it. He had been her husband, that was all. They had 'to do' all life long one alongside the other, and there had been no time for nonsense. Nor any need to probe the heart and loins. She mourned for him in her heart. But she was still 'doing', because there was plenty to do, you didn't ask questions about it, doing was perceiving, handling, rejoicing, laughing, crying. Keeping one's heart alive, in short. Her heart was alive because she had been married.

But Nadia, she was not married to her husband. There lay between them a labyrinth so wide Dedalus himself could have claimed it, rancour for having spent her youth scurrying from one invisible/unimportant task to another, and contempt passed down to her by generations of women for man the provider and procreator, but riddled with petty cares, hollow at the centre, whom it was women's task to deceive. 'The way to hold a man is by his stomach and his sex. A clever woman manages her husband like a crafty minister his king, makes him do what she wants and lets him believe he's had the idea.' Only she, all comforts ruptured by her need to be a bread-winner too, dazed by the continuous rush, has the Machiavellian's detachment without the art let alone relish for the policy. She is only 'married' because something in her has obeyed the law of the species. Reproduce.

Besides, it would have been ridiculous for her to try and become a peasant. They were a dying race. Of the five farms on that side of the mountain, only two were still inhabited, and those by one person alone. So that when the ewes which spent the winter in Mme Blaise's great arched stable lambed at night, Mme Blaise stood at the window and blew her late husband's regimental trumpet to call Gaston, the other farmer who persisted in tilling these deserted fields, and he plodded through the snow to help her, with his lantern. And then, how was she to shed city habits, consumer's appetites, and all the twisted rhetoric of the age which kept her apart from a world in which you are what you do?

Yet she, the fallen daughter of a fallen race, can touch the peasant woman by putting her hand in the drawer. She can know her by the way the marrow rests on the vegetable bowl. The crab in her, despite its lost shell, knows with sub-marine knowledge that here lies hidden a deep-sea world where she could move at ease.

The door, noisily banged open, makes her jump. She has not heard the warning noises, the dog's chain clicking on the paving-stones, the rumbling throat warming to a bark, soon swallowed because here's someone he knows. Vassili. Defiant, aggressive. Drunk too much, as so often these days.

'You've come back early. Is anything wrong?'

'I thought I'd come back to see *you*.'

He must have been sent packing.

'I am flattered.'

'What's up with you? You've no need to adopt such a tone.'

'I'll adopt the tone I please.'

'Let me warn you, my dear wife, don't you use that tone with me. No one speaks to me like that.'

'One has the rights one takes.'

There are two possible readings of this scene. Others too, perhaps, inside the spectrum. But there are two extremes whose opposition is created by contrasting faiths. And charities.

Black Version

He grabs her by the collar. His eyes are bloodshot. Her heart fills her ears and drains her belly. He has only ever beaten her twice, once she had spoken ill of his father, the other time he was drunk. Like now. Why couldn't she have held her tongue? His eyes are two black slits with red round the edges. He is breathing noisily, as noisily as her heart thumps in her ears, no, it's his breathing that makes her heart thump.

'You're going to apologize. No one, do you hear me, no one ever, do you hear, ever talks to me like that. So you can swallow your puny rights because if you don't I'm going to kill you do you hear do you hear you bitch.'

'Yes Vassili Vassili I'm sorry I didn't mean to insult you I beg you Vassili calm down'

and oh how she despises herself for being so abject.

'Because your rights do you hear your rights you can stick them up your arse and besides besides I'm going to stick them up your arse bugger your rights come on go upstairs.'

'Vassili Vassili I beg you don't be like that.'

'Upstairs do you hear do you hear you bitch upstairs no one is ever going to tell me what to do I'm going to give you rights for your money you plaintive mealy-mouthed hysterical bitch if you dare speak to me like that I'm not going to let myself be dragged down into your miasma your dank cell I'm going to give you something to feel resentful about. Upstairs.'

'Don't do it Vassili I swear I won't do it again.'

'Upstairs.'

Will you come down or shall I come upstairs. Bluebeard shouted to his wife. She wriggles away she moans don't wake the children and she hates him, lord how she hates him. He is all wet, and she's all dry.

He's twice her weight. Under her the cold creased sheet is part of the hatred. He is crushing her, all women dream of it all women dream of being raped you'll see it'll satisfy you. He's got hold of her Nivea cream rubs it into her behind and oh the hatred for desire which is there but elsewhere everything the wrong way round. The wrong way round world explodes into pain (I shit you I shit you) she screams he puts his hand across her mouth shsh it's good he says going up and down biting her ear with his other hand he's kneading one of her breasts she cries screams fights him off he says stop it stop it if you don't stop it I'm going to kill you do you hear see how good how good saliva runs into her ear her legs paralyzed pain shoots down her ailing back he's finally breaking my spine for good this time (oh how I shit you I shit the universe) she wriggles away he pushes her down violently and up and down goes comes she would like to vomit he says how good she is being torn apart as by the children but where you shit he's getting excited he's beginning to groan how good goooooood.

He has slipped off her. He's lying on his side. He has given her. A sated kiss. He has fallen asleep. She goes on sobbing, short sobs. Her teeth chatter. But she does not cover herself up, she's glad she's cold, not under the same sheet as this bastard. She wipes herself on the sheet, raises it up to the moonlight, but it's too dark for her to be able to see whether it's blood. She bites her pillow, right, left, wipes her nose on it, everything is snot, everything is shit. And she's throbbing. So she makes herself come, three, four times, to expel, exorcize him. You're nothing but a bag full of shit. And all the times to expel to exorcize him. You're nothing but a bag full of shit. And all the other bastards the senior bastards all the chairmen headmen all buggerers bags full of shit. But no release. Nothing but bags full of shit looking for bags to pour their shit into because that's all they are all they can do. Grind to pieces poor invertebrates who have already lost their shells. The hard laying into the soft. Is there no justice? But neither masturbation nor tears which now stream down both sides of her face, she is lying on her back and he is snoring close to her, he masticates like a toothless old man a baby that air of innocence, neither masturbation nor words all the words can drain away her rage. She would like to get hold of the wardrobe and bash his head in but she shrinks from the certainty of her own weakness, she does not know how to aim her violence outwards, she does not belong to the race of the vertebrates. Something's running down from her is it blood or mislaid semen, she frantically wipes herself on the sheet. Already wet in patches. Anyone can lay into me a piece of cake. All laughing at me I'm the poor fool the soft touch. Is she bleeding and she thinks of that dream, a jet-black crow was furiously assaulting its mate, plucking feather after feather with its beak. Every time he pulled a feather off blood seeped to the surface red liquid red. Red like the cactus flowers which bloom on the small nipples which in the spring swell on the pores of the stem. And the she-bird was nearly stripped of her feathers, grotesque, defenceless against the predatory beak, and she had, how funny, fowl that she was, goose pimples all over her. Like her now, still bleeding from the last assault. Plucked like a chicken, she is cold and can no longer fly. Nor take shelter from the rain. Nor from looks. Voles's look, 'let me have a look at this essay will you point out to me the mistakes in grammar.' Vole's the vole the rat they're all in a league those rodents those destroyers voles Vassili. They gnaw gnaw gnaw at you there's a million of them. The unclean the plague-bearers they gnaw at me with their million little tasks little perceptions little humiliations take one bite after another. And I am nothing any more. But a prey to all the violence. And the little vermin, my children, the unclean offspring of an unclean race, the race of rodents, planted there who knows by what magic trick what conspiracy to devour my inside drain my calcium from me then tear my cunt open while the big voles the father senior voles gnaw at my feathers my shell tear me apart with their sharp teeth.

And when I think. That a little while ago. Centuries generations ago. In the kitchen. And the vole who is my bastard of a lord and master. Has buggered me. In the bed. In which Mme Blaise conceived her children.

But they won't get away with it. They won't get away with it. For no pulsing no chattering of teeth no verbal violence. Can drain the rage which festers in her heart.

And the thought of Mme Blaise makes her go down into the kitchen again.

When I think I regretted not being 'married' to him. Flesh of my flesh. Pahhh.

She has slipped on thick socks and wellingtons, has wrapped herself up in her anorak. She paces up and down, teeth chattering, muttering on and on. I must find a release or I'm going to go mad I must. She goes to the drawer. She barely dares touch it with her leper's flesh. Have faith. She opens it. Slowly opens it. Dips her forearms into it as if into a bowl, resting her hands on the curved spoons without caressing them, for caresses are disgusting. She tries to calm herself down. She bangs her head against the edge of the drawer, she says please help please help or I'm going to go mad. She bangs her head harder and harder, accompanying the beat of the clock, to free herself from the pain down there, and from the beat of her own blood.

She pulls the drawer further out, takes it out altogether, carefully, so as not to disturb the arrangement of the cutlery. She puts it on the wooden floor. All that wood, which you must work with the grain, sweep with the grain. She sits on the drawer, astride first, as on a bidet, so that the coolness of the metal, the order, should cure her poor flesh. She looks at the knives between her thighs, she thinks of that woman, where was the memory buried in her, who slit herself with pieces of glass to be freed once and for all from her husband's advances. But she has no violence to aim at herself. She is enough of a mess as it is, a poor old ship plundered by Vassilis and Voles. What she needs are creative forces. Like being coffined in a drawer. She places her legs inside it, carefully, one after the other. She is now a crouching mummy, knees girded by her arms, wrapped in the bandages of her closed lids. She is sailing away in a square ship in which she is untouchable, because the forces that prevail here are kindly spirits, they have beckoned to her, she alone knows they're there. If all those cretins could see her, crouching inside a drawer bare arse on cutlery, they would get her certified. Whereas for the first time in years she is being. Sane. Hale, whole, holy.

She sails for a long time, rocked by the sea-swell.

Then she runs ashore again, for a new throbbing makes her feel her rage is unappeased.

There is blood on the spoons. She takes a cloth and rubs them, rubs, terrified. Bluebeard, is blood going to appear on the other side? As on the little key to the cupboard where the seven murdered wives were hanging.

What she needs are things on which to stand. There is the drawer. And there is the marrow. She takes it in her arms, like an infant, like a hot-water bottle, she rocks it from left to right, eyes closed. Let the green impregnate me, let it make me a daughter and mother of greenness. And there is the mint. One drives vampires away with garlic, and evil spirits with fumigations of aromatic herbs. She gently lifts the latch of the kitchen door, slides open the big oiled bolts of the entrance door. Under her wellingtons now the uneven roundness of the paving-stones, and in her ears the clicking of the dog's chain. She gropes, feels the tousled mane, smells the sweet warm breath. Hears the murmur of the fountain, gradually visible, a massive shape in the centre of the courtyard. Mint grows at the edge of the brook, behind the barn. To the right.

It is by its scent she makes it out, and by the discreet song of the brook. She throws herself into all that green scent. Rolls herself in it, her anorak flung aside, rubs her arse in it to clean it up to cure it, rubs the leaves on her cheeks her belly her thighs. Let them dye me green, let them shield me with greenness. I want to become the green knight, the one whose head grows again after it's been severed. She closes the tufts over her head, a leafy dais between the stars and herself, and she lies there, shivering, one hand trailing in the brook, she sails away in her boat of freshness, inhaling freshness with all the might of her lungs. I am the child of mint. I have the power to destroy evil spirits.

Back in the kitchen. Her body is mottled with green and she still shivers in her anorak. But the coolness she feels is hers, her teeth are no longer chattering against the world. She opens the drawer, gets hold of one of the black handled knives with the steel blades. Well sharpened. She takes potatoes from the vegetable bowl. On the largest two she carves *V*s. She is erect leaning against the night thighs mottled with green. She has strewn the table with handfuls of mint. Some has fallen into the cup, at the bottom of which left-over chocolate from a long time ago has dried up, brown sand from which the tide is ebbing. She clasps the black handle with both hands, raises the blade as they do for sacrifices. And brings it down, down, stabs, stabs the potatoes, take that, and that, and that and that again, bastards. I hate you, rats, I hate you. White juice spittles from the yellow flesh, quickly soaked up by the clinging earth. Go and bleed your sperm into the earth. You bastards I shall open as many gashes in your flesh as the conspirators did in the body of Julius Caesar. I'm going to split you up as you've split me up. Take that and that and that.

'You're cooking? At four in the morning?'

She turns. Knife in her fist sticky with earthy juice. Dishevelled.

What can be seen of her legs between the anorak and the wellingtons mottled with green. Triumphant at seeing him, pitiful, hungover, ashamed of what he's done, wrapped in his maroon dressing-gown. A hundred to one he's going to apologize now he's worked off his violence. But mine is only beginning. I have discovered my strength. Greenness. The magic order that makes heads grow again.

'Nadia. My poor darling. You look you look . . . as if you've gone mad. Have you seen yourself? You poor sweetheart. It's all my fault. The drink. It wasn't me, it was the drink that was acting. I have to get it out of my system. I am sorry. My poor darling. Come back to bed.'

She says, 'Can you see that knife? Don't you come near me. See that potato? Well, you're that potato. See what I do to that potato? Well it works. You woke up didn't you? You feel rotten don't you? Well you'll feel even worse when I'm finished with you.'

'Nadia. Stop pretending to be mad.'

'Don't you come near me. If you come nearer, that's what you'll get. And that.'

She stabs the potato, again and again.

'I'm not coming any nearer, look I won't move. It must have gone to your head, Nadia, come back to bed, tomorrow things'll be better.'

She sees he is afraid. Oh, she knows he's not afraid of the knife, he's ten times stronger than her. But he's afraid of what she looks like. He's afraid of her gesture when she digs the knife into the potato.

She says, 'I will go to bed. But not with you. With the marrow. You can sleep here. If you come upstairs, I'll stay here. With my knife. And my potatoes.'

She knows that at any other time he would try to slap her, force her to speak 'normally', he'd say 'now I've had enough of this farce.' But he is gutted. And she, triumphant. She is the green knight.

'All right. Go to bed. I'll sleep here. You mustn't resent me like this, Nadia, you mustn't hate me. You'll see, tomorrow things'll be better.'

She hugs the marrow. Green and round against her belly. She smiles at him. Tomorrow. She knows very well that tomorrow won't be another day. That she won't leave the farm. Won't go back to Paris like a good girl good mother good wife responsible teacher.

'I won't go. I won't let go of the wood. Nor the green. Go without me. I don't want to see you any more. Don't touch me. I know what you are. I know what they are. Take them away.' She will face them, husband and children, uneasy, who will leave her alone perhaps because of that unease. She will have her back to the table, and on the table there will be the marrow, and her hands will be behind her back, and she will be stroking the marrow. On her right she will feel the presence of the drawer.

Perhaps if they let her be long enough. Perhaps if they let her recover here, in this virgin place, full of the whispers of magic. If they leave her at peace with all this wood you must sweep with the grain, water you have to fetch from the fountain, this farmyard where the wind blows, having swept over the mint and the crocuses of the sloping meadows, these aluminium saucepans smooth with patient scouring. Perhaps if they let her lie at peace inside the drawer, alongside the spoons and forks. Perhaps then she will go back to them. But for the time being, the marrow is more important.

White Version

'You and your puny declaration of women's rights. What's the matter with you?'

The matter with me is that I am sick to death of you, of marriage, of our mutual hypocrisy. If you think I don't know you go with other women. Liar. Philanderer. You think you're Casanova because you lay a few secretaries who're all but too happy to open their legs to any fourth-rate aspiring manager of bloody rubbish. Only don't come playing the tender devoted husband to me. You make me want to spit.'

'Nadia.'

'You make me sick do you hear sick. Conceited prick. You're farcical, that's what you are. Farcical.'

He remains, gaping. Goes and sinks into the only armchair in the room. That again is typical, when his lordship collapses he makes sure it's on something comfortable.

The silence crackles with background noises, as when you've forgotten to switch off the radio after all programmes are over. The clock strikes, half past. What. Vassili sits with head bowed, palms joined, as if he were praying. She can only see his curls, curly like John the Baptist, and that mop of hair is so like Robert's, their youngest, it fills her with tenderness.

He clears his throat, his voice is hoarse.
I don't know where this hurricane has come from. I don't know where you got the idea that I sleep around. I suppose there's no point in denying it if you're not going to believe me.'

'You flatter yourself if you think I'm jealous. It's your lies I can't bear.'

'But what the hell makes you think I'm lying?'

'There's no need to shout. The last resort of men, shouting their big mouths and then brute force. Fine animal superiority.'

He shrugs. He looks like a dog that's been beaten. You'd think he was trying not to cry. She feels elated. The air has become sheer ease to her. She could abolish the space that separates her from this man with one stride of her seven-league boots.

'I'm going to bed.'

'I thought you wanted to spend the evening with me.'

'Oh shut up.'

He slams the door after him. His footsteps give away his weight, creaking on the wooden steps, one after the other. She feels frustrated. Without purpose. Swallows dregs of cold chocolate, floury, with strips of skin in it. Puts out the light. Climbs upstairs too, with smaller creakings, and against her palms, in the dark, occasionally the uneven lukeward feel of the white-washed walls.

He is huddled on the edge of the bed. The unusual meekness touches her. How hard I am. He had come back home, all readiness all affection, and that's how you welcome him. How mean you are. What's the good of revenge, what's the point of destroying him. In any case, it's all in my head. My head's full of rancour, spider's webs out of thin air. Be kind. Be generous. Fashion the world to the image of love. She thinks of the beauty of the cutlery in the drawer, the serenity, and she feels ashamed of this storm in a teacup she has created. Just my spine screeching, that's all it was. Be bountiful like the gestures which have made the kitchen downstairs such a haven of peace. She clasps his back, pressing her breasts hard against it. Showers kisses on his nape.

'Nadia Nadia.'

He turns over, clasps her in his turn, with violence viciousness? Latching on to her as on to a life raft? A rebellious servant to be punished? She comes before him, crying out, longing for further heights, further, further up, carry me up my seven-league boots, but he, a brief spasm, withdraws. Turns his back to her. And falls asleep.

Blackness is full of whispers. Swarms with luminous dots. Vassili, warm, heavy. Snores. Glutted. Cold, down both temples, Nadia's tears are running. A huge nervous force lifts her up, she is a non-happening, nothing but the need to howl. I've been had, as usual. But this time it was my fault. The pig. Fancy my wanting to be 'generous', the madness of it, what has Christian love got to do with marriage I ask you. And all the time she knows she wants him. She even knows she likes him. Marriage is war, it's only bearable on either side of a Berlin wall. She could kick herself, 'generous', what a joke, and her rage circles round and round without finding a way out, a tiger behind bars. What have I got to cling to since my rock my supposed inner strength is nothing but an interminable bleeding. For a while she tries to imagine that it is not Vassili who is resting there but the marrow, green, monumental, and she lies alongside its vegetable coolness, the peace of its curves, like the forks against the spoons, but Vassili's snoring stops, he moans, turns on to his back, brushes against her. She starts wanting the marrow too. The pig. I hate him. Is there anything more grotesque in creation than a glutted male snoring in bed? And all the time she likes him. The ignoble fumblings of this degenerate race which rules the world, let the time of the hive come back, we'll turn them into bumble-bees again, only used for procreation which is all they're good for anyway, then whamm! exterminated. And the universe will be ruled by the minute rigour of the bees.

In order not to touch him she is now on the edge of the bed, where the sheets are cold. About to tip into the void. She says aloud 'you pig', but a satisfied grunt answers her. She throws the sheets aside viciously, gets up, slips into Vassili's thick pullover, his socks, her wellingtons, climbs down the stairs which creak again, board after board; draws open the well-oiled bolts. And then the night.

His chain tinkling, the dog comes and frolics around her. She says shhh, rubs his head, his back, the tousled mane is damp with the night dew. Gropes her way between the piles of logs drying for winter, through the door with the wooden latch; beyond the rickety stone step, worn hollow in its centre, space tumbles as far as the night will go.

On her left: the loo.

Sits, amidst darkness peopled by sounds and smells. Eyes raised to the lozenge of the peephole, blue-black in the surrounding pitch black, nostrils dilated by the smell of ammonia, warm in the cold night, she shits more warmly still on the soft spider's webs, dreaming of Gargantua or was it Pantagruel who of all things to wipe one's arse on favoured gosling down. And of Keats who found it repulsive that his beloved should be made of flesh solid enough to need daily to let out turds. You're a literary lady or you're not. What decadence, from the hale heartiness of the one to the squeamishness of the other. A fallen sex. The sounds open space out. A cricket nearby, frogs in the distance as evocative of water as the cricket is of sun stored in the earth, and also, much further away, the sustained barkings of dogs. They expand space into fixed directions, Gaston's farm, the forest, the hamlet of Conches. Whereas the intermittent reving of cars down in the valley makes her tip into a vertigo of mobility. They're only audible as they come near, they cease to be when they've moved away: they give away the surrounding geography, Les Thuiles on the left, Jauziers on the right, and beyond them the passes, Larche and its Piedmontese buttresses, Vars from which you can see the white and the black glaciers, and Les Caillols which are the gateway to the coast where for a long time now the mimosas have ceased to be in bloom. And in the contrast between the moored barkings of the dogs, which tell of rhythms of living in which everything matters, the precise wanderings of tinkling bells on the mountain pastures in summer, warm flocks parked in the great sheep-folds of vaulted stone during the snows of winter, and on the other hand down in the valley the burring of those cars which are pure movement, dissipated energy, and endless flight from nothing, she is gripped again by the dilemma which faced her in the kitchen. How could she ever cast her anchor in the space which is heralded by a chained dog when she belongs to spaces which only exist because they are being run through? Here, here only. There is no shelter left for the intellectuals of the diaspora save in the outdoor loos of the countryside.

A gust of wind sweeps over the human manure, freezing her buttocks. Rocking back and forth, her palms against the warm wood, she relishes being thus exposed to the elements. Perhaps one must speed up the pace of wandering to alter its course. One must be had in order not to be had. Rejoice in belonging to the losers' camp. The female camp. But free, free from rancour. The peasant woman treats her tin-plate knives and forks as if they were silver. Thus making them into something better than king's silver.

When she climbs back into the squeaking bed, she perceives, from his breathing, that he is awake. They lie side by side for a long time, in pitch black, neither of them ready to risk the first word. But she, strengthened by her fine meditation:

'Did I wake you up? I tried to be quiet.'

'Are you feeling ill?'

'I only wanted to go to the loo.'

Blackness again, thick with the consciousness each has of the other. She nestles close to him, he is warm, the tawny smell of his sweat, his breath still sweet with alcohol.

'You're frozen, your teeth are chattering.'

He squeezes her against him, and she feels him go hard.

'Vassili. Make love to me.'

'Didn't you come? I thought you had one.'

'I want another.'

'Messalina.'

Later on, she is smiling. In the black, which is beginning to whiten. His shoulder is hard, she hears the muscles crunch under her weight. A lovely hushed sound, the distant echo of gravel in one's childhood. Her nape is comfortable there.

'I like it when you're like this. Usually I feel as if I'm annoying you.'

'It's that I feel ashamed to ask.'

'Silly. I like you to want me.'

Feet forward, she feels herself slide into a warm sea. Outside, a lark bursts into song. It must be soaring, soaring towards the whitening sky, and grass in the sloping meadows must be dripping with dew.

GRANTA

MARTIN AMIS
LET ME COUNT THE TIMES

Vernon made love to his wife three and a half times a week, and this was all right.

For some reason, making love always averaged out that way. Normally—though by no means invariably—they made love every second night. On the other hand Vernon had been known to make love to his wife seven nights running; for the next seven nights they would not make love—or perhaps they would once, in which case they would make love the following week only twice but four times the week after that—or perhaps only three times, in which case they would make love four times the next week but only twice the week after that—or perhaps only once. And so on. Vernon didn't know why, but making love always averaged out that way; it seemed invariable. Occasionally—and was it any wonder?—Vernon found himself wishing that the week contained only six days, or as many as eight, to render these calculations (which were always blandly corroborative in spirit) easier to deal with.

It was, without exception, Vernon himself who initiated their conjugal acts. His wife responded every time with the same bashful alacrity. Oral foreplay was by no means unknown between them. On average—and again it always averaged out like this, and again Vernon was always the unsmiling ring master—fellatio was performed by Vernon's wife every third coupling, or 60.8333 times a year, or 1.1698717 times a week. Vernon performed cunnilingus rather less often: every fourth coupling, on average, or 45.625 times a year, or .8774038 times a week. It would also be a mistake to think that this was the extent of their variations. Vernon sodomized his wife twice a year, for instance—on his birthday, which seemed fair enough, but also, ironically (or so *he* thought), on hers. He put it down to the expensive nights out they always had on these occasions, and more particularly to the effects of champagne. Vernon always felt desperately ashamed afterwards, and would be a limp spectre of embarrassment and remorse at breakfast the next day. Vernon's wife never said anything about it, which was something. If she ever did, Vernon would probably have stopped doing it. But she never did. The same sort of thing happened when Vernon ejaculated in his wife's mouth, which on average he did 1.2 times a year. At this point they had been married for ten years. That was convenient. What would it be like when they had been married for eleven years—or thirteen. Once, and only once,

Vernon had been about to ejaculate in his wife's mouth when suddenly he had got a better idea: he ejaculated all over her face instead. She didn't say anything about that either, thank God. Why he had thought it a better idea he would never know. He didn't think it was a better idea now. It distressed him greatly to reflect that his rare acts of abandonment should expose a desire to humble and degrade the loved one. And she was the loved one. Still, he had only done it once. Vernon ejaculated all over his wife's face .001923 times a week. That wasn't very often to ejaculate all over your wife's face, now was it?

Vernon was a businessman. His office contained several electronic calculators. Vernon would often run his marital frequencies through these swift, efficient, and impeccably discrete machines. They always responded brightly with the same answer, as if to say, 'Yes, Vernon, that's how often you do it,' or 'No, Vernon, you don't do it any more often than that.' Vernon would spend whole lunch-hours crooked over the calculator. And yet he knew that all these figures were in a sense approximate. Oh, Vernon knew, Vernon knew. Then one day a powerful white computer was delivered to the accounts department. Vernon saw at once that a long-nursed dream might now take flesh: leap years. 'Ah, Alice. I don't want to be disturbed, do you hear?' he told the cleaning lady sternly when he let himself into the office that night. 'I've got some very important calculations to do in the accounts department.' Just after midnight Vernon's hot red eyes stared up wildly from the display screen, where his entire sex life lay tabulated in recurring prisms of threes and sixes, in endless series, like mirrors placed face to face.

Vernon's wife was the only woman Vernon had ever known. He loved her and he liked making love to her quite a lot; certainly he had never craved any other outlet. When Vernon made love to his wife he thought only of her pleasure and her beauty: the infrequent but highly flattering noises she made through her evenly parted teeth, the divine plasticity of her limbs, the fever, the magic, and the safety of the moment. The sense of peace that followed had only a little to do with the probability that tomorrow would be a night off. Even Vernon's dreams were monogamous: the woman who strode those slipped but essentially quotidian landscapes were mere icons of the self-sufficient female kingdom, nurses, nuns, bus-conductresses, parking wardens, policewomen. Only every now and then, once a week, say, or less, or not calculably, he saw things that made him suspect that life might have room for more inside—a luminous ribbon dappling the under-curve of a bridge, certain cloudscapes, intent figures hurrying through changing light.

All this, of course, was before Vernon's business trip. It was not a particularly important business trip: Vernon's firm was not a particularly important firm. His wife packed his smallest suitcase and drove him to the station. On the way she observed that they had not spent a night apart for over four years—when she had gone to stay with her mother after that operation of hers. Vernon nodded in surprised agreement, making a few brisk calculations in his head. He kissed her good-bye with some passion. In the restaurant car he had a gin and tonic. He had another gin and tonic. As the train approached the thickening city Vernon felt a curious lightness play through his body. He thought of himself as a young man, alone. The city would be full of cabs, stray people, shadows, women, things happening.

Vernon got to his hotel at eight o'clock. The receptionist confirmed his reservation and gave him his key. Vernon rode the elevator to his room. He washed and changed, selecting, after some deliberation, the more sombre of the two ties his wife had packed. He went to the bar and ordered a gin and tonic. The cocktail waitress brought it to him at a table. The bar was scattered with city people: men, women who probably did things with men fairly often, young couples secretively chuckling. Directly opposite Vernon sat a formidable lady with a fur, a hat, and a cigarette holder. She glanced at Vernon twice or perhaps three times. Vernon couldn't be sure.

He dined in the hotel restaurant. With his meal he enjoyed half a bottle of good red wine. Over coffee Vernon toyed with the idea of going back to the bar for a creme de menthe—or a champagne cocktail. He felt hot; his scalp hummed; two hysterical flies looped round his head. He rode back to his room, with a view to freshening up. Slowly, before the mirror, he removed all his clothes. His pale body was inflamed with the tranquil glow of fever. He felt deliciously raw, tingling to his touch. What's happening to me? he wondered. Then, with relief, with shame, with rapture, he keeled backwards on to the bed and did something he hadn't done for over ten years.

Vernon did it three more times that night and twice again in the morning.

Four appointments spaced out the following day. Vernon's mission was to pick the right pocket calculator for daily use by all members of his firm. Between each demonstration—the Moebius strip of figures, the repeated wink of the decimal point—Vernon took cabs back to the hotel and did it again each time. 'As fast as you can, driver,' he found himself saying. That night he had a light supper sent up to his room. He did it five more times—or was it six? He could no longer be absolutely sure. But he was sure he did it three more times the next morning, once before breakfast and twice after. He took the train back at noon, having done it an incredible 18 times in 36 hours: that was—what?—84 times a week, or 4,368 times a year. Or perhaps he had done it 19 times! Vernon was exhausted, yet in a sense he had never felt stronger. And here was the train giving him an erection all the same, whether he liked it or not.

'How was it?' asked his wife at the station.

'Tiring. But successful,' admitted Vernon.

'Yes, you do look a bit whacked. We'd better get you home and tuck you up in bed for a while.'

Vernon's red eyes blinked. He could hardly believe his luck.

Shortly afterwards Vernon was to look back with amused disbelief at his own faint-heartedness during those trail-blazing few days. Only in bed, for instance! Now, in his total recklessness and elation, Vernon did it everywhere. He hauled himself roughly on to the bedroom floor and did it there. He did it under the impassive gaze of the bathroom's porcelain and steel. With scandalized laughter he dragged himself out protesting to the garden tool shed and did it there. He did it lying on the kitchen table. For a while he took to doing it in the open air, in windy parks, behind hoardings in the town, on churned fields; it made his knees tremble. He did it in corridorless trains. He would rent rooms in cheap hotels for an hour, for half an hour, for ten minutes (how the receptionists stared). He thought of renting a little love-nest somewhere. Confusedly and very briefly he considered running off with himself. He started doing it at work, cautiously at first, then with nihilistic abandon, as if discovery was the very thing he secretly craved. Once, giggling coquettishly before and afterwards (the danger, the danger), he did it while dictating a long and tremulous letter to the secretary he shared with two other senior managers. After this he came to his senses somewhat and resolved to try only to do it at home.

'How long will you be, dear?' he would call over his shoulder as his wife opened the front door with her shopping-bags in her hands. An hour? Fine. Just a couple of minutes? Even better! He took to lingering sinuously in bed while his wife made their morning tea, deliciously sandwiched by the moist uxoriousness of the sheets. On his nights off from love-making (and these were invariable now: every other night, every other night) Vernon nearly always managed one while his wife, in the bathroom next door, calmly readied herself for sleep. She nearly caught him at it on several occasions. He found that especially exciting. At this point Vernon was still trying hectically to keep count; it was all there somewhere, gurgling away in the memory banks of the computer in the accounts department. He was averaging 3.4 times a day, or 23.8 times a week, or an insane 1,241 times a year. And his wife never suspected a thing.

Until now, Vernon's 'sessions' (as he thought of them) had always been mentally structured round his wife, the only woman he had ever known—her beauty, the flattering noises she made, the fever, the safety. There were variations, naturally. A typical 'session' would start with her undressing at night. She would lean out of her heavy brassière and submissively debark the tender checks of her panties. She would give a little gasp, half pleasure, half fear (how do you figure a woman?), as naked Vernon, obviously in sparkling form, emerged impressively from the shadows. He would mount her swiftly, perhaps even rather brutally. Her hands mimed their defencelessness as the great muscles rippled and plunged along Vernon's powerful back. 'You're too big for me,' he would have her say to him sometimes, or 'That hurts, but I like it.' Climax would usually be synchronized with his wife's howled request for the sort of thing Vernon seldom did to her in real life. But Vernon never did the things for which she yearned, oh no. He usually just ejaculated all over her face. She loved that as well of course (the bitch), to Vernon's transient disgust.

And then the strangers came.

One summer evening Vernon returned early from the office. The car was gone: as Vernon had shrewdly anticipated, his wife was out somewhere. Hurrying into the house, he made straight for the bedroom. He lay down and lowered his trousers—and then with a sensuous moan tugged them off altogether. Things started well, with a compelling preamble that had become increasingly popular in recent weeks. Naked, primed, Vernon stood behind the half-closed bedroom door. Already he could hear his wife's preparatory truffles of shy arousal. Vernon stepped forward to swing open the door, intending to stand there menacingly for a few seconds, his restless legs planted well apart. He swung open the door and stared. At what? At his wife sweatily grappling with a huge bronzed gypsy, who turned incuriously towards Vernon and then back again to the hysteria of volition splayed out on the bed before him. Vernon ejaculated immediately. His wife returned home within a few minutes. She kissed him on the forehead. He felt very strange.

The next time he tried, he swung open the door to find his wife upside down over the headboard, doing scarcely credible things to a hairy-shouldered Turk. The time after that, she had her elbows hooked round the back of her knee-caps as a 15 stone Chinaman feasted at his leisure on her imploring sobs. The time after that, two silent, glistening negroes were doing what the hell they liked with her. The two negroes, in particular, wouldn't go away; they were quite frequently joined by the Turk, moreover. Sometimes they would even let Vernon and his wife get started before they all came thundering in on them. And did Vernon's wife mind any of this? Mind? She liked it. Like it? She *loved* it! And so did Vernon, apparently. At the office Vernon soberly searched his brain for a single neutrino of genuine desire that his wife should do these things with these people. The very idea made him shout with revulsion. Yet, one way or another, he didn't mind it really, did he? One way or another, he liked it. He loved it. But he was determined to put an end to it.

His whole approach changed. 'Right, my girl,' he muttered to himself, 'two can play at that game.' To begin with, Vernon had affairs with all his wife's friends. The longest and perhaps the most detailed was with Vera, his wife's old school chum. He sported with her bridge-partners, her co-workers in the Charity. He fooled around with all her eligible relatives—her younger sister, that nice little niece of hers. One mad morning Vernon even mounted her hated mother. 'But Vernon, what about . . .?' they would all whisper fearfully. But Vernon just shoved them on to the bed, twisting off his belt with an imperious snap. All the women out there on the edges of his wife's world—one by one, Vernon had the lot.

Meanwhile, Vernon's erotic dealings with his wife herself had continued much as before. Perhaps they had even profited in poignancy and gentleness from the pounding rumours of Vernon's nether life. With this latest development, however, Vernon was not slow to mark a new dimension, a disfavoured presence, in their bed. Oh, they still made love all right; but now there were two vital differences. Their acts of sex were no longer hermetic; the safety and the peace had gone: no longer did Vernon attempt to apply any brake to the chariot of his thoughts. Secondly—and perhaps even more crucially—their love-making was, without a doubt, *less frequent*. Six and a half times a fortnight, three times a week, five times a fortnight . . . : they were definitely losing ground. At first Vernon's mind was a chaos of back-logs, short-falls, restructured schedules, recuperation schemes. Later he grew far more detached about the whole business. Who said he had to do it three and a half times a week? Who said that this was all right? After ten nights of chaste sleep (his record up till now) Vernon watched his wife turn sadly on her side after her diffident goodnight. He waited several minutes, propped up on an elbow, glazedly eternalized in the potent moment. Then he leaned forward and coldly kissed her neck, and smiled as he felt her body's axis turn. He went on smiling. He knew where the real action was.

For Vernon was now perfectly well aware that any woman was his for the taking, any woman at all, at a nod, at a shrug, at a single convulsive snap of his peremptory fingers. He systematically serviced every woman who caught his eye in the street, had his way with them, and tossed them aside without a second thought. All the models in his wife's fashion magazines—they all trooped through his bedroom, too, in their turn. Over the course of several months he worked his way through all the established television actresses. An equivalent period took care of the major stars of the Hollywood screen. (Vernon bought a big glossy book to help him with this project.

For his money, the girls of the Golden Age were the most daring and athletic lovers: Monroe, Russell, West, Dietrich, Dors, Ekberg. Frankly, you could keep your Welches, your Dunaways, your Fondas, your Keatons.) By now the roll-call of names was astounding. Vernon's prowess with them epic, unsurpassable. All the girls were saying that he was easily the best lover they had ever had.

One afternoon he gingerly peered into the pornographic magazines that blazed from the shelves of a remote newsagent. He made a mental note of the faces and figures, and the girls were duly accorded brief membership of Vernon's thronging harem. But he was shocked; he didn't mind admitting it: why should pretty young girls take their clothes off for money like that, like *that*? Why should men want to buy pictures of them doing it? Distressed and not a little confused, Vernon conducted the first great purge of his clamorous rumpus rooms. That night he paced through the shimmering corridors and becalmed ante-rooms dusting his palms and looking sternly this way and that. Some girls wept openly at the loss of their friends; others smiled up at him with furtive triumph. But he stalked on, slamming the heavy doors behind him.

Vernon now looked for solace in the pages of our literature. Quality, he told himself, was what he was after—quality, quality. Here was where the high-class girls hung out. Using the literature shelves in the depleted local library, Vernon got down to work. After quick flings with Emily, Griselda, and Criseyde, and a strapping weekend with the Good Wife of Bath, Vernon cruised straight on to Shakespeare and the delightfully wide eyed starlets of the romantic comedies. He romped giggling with Viola over the Illyrian hills, slept in a glade in Arden with the willowy Rosalind, bathed nude with Miranda in a turquoise lagoon. In a single disdainful morning he splashed his way through all four of the tragic heroines: cold Cordelia (this was a bit of a frost, actually), bitter-sweet Ophelia (again rather constricted, though he quite liked her dirty talk), the snake-eyed Lady M. (Vernon had had to watch himself there) and, best of all, that sizzling sorceress Desdemona (Othello had *her* number all right. She *stank* of sex!). Following some arduous, unhygienic yet relatively brief dalliance with Restoration drama, Vernon soldiered on through the prudent matrons of the Great Tradition. As a rule, the more sedate and respectable the girls, the nastier and more complicated were the things Vernon found

Martin Amis

himself wanting to do to them (with lapsed hussies like Maria Bertram, Becky Sharp, or Lady Dedlock, Vernon was in, out, and away, darting half-dressed over the rooftops). Pamela had her points, but Clarissa was the one who turned out to be the true cot-artist of the *oeuvre*; Sophie Western was good fun all right, but the pious Amelia yodelled for the humbling high points in Vernon's sweltering repertoire. Again, he had no very serious complaints about his one-night romances with the likes of Elizabeth Bennett and Dorothea Brooke; it was adult, sanitary stuff, based on a clear understanding of his desires and his needs; they knew that such men will take what they want ; they knew that they would wake the next morning and Vernon would be gone. Give him a Fanny Price, though, or better, much better, a Little Nell, and Vernon would march into the bedroom rolling up his sleeves; and Nell and Fan would soon be ruing the day they'd ever been born. Did they mind the horrible things he did to them? Mind? When he prepared to leave the next morning, solemnly buckling his belt before the tall window—how they howled!

The possibilities seemed endless. Other literatures dozed expectantly in their dormitories. The sleeping lion of Tolstoy—Anna, Natasha, Masha, and the rest. American fiction—those girls would show even Vernon a trick or two. The sneaky Gauls—Vernon had a hunch that he and Madame Bovary, for instance, were going to get along just fine . . . . One puzzled weekend, however, Vernon encountered the writings of D. H. Lawrence. Snapping *The Rainbow* shut on Sunday night, Vernon realized at once that this particular avenue of possibility—sprawling as it was, with its intricate trees and their beautiful diseases, and that distant prospect where sandy mountains loomed—had come to an abrupt and unanswerable end. He never knew women behaved like *that* . . . . Vernon felt obscure relief and even a pang of theoretical desire when his wife bustled in last thing, bearing the tea-tray before her.

Vernon was now, on average, sleeping with his wife 1.15 times a week. Less than single figure love-making was obviously going to be some sort of crunch, and Vernon was making himself vigilant for whatever form the crisis might take. She hadn't, thank God, said anything about it, yet. Brooding one afternoon soon after the Lawrence débâcle, Vernon suddenly thought of something that made his heart jump. He blinked. He couldn't believe it. It was true.

Not once since he had started his 'sessions' had Vernon exacted from his wife any of the sly variations with which he had used to space out the weeks, the months, the years. Not once. It had simply never occurred to him. He flipped his pocket calculator on to his lap. Stunned, he tapped out the figures. She now owed him . . . . Why, if he wanted, he could have an entire week of . . . . They were behind with *that* to the tune of . . . . Soon it would be time again for him to . . . . Vernon's wife passed through the room. She blew him a kiss. Vernon resolved to shelve these figures but also to keep them up to date. They seemed to balance things out. He knew he was denying his wife something she ought to have; yet at the same time he was withholding something he ought not to give. He began to feel better about the whole business.

For it now became clear that no mere woman could satisfy him—not Vernon. His activities moved into an entirely new sphere of intensity and abstraction. Now, when the velvet curtain shot skywards, Vernon might be astride a black stallion on a mammoreal dune, his narrow eyes fixed on the caravan of defenceless Arab women straggling along beneath him; then he dug in his spurs and thundered down on them, swords twirling in either hand. Or else Vernon climbed from a wriggling human swamp of tangled naked bodies, playfully batting away the hands that clutched at him, until he was tugged down once again into the thudding mass of membrane and heat. He visited strange planets where women were metal, were flowers, were gas. Soon he became a cumulus cloud, a tidal wave, the East Wind, the boiling Earth's core, the air itself, wheeling round a terrified globe as whole tribes, races, ecologies fled and scattered under the continent-wide shadow of his approach.

It was after about a month of this new brand of skylarking that things began to go rather seriously awry.

The first hint of disaster came with sporadic attacks of *ejaculatio praecox*. Vernon would settle down for a leisurely session, would just be casting and scripting the cosmic drama about to be unfolded before him—and would look down to find his thoughts had been messily and pleasurelessly anticipated by the roguish weapon in his hands. It began to happen more frequently, sometimes quite out of the blue: Vernon wouldn't even notice until he saw the boyish, tell-tale stains on his pants last thing at night. (Amazingly, and rather hurtfully too, his wife didn't seem to detect any real difference. But he was making love to her only every ten or eleven days by that time.) Vernon made a creditable attempt to laugh the whole thing off, and, sure enough, after a while the trouble cleared itself up. What followed, however, was far worse.

To begin with, at any rate, Vernon blamed himself. He was so relieved, and so childishly delighted, by his newly recovered prowess that he teased out his 'sessions' to unendurable, unprecedented lengths. Perhaps that wasn't wise . . . . What was certain was that he overdid it. Within a week, and quite against his will, Vernon's 'sessions' were taking between thirty and forty-five minutes; within two weeks, up to an hour and a half. It wrecked his schedules: all the lightning strikes, all the silky raids, that used to punctuate his life were reduced to dour campaigns which Vernon could perforce never truly win. 'Vernon, are you ill?' his wife would say outside the bathroom door. 'It's nearly *tea*-time.' Vernon—slumped on the lavatory seat, panting with exhaustion—looked up wildly, his eyes startled, shrunken. He coughed until he found his voice. 'I'll be straight out,' he managed to say, climbing heavily to his feet.

Nothing Vernon could summon would deliver him. Massed, maddened, cart-wheeling women—some of molten pewter and fifty feet tall, others indigo and no bigger than fountain-pens—hollered at him from the four corners of the universe. No help. He gathered all the innocents and subjected them to atrocities of unimaginable proportions, committing a million murders enriched with infamous tortures. He still drew a blank. Vernon, all neutronium, a supernova, a black sun, consumed the Earth and her sisters in his dead fire, bullocking through the solar system, ejaculating the Milky Way. That didn't work either. He was obliged to fake orgasms with his wife (rather skilfully, it seemed: she didn't say anything about it). His testicles developed a mighty migraine, whose slow throbs all day timed his heartbeat with mounting frequency and power, until at night Vernon's face was a sweating parcel of lard and his hands shimmered deliriously as he juggled the aspirins to his lips.

Then the ultimate catastrophe occurred. Paradoxically, it was heralded by a single, joyous, uncovenanted climax—again out of the blue, on a bus, one lunchtime. Throughout the afternoon at the office Vernon chuckled and gloated, convinced that finally all his troubles were at an end. It wasn't so. After a week of ceaseless experiment and scrutiny Vernon had to face the truth. The thing was dead. He was impotent.

'Oh my God,' he thought, 'I always knew something like this would happen to me some time.' In one sense Vernon accepted the latest reverse with grim stoicism (by now the thought of his old ways filled him with the greatest disgust); in another sense, and with terror, he felt like a man suspended between two states: one is reality, perhaps, the other an unspeakable dream. And then when day comes he awakes with a moan of relief; but reality has gone and the nightmare has replaced it: the nightmare was really there all the time. Vernon looked at the house where they had lived for so long now, the five rooms through which his calm wife moved along her calm tracks, and he saw it all slipping away from him forever, all his peace, all the fever and the safety. And for what, for what?

'Perhaps it would be better if I just told her about the whole thing and made a clean breast of it,' he thought wretchedly. 'It wouldn't be easy, God knows, but in time she might learn to trust me again. And I really *am* finished with all that other nonsense. God, when I . . .'. But then he saw his wife's face—capable, straightforward, confident—and the scar of dawning realization as he stammered out his shame. No, he could never tell her, he could never do that to her, no, not to her. She was sure to find out soon enough anyway. How could a man conceal that he had lost what made him a man? He considered suicide, but—'But I just haven't got the guts,' he told himself. He would have to wait, to wait and melt in his dread.

A month passed without his wife saying anything. This had always been a make-or-break, last-ditch deadline for Vernon, and he now approached the coming confrontation as a matter of nightly crisis. All day long he rehearsed his excuses. To kick off with Vernon complained of a headache, on the next night of a stomach upset. For the following two nights he stayed up virtually until dawn—'preparing the annual figures,' he said. On the fifth night he simulated a long coughing fit, on the sixth a powerful fever. But on the seventh night he just helplessly lay there, sadly waiting. Thirty minutes passed, side by side. Vernon prayed for her sleep and for his death.

'Vernon?' she asked.

'Mm-hm?' he managed to say—God, what a croak it was.

'Do you want to talk about this?'

Vernon didn't say anything. He lay there, melting, dying. More minutes passed. The he felt her hand on his thigh.

Quite a long time later, and in the posture of a cowboy on the

Martin Amis

back of a bucking steer, Vernon ejaculated all over his wife's face. During the course of the preceding two and a half hours he had done to his wife everything he could possibly think of, to such an extent that he was candidly astonished that she was still alive. They subsided, mumbling soundlessly, and slept in each other's arms.

Vernon woke up before his wife did. It took him thirty-five minutes to get out of bed, so keen was he to accomplish this feat without waking her. He made breakfast in his dressing-gown, training every cell of his concentration on the small, sacramental tasks. Every time his mind veered back to the night before, he made a low growling sound, or slid his knuckles down the cheese-grater, or caught his tongue between his teeth and pressed hard. He closed his eyes and he could see his wife crammed against the headboard with that one leg sticking up in the air; he could hear the sound her breasts made as he two-handedly slapped them practically out of alignment. Vernon steadied himself against the refrigerator. He had an image of his wife coming into the kitchen—on crutches, her face black and blue. She couldn't very well not say anything about *that*, could she? He laid the table. He heard her stir. He sat down, his knees cracking, and ducked his head behind the cereal packet.

When Vernon looked up his wife was sitting opposite him. She looked utterly normal. Her blue eyes searched for his with all their light.

'Toast?' he bluffed.

'Yes please. Oh Vernon, wasn't it lovely?'

For an instant Vernon knew beyond doubt that he would now have to murder his wife and then commit suicide—or kill her and leave the country under an assumed name, start all over again somewhere, Romania, Iceland, the Far East, the New World.

'What, you mean the—?'

'Oh yes. I'm so happy. For a while I thought that we . . . . I thought you were—'

'I—'

'—Don't, darling. You needn't say anything. I understand. And now everything's all right again. Ooh,' she added. 'You were naughty, you know.'

Vernon nearly panicked all over again. But he gulped it down and said, quite nonchalantly, 'Yes, I was a bit, wasn't I?'

206

'Very naughty. So *rude*. Oh Vernon . . .'.

She reached for his hand and stood up. Vernon got to his feet too—or became upright by some new hydraulic system especially devised for the occasion. She glanced over her shoulder as she moved up the stairs.

'You mustn't do that too often, you know.'

'Oh really?' drawled Vernon. 'Who says?'

'*I* say. It would take the fun out of it. Well, not *too* often, anyway.'

Vernon knew one thing: he was going to stop keeping count. Pretty soon, he reckoned, things would be more or less back to normal. He'd had his kicks: it was only right that the loved one should now have hers. Vernon followed his wife into the bedroom and softly closed the door behind them.

GRANTA

KENNETH BERNARD
SHERRY FINE: CONCEPTUALIST

When Jimmy Dellapiccolo first met her, she was in a SoHo gallery masturbating. She was the only exhibit. Every hour on the hour, from eleven to four, she masturbated. She drew quite a crowd, and Jimmy saw her twice. In between her sessions she rolled herself up in a rug and seemed to sleep, although no one could be sure since only her feet were visible. Each session took five to ten minutes, and she seemed to have a set procedure. Jimmy was fascinated. She had a fine but not stupendous body and a truly lovely face. Again and again, he found himself straying from the mechanics of her ritual to her face, which she kept expressionless as she stared directly at her audience. The only change was when she had, or seemed to have, an orgasm. Her face cracked into a brief moment of pain, she emitted a few short goatlike cries, which Jimmy found hair-raising, rolled her nude body in the rug, and was still. Jimmy wondered how she knew when the next session was, for no bell or signal sounded. The crowd, of course, built up each time, buzzing with high and low talk of art, snickering, manoeuvering for good sight lines. Promptly on schedule the rug began to move. She unrolled herself, leaned up on one elbow, and did her thing. She was billed as Sherry Fine, or more precisely, Sherry Fine Masturbates, to March 24. By Jimmy's count, she masturbated six times a day, thirty times a week, and would, by the end of the exhibit, have achieved, presumably, one hundred and twenty orgasms in a month's time, not counting outside sex, if any. This did not seem excessive according to what he had been reading. As he left the gallery he wondered what her last exhibit had been and what her next would be. Sherry Fine intrigued him.

They Meet and Sherry Explains Her Art to Jimmy

In the next ten days, Jimmy saw Sherry seven more times, once three hours in a row and twice two hours in a row. Then he *met* her in a natural food restaurant on Spring Street. He couldn't believe his eyes. The first thing he said was, 'My god, is it really you?' The first thing she said was, 'Not while eating.' She was eating steamed vegetables over brown rice, and he ordered lentil soup and yogurt delight. Then they got acquainted. Jimmy told her that he lived in Queens with his mother and was an accountant but broad-minded. Sherry told him that she was opening in Rome in six weeks and that her show had good parameters. 'What are parameters?' Jimmy asked. And she told him. For example, had he noticed that each time she unrolled from her rug she was never precisely in the same place? He had. Was he certain that she in fact had an orgasm each time? He was not. When she unrolled herself, was he ever certain which way she would be facing? No, in fact twice he had been in back of her. 'And you didn't mind, did you?' 'That's right,' Jimmy said with some surprise, 'I didn't mind at all. In fact, it was just as interesting as being in front. I mean—well, of course I had *already* been in front.' 'Precisely,' Sherry said. 'And even if you hadn't?' 'Hmmm,' Jimmy mused. When he stayed between showings, Sherry continued, what did he do? Jimmy thought a bit. Well, he watched her toes a lot, wondered which people were going to stay over for the next unrolling, talked to some of them, imagined wild things about the women who came, especially more than once, wondered how she knew when the hour had come, whether she slept, did she come out for her first showing of the day nude, in a robe, or what, were people there, which people (e.g. gallery people?), how did she leave after her last showing, did it all interfere with her sex life, was she embarrassed, had her mother come, had any spectators come while watching her, did she take breaks to urinate, eat, smoke a cigarette—Sherry Fine interrupted to say that she didn't smoke. There was a pause. 'Parameters,' she said. 'All parameters.' '*Wow*,' responded Jimmy slowly. 'That is *terrific*. You mean it's all part of your show?' She nodded. 'It's a grid, with astronomical but nevertheless finite (human) possibilities. Theoretically,' she said, 'you could keep coming to my show as long as I (and you, of course) lived. And it would never be the same. I think that's wonderfully human.' Jimmy pondered. He lost himself in *Sherry Fine Still Masturbates*, Sherry eighty years old. The parameters would be unbelievable. 'What about temperature?' he asked. 'Of course,' she said. 'Seasons, light everything.' 'You know,' Jimmy said, 'I feel I know you intimately.' 'Exactly.' 'Would you like to make love?' 'Men bore me.' 'How about a movie?' They went to the movies. Later Sherry told him she was thinking of getting into epicycles. Even with astronomical parametrical possibilities, she was still too *visible*, trapped in fact. 'Epicycles are different?' Jimmy asked. Sherry didn't answer.

Kenneth Bernard

Sherry Fine Explains about the Men in her Life

During the last week of her exhibit, Sherry was angry. The crowds had increased each week, with many more hold-overs from showing to showing. This was expected. It was one of the of the parameters. Then the gallery interfered. Because of the crowd they put up platforms so that those in back could see more easily. This changed her space and her options. The gallery also made the viewers wait in line before each viewing, and after it they were ushered out like stale air instead of being allowed to mill about and wait, if they wished, for the next viewing. A good many nevertheless went out and stood in line again. Even so, Sherry thought, it was a bad parameter. She felt constricted, she felt vulgar, like a peep show. It defused her rug roll. She felt manipulated. 'They wouldn't do this to me,' she said, 'if I were a man, if I had a cock.' And with this comment, she began telling Jimmy about the men in her life. The most serious had been Archie Baldour, who had since disappeared from the downtown art scene. He had made a modest reputation mutilating himself in minor ways, but during their courtship he had become very *heavy* and announced a major mutilation. He would castrate or otherwise emasculate himself the opening day of the exhibit and after a day or two in the hospital would be on view in the gallery. 'Why?' Sherry had asked. 'Why what?' Baldour had asked back. 'Why the hospital? Why not just lie there and bleed?' Jimmy felt the hair on his head rise. 'What did he say?' he asked. 'Nothing. It was all academic anyway. A week later a German beat him to it. After that he just disappeared. It was ironic, in a way,' she continued. 'It was Baldour that really started me out. He got me a part in a play where all I had to do was sit on a toilet through the whole play. The audience only saw my legs. But I really had my pants down and it was a real toilet, though without plumbing. I really felt *there*, you know. I could feel the audience thinking about me. When we took our curtain call each night, they had eyes only for me. Seeing me finally made them orgasmic. It made the play, really. That *was* the play.' 'What was the play?' Jimmy asked. 'I forget. What I do now, that's not orgasmic at all. For you, I mean, for the viewer. It's all very intellectual.' 'Parameters?' Jimmy suggested. 'Exactly,' she said. 'For me it's extremely beautiful—passionate and spiritual. I had an affair with the stage manager, but only briefly. He had to check everything before the curtain went up. Every night he would peek over the toilet door and say, 'Got your pants down, honey?' And if I hadn't, he would keep looking until I did. Finally he couldn't stand it. He practically raped me one night after the show, said he had been masturbating every night after the curtain went up. He wasn't too bad once I go to know him. But by the time the show closed, I had already thought out a few things. One night, for example, I left something in the toilet. I knew where I wanted to go. And *he* definitely wasn't a part of *it*.' 'How old were you?' Jimmy asked. 'Why?' 'Just curious.' 'Eighteen,' Sherry said. 'I was a Bayside dropout. Then I got involved with a burn freak, a gun-wound freak, and a woman in rapid succession. It wasn't until I met Mel that I really hit my stride. Mel is into multi-media, among other things. He builds these terrific moments around long silences. He has these fantastic movements also, but you don't see them. They're all *inside* him. But, oh god, how you *feel* them. Silence and immobility, those are his things. He's very beautiful and is making a tremendously powerful statement.' 'What?' Jimmy asked. 'I couldn't live with his integrity,' Sherry said. 'I wasn't ready. It was too much, though I'm coming to appreciate him more.' 'Where can I get to see him?' Jimmy asked. 'He sounds interesting.' 'That's difficult. He doesn't perform much. I don't even know whether he's alive. No one does. Every once and a while you hear from someone that he's done something, made a telephone call, you know, from a public booth on Fourteenth Street, and you feel good, you know, because the vibes are still there, working.' 'Yeah. Yeah,' Jimmy said slowly. 'But he's hard to catch,' Sherry went on. 'I mean you've really got to be *alert*.' 'Listen,' said Jimmy, '*I'd* like to make a few statements to *you*.' 'Jimmy,' she said, 'you don't know shit, but you're kinda cute.'

Sherry Meets Mrs Dellapiccolo

When Jimmy told his mother he had met a nice girl, she said it was about time and asked whether she was Italian. 'No,' she's an artist,' Jimmy told her. When Sherry returned from Italy, Jimmy told her excitedly that he was reading Proust. 'Who's he?' Sherry asked. She was disillusioned with Rome. Her parameters had been totally destroyed. The Italians had stampeded her and broken three ribs. 'It's their economy,' she said. 'What about the critics?'

Jimmy asked. 'They all had cameras.' He changed the subject. 'I think I saw Mel,' he said. 'Is he about five-nine, wears fatigues, wild hair, a beard, gas-mask bag, combat boots, glasses and Hopi Indian hat?' 'Harelip?' Sherry asked. 'Right.' 'That's Mel. Where?' 'Going east on Twelfth and Avenue B. He went into an alley, then into a basement.' 'Did he see you?' 'No.' 'What did he do?' 'Well, I thought he was urinating against a wall.' 'Was he?' 'I waited until he left, then I lit a match and looked.' 'And?' 'There was a puddle.' 'That all?' 'No. On the wall he had written something.' 'What?' '*Mel*.' A long pause, then Sherry said, '*Goddam!*' and '*Fantastic*.' Three days later she met Mrs Dellapiccolo who called her Cherry, kept an emaculate house, and asked what kind of art she did. 'Right now,' Sherry said, 'I masturbate in public.' 'Ahhh,' said Mrs Dellapiccolo, 'that's a nice. My Jimmy, he used to paint too when he's a little boy.' Privately she thought, 'Better an artist than Jewish.' They became friends.

Sherry and Jimmy Copulate

Jimmy finally got into Sherry's apartment in mid-July. It was a mess. Her ribs were nearly healed, and she was thinking about going to South Hampton. 'I hate it,' she said. 'Never been there,' Jimmy answered. 'I'm thinking about changing galleries. They won't let me tear out the walls.' 'Don't you ever make your bed?' 'Listen, why is your mother so fucken interested in my *hips?* And why is she always muttering to me what a good boy you are? Where the hell is your father?' 'Dead,' Jimmy said. 'Why the hell didn't you say so?' She was not in a very good mood. Her creativity level was low. She also had been turned down for a Guggenheim. 'Do you know they sent a *hunchback* to see me in March?' 'I think I saw him,' Jimmy said. 'What the fuck do *you* know?' Sherry snarled. Jimmy stood up. 'Well, I better be going.' He was getting pretty sensitive to her moods. 'Who said?' Sherry challenged. Jimmy shifted on his feet. 'I think I'm a little confused,' he said. Sherry cackled loudly. She came up close to him. 'Listen, come tell me about Queens. I hear it stinks—How old do you think I am?' Jimmy looked at her uncertainly. 'Thirty?' Sherry's eyes glistened. '*Tell me about Queens, you fucken philistine!*' So Jimmy put his hands around to her buttocks and told her about Queens. And Sherry listened.

GRANTA

RAYMOND CARVER
VITAMINS

I had a job and Patti didn't. I worked a few hours a night for the hospital. It was a nothing job. I did some work, signed the card for eight hours, went drinking with the nurses. After a while Patti wanted a job. She said she needed a job for her self-respect. So she started selling multiple vitamins and minerals door-to-door.

For a while she was just another girl who went up and down blocks in strange neighbourhoods knocking on doors. But she learned the ropes. She was quick and had excelled at things in school. She had personality. Pretty soon the company gave her a promotion. Some of the girls who weren't doing so hot were put to work under her. Before long she had herself a crew and a little office out in the mall. But the names and faces of the girls who worked for her were always changing. Some girls would quit after a few days, after a few hours sometimes. One or two of the girls were good at it. They could sell vitamins. These girls stuck with Patti. They formed the core of the crew. But there were girls who couldn't give away vitamins.

The girls who couldn't cut it would last a week or so and then quit. Just not show for work. If they had a phone they'd take it off the hook. They wouldn't answer their door. At first Patti took these losses to heart, like the girls were new converts who had lost their way. She blamed herself. But she got over that. Too many girls quit. Once in a while a girl would quit on her first day in the field. She'd freeze and not be able to push the doorbell. Or maybe she'd get to the door and something would happen to her voice. Or she'd get the opening remarks mixed up with something she shouldn't be saying until she got inside. Maybe it was then the girl would decide to bunch it, take the sample case, and head for the car where she hung around until Patti and the others had finished. There'd be a hasty one-on-one conference. Then they'd all ride back to the office. They'd say things to buck themselves up. 'When the going gets tough, the tough get going.' And, 'Do the right things and the right things will happen.' Stuff like that. Now and then a girl disappeared in the field, sample case and all. She'd hitch a ride into town, then beat it. Just disappear. But there were always girls to take their places. Girls were coming and going. Patti had a list. Every few weeks or so she ran a little ad in the *Pennysaver* and more girls showed up and another training session was in order. There was no end of girls.

The core group was made up of Patti, Donna, and Sheila. My

Patti was a beauty. Donna and Sheila were medium-pretty. One night Sheila confessed to Patti that she loved her more than anything on earth. Patti told me she used those words. Patti had driven her home and they were sitting in front of Sheila's apartment. Patti said she loved her too. She loved all her friends. But not in the way Sheila had in mind. Then Sheila touched Patti's breast. She brushed the nipple through Patti's blouse. Patti took Sheila's hand and held it. She told her she didn't swing that way. Sheila didn't bat an eye. After a minute, she nodded. But she kept Patti's hand. She kissed it, then got out of the car.

That was around Christmas. The vitamin business was off, and we thought we'd have a party to cheer everybody up. It seemed like a good idea at the time. But Sheila got drunk early and passed out. She passed out on her feet, fell over, and didn't wake up for hours. One minute she was standing in the middle of the living room, laughing. Then her eyes closed, the legs buckled, and she went down with a glass in her hand. The hand holding the drink smacked the coffee table as she fell. She didn't make a sound otherwise. The drink poured into the rug. Patti and I and somebody else lugged her out to the back porch and put her down on a cot and tended to forget about her.

Everybody got drunk and went home. Patti went to bed. I wanted to keep on, so I sat at the table with a drink until it started to get light out. Then Sheila came in from the porch and began complaining. She said she had this headache that was so bad it was like somebody was sticking hot wires into her temples. It was such a headache, she said, she was afraid it might leave her with a permanent squint. And she was sure her little finger was broken. She showed it to me. It looked purple. She bitched that we'd let her sleep all night with her contacts in. She wanted to know didn't anybody give a shit. She brought the finger up close and looked at it. She shook her head. She held the finger as far away as she could and looked some more. It was as if she couldn't believe the things that must have happened to her that night. Her face was puffy, and her hair was all over. She looked hateful and half-crazy. She ran cold water over her finger. 'God, oh God,' she said and cried some over the sink.

But she'd made a serious pass at Patti, a declaration of love, and I didn't have any sympathy.

I was drinking scotch and milk with a sliver of ice. Sheila leaned against the drainboard. She watched me from little slits of eyes. I took some of my drink. I didn't say anything. She went back to telling me how bad she felt. She said she needed to see a doctor. She said she was going to wake Patti. She said she was quitting, leaving the state, going to Portland, and she had to say goodbye to Patti. She kept on. She wanted Patti to drive her to the emergency room.

'I'll drive you,' I said. I didn't want to do it, but I would.

'I want Patti to drive me,' she said. She was holding the wrist of her bad hand with her good hand, the little finger as big as a pocket flashlight. 'Besides, we need to talk. I want to tell her I'm leaving. I need to tell her I'm going to Portland. I need to say goodbye.'

I said, 'I guess I'll have to tell her for you. She's asleep.'

She turned mean. 'We're *friends*,' she said. 'I have to talk to her. I have to tell her myself.'

I shook my head. 'She's asleep. I just said so.'

'We're friends and we love each other,' she said. 'I have to say goodbye to her.' She made to leave the kitchen.

I started to get up. I said, 'I told you I'll drive you.'

'You're drunk! You haven't even been to bed yet.' She looked at her finger again and said, 'Goddamn, why'd this have to happen?'

'Not too drunk to drive you to the hospital,' I said.

'I won't ride with you, you bastard!' Sheila yelled.

'Suit yourself. But you're not going to wake Patti. Lesbo bitch,' I said.

'Fucker bastard,' she said. She said that and then she went out of the kitchen and out the front door without using the bathroom or even washing her face. I got up and looked out the window. She was walking down the road toward Fulton Avenue. Nobody else was up. It was too early.

I finished my drink and thought about fixing another one. I fixed one.

Nobody saw any more of Sheila. None of us vitamin-related people anyway. She walked to Fulton Avenue and out of our lives. Later on that day Patti said, 'What happened to Sheila?' and I said, 'She went to Portland.' That was that. Patti didn't ask the details.

I had the hots for Donna, the other member of the core group. We'd danced to some Duke Ellington records that night. I'd held her pretty tight, smelled her hair, and kept a hand at the small of her back as I guided her over the rug. I got turned on dancing with her. I was the only guy at the party and there were six or seven girls dancing with each other. It was a turn on to look around the living room. I was in the kitchen when Donna came in with her empty glass. We were alone for a minute. I got her into a little embrace. She hugged me back. We stood there and hugged.

Then she said, 'Don't. Not now.' When I heard that 'not now' I let go and figured it was money in the bank.

So I'd been at the table reconstructing that hug, Donna on my mind, when Sheila came in with her bum finger.

I thought some more on Donna. I finished the drink. I took the phone off the hook and headed for the bedroom. I took off my clothes and got in beside Patti. I lay for a minute, winding down. Then I started in. But she didn't wake up. Afterwards, I closed my eyes.

It was afternoon when I opened them again, and I was in bed alone. Rain was blowing against the window. A sugar doughnut lay on Patti's pillow, and a glass of old water sat on the nightstand. I was still drunk and couldn't figure anything out. I knew it was Sunday and close to Christmas. I ate the doughnut and drank the water. I went back to sleep until I heard Patti running the vacuum. She came into the bedroom and asked about Sheila. That's when I told her, said she'd gone to Portland.

A week or so into the New Year Patti and I were having a drink. She'd just come home from work. It wasn't so late, but it was dark and rainy. I was going to work in a couple of hours. But first we were having us some scotch and talking. Patti was tired. She was down in the dumps and onto her third drink. Nobody was buying vitamins. She was reduced to Donna, core, and Sandy, a semi-new girl and a kleptomaniac. We were talking about things like negative weather and the number of parking tickets Patti had accumulated and let go. Finally, how maybe we'd be better off if we moved to Arizona, some place like that.

I fixed us another one. I looked out the window. Arizona wasn't a bad idea.

Patti said, 'Vitamins.' She picked up her glass and swirled the ice. 'For shit sake! I mean, when I was a girl this is the last thing I ever saw myself doing. Jesus, I never thought I'd grow up to sell vitamins. Door-to-door vitamins. This beats everything. This blows my mind.'

'I never thought so either, honey,' I said.

'That's right,' she said. 'You said it in a nutshell.'

'Honey.'

'Don't honey me,' she said. 'This is hard, brother. This life is not easy, anyway you cut it.'

She seemed to think things over for a minute. She shook her head. Then she finished her drink. She said, 'I even dream of vitamins when I'm asleep. I don't have any relief. There's no relief! At least you can walk away from your job after work and leave it behind. Forget about it. I'll bet you haven't had one dream about your job. You don't come home dead tired and fall asleep and dream you're waxing floors or whatever you do down there. Do you? After you've left the fucking place, you don't come home and dream about the fucking job!' she screamed.

I said, 'I can't remember what I dream. Maybe I don't dream. I don't remember anything when I wake up.' I shrugged. I didn't keep track of what went on in my head when I was asleep. I didn't care.

'You dream!' Patti said. 'Even if you don't remember. Everybody dreams. If you didn't dream, you'd go crazy. I read about it. It's an outlet. People dream when they're asleep. Or else they'd go nuts. But when I dream I dream of vitamins. Do you see what I'm saying?' She had her eyes fixed on me.

'Yes and no,' I said. It wasn't a simple question.

'I dream I'm pitching vitamins,' she went on. 'I dream I've run out of vitamins and I have a dozen orders waiting to be written if I can just show them the fucking *product*. Understand? I'm selling vitamins day and night. Jesus, what a life,' she said. She finished her drink.

'How's Sandy doing? She still have sticky fingers?' I wanted to get us off this subject. But there wasn't anything else.

Patti said, 'Shit,' and shook her head as if I didn't know anything.

We listened to it rain.

'Nobody is selling vitamins,' Patti said. She picked up her glass. But it was empty. 'Nobody is buying vitamins. That's what I'm telling you. I just told you that. Didn't you hear me?'

I got up to fix us another one. 'Donna doing anything?' I read the label on the bottle and waited.

Patti said, 'She made a little sale a few days ago. That's all. That's all that's happened this week. It wouldn't surprise me if she quit. I wouldn't blame her,' Patti said. 'If I was in her place, I'd think of quitting. But if she quits, then what? Then I'm back at the start, that's what. Ground zero. The middle of winter, people sick all over the state, people dying, and nobody thinks they need vitamins. I'm sick as hell myself.'

'What's wrong, honey?' I put the drinks on the table and sat down. She went on as if I hadn't said anything. Maybe I hadn't.

'I'm my own best customer,' she said. 'I've taken so many vitamins I think they may be doing something to my skin. Does my skin look okay to you? Can a person O.D. on vitamins? I'm getting to where I can't even go to the bathroom like a normal person.'

'Honey,' I said.

Patti said, 'You don't care if I take vitamins or don't take vitamins. That's the point. You don't care. You don't care about anything. The windshield wiper quit this afternoon in the rain. I almost had a wreck. I came this close.'

We went on drinking and talking until it was time for me to go to work. Patti said she was going to soak in a hot tub, if she didn't fall asleep first. 'I'm asleep on my feet,' she said. She said, 'Vitamins, for shit's sake. That's all there is any more.' She looked around the kitchen. She looked at her empty glass. 'Why in hell aren't you rich?' She laughed. She was drunk. But she let me kiss her. Then I left for work.

There was a place I went to after work. I'd started going for the music and because I could get a drink there after closing hours. It was a place called the Off-Broadway. It was a spade place in a spade neighbourhood. It was run by a spade named Khaki and was patronized by spades, along with a few whites. People would show up after the other places in town had stopped serving. They'd ask for house specials—RC Colas with a belt of whisky—or else they'd bring their own stuff in under their coats or in the women's ditty bags, order RC and build their own. Musicians showed up to jam, and the drinkers who wanted to keep drinking came to drink and listen to the music. Sometimes people danced on the little dance floor. But usually they sat in the booths and drank and listened to the music.

Now and then a spade hit another spade in the head with a bottle. Once a story went around that somebody had followed another somebody into the Gents and cut the man's throat while he stood in front of the urinal. But I never saw any trouble. Nothing that Khaki couldn't handle. Khaki was a big spade with a bald head that gleamed under the fluorescents. He wore Hawaiian print shirts that hung over his pants. I think he carried a pistol inside his waistband. At least a sap. If somebody started to get out of line, Khaki would walk over to where it was beginning, some voice rising over the other voices and the music. He'd rest his big hand on the party's shoulder and say a few words and that was that. I'd been going there off and on for months. I was pleased that he'd say things to me like, 'How're you doing tonight, friend?' Or, 'Friend, I haven't seen you for a spell. Glad to see you. We're here to have fun.'

The Off-Broadway is where I took Donna on our first and last date.

I walked out of the hospital just after midnight. It'd cleared up and stars were out. I still had this buzz from the scotch I'd had with Patti. But I was thinking to hit New Jimmy's for a quick one on the way home. Donna's car was parked in the space beside my car. Donna was inside the car. I remembered that hug we'd had in the kitchen. Not now, she'd said.

I walked over to her door. She rolled the window down and knocked ashes from her cigarette.

'I couldn't sleep,' she said. 'I have things on my mind, and I couldn't sleep.'

I said, 'Donna. Hey, I 'm glad to see you.'

'I don't know what's wrong with me,' she said.

'You want to go some place for a drink? I could have been out of this place an hour ago,' I said.

'I haven't been here long. Anyway, I needed time to think. I guess one drink can't hurt. Patti's my friend,' she said. 'You know that.'

'She's my friend too,' I said. Then I said, 'Let's go.'

'Just so you know,' she said.

'There's this place. It's a spade place,' I said. 'They have music. We can get a drink, listen to some music.'

'You want to drive me?' Donna said.

'Scoot over.'

She started in about vitamins. Vitamins were in a skid, vitamins had taken a nosedive. The bottom had fallen out of the vitamin market.

Donna said, 'I hate to do this to Patti. She's my best friend, and she's trying to build things up for us. But I may have to quit. This is between us. Swear it! But I have to eat. I have to pay rent. I need new shoes and a new coat. Vitamins can't cut it,' she said. 'I don't think vitamins is where it's at any more. I haven't said anything to Patti. Like I said, I'm still just thinking about it.'

Donna's hand lay next to my leg. I reached down and squeezed her fingers. She squeezed back. Then she took her hand away and pushed in the lighter. After she had her cigarette going, she put the hand back on the seat next to my leg. 'Worse than anything, I hate to let Patti down. You know what I'm saying? We were a team.' She handed me her cigarette. 'I know it's a different brand,' she said, 'but try it, you might like it.'

I pulled into the lot for the Off-Broadway. Three spades leaned against an old Chrysler that had a cracked front windshield. They were just lounging, passing a bottle in a paper sack. They looked us over. I got out and went around to open the door for Donna. I checked the doors, took her arm, and we headed for the street. The spades watched but didn't say anything.

'You're not thinking about moving to Portland?' I said. We were on the sidewalk. I put my arm around her waist.

'I don't know anything about Portland. Portland hasn't once crossed my mind.'

The front half of the Off-Broadway was like a regular spade cafe and bar. A few spades sat at the counter and a few more worked over plates of food at tables covered with red oilcloth. We passed through the cafe and into a big room in back. There was a long counter with booths against the wall. But at the back of the room was a platform where musicians could set up. In front of the platform was something that could pass for a dance floor. Bars and nightclubs were still serving, so people hadn't turned up at the Off-Broadway in any large numbers yet. I helped Donna take off her coat. We settled ourselves in a booth and put our cigarettes on the table. The spade waitress named Hannah came over. Hannah and me nodded. She looked at Donna. I ordered us two RC Cola specials and decided to feel good about things.

After the drinks came and I'd paid and we'd each had a sip, we started hugging. We carried on lightly for a while, squeezing and patting, kissing each other's face. Every so often Donna would stop and draw back, push me away a little, then hold me by the wrists. She'd gaze into my eyes. Then her lids would close slowly and we'd fall to kissing again. Pretty soon the place began to fill. We stopped kissing. But I kept my arm around her. She ran her fingers up and down my thigh. A couple of spade horn players and a white drummer began fooling around with a piece. I figured Donna and me would have another drink and listen to the set. Then we'd leave and go to her place to finish what we'd started.

I'd just ordered two more from Hannah when this spade named Benny came over with this other spade, a big dressed-up spade. The big spade had little red eyes amd was wearing a three-piece grey pinstripe that looked new but was tight in the shoulders, a rose-coloured shirt, a tie, topcoat, a fedora. All of it.

'How's my man?' said Benny. Benny stuck out his hand for a brother handshake. Benny and I had talked. He knew I liked jazz and he used to come over to the booth and talk whenever he and I were in the place at the same time. He liked to talk about Johnny Hodges, how he had played sax accompaniment for Johnny. He'd say things like, 'When Johnny and me had this gig in Mason City.'

'Hi, Benny,' I said.

'I want you to meet Nelson,' Benny said. 'He just back from Vietnam today. This morning. He here to listen to some of these good sounds. He got his dancing shoes on in case.' He looked at Nelson and nooded. 'This here is Nelson.'

I was looking at Nelson's shiny black shoes, and then I looked at Nelson. He seemed to want to place me from somewhere. He studied me. Then he let loose a rolling grin that showed his teeth. He looked down the booth.

'This is Donna,' I said. 'Donna, this is Benny, and this is Nelson.

Nelson, this is Donna.'

'Hello, girl,' Nelson said and Donna said right back, 'Hello there, Nelson. Hello, Benny.'

'Maybe we'll just slide in and join you folks?' Benny said. 'Okay?'

I said, 'Sure'. But I was sorry they hadn't found some place else. 'We're not going to be here long,' I said. 'Long enough to finish this drink is all.'

'I know man, I know,' Benny said. He sat across from me after Nelson had let himself down into the booth. 'Things to do, places to go. Yes, sir, Benny knows,' he said and winked.

Nelson looked across the booth to Donna. He stared at her. Then he took off the hat. He seemed to be examining the brim as he turned the hat around in his big hands. He made room for the hat on the table. He looked up at Donna. He grinned and squared his shoulders. He had to square his shoulders every few minutes. It was like he was very tired. I wished they'd have landed some place else.

'You real good friends with him, I bet,' Nelson said to Donna, not wasting a minute.

'We're good friends,' Donna said.

Hannah came over. Benny asked for RC's. Hannah went away and Nelson worked a pint of whisky from his top-coat pocket.

'Good friends,' Nelson said. 'Real good friends.' He unscrewed the lid.

'Watch out, Nelson,' Benny said. 'Keep that bottle out of sight. Nelson just got off the plane from Vietnam,' Benny said.

Nelson raised the bottle and drank some of his whisky. He screwed the lid back, laid the bottle on the table, and tried to cover it with his hat. 'Real good friends,' he said.

Benny looked at me and rolled his eyes. But he was drunk too. 'I got to get into shape,' he said to me. He drank RC from both of their glasses and then held the glasses under the table and poured whisky. He put the bottle in his coat pocket. 'Man, I ain't put my lips to a reed for a month now. I got to get with it.'

We were bunched in the booth, glasses in front of us, Nelson's hat on the table. 'You,' Nelson said to me. 'You with somebody else, ain't you? This beautiful woman, she ain't your wife. I know that. But you real good friends with this woman. Ain't I right?'

I had some of my drink. I couldn't taste the whisky. I couldn't taste anything. I said, 'Is all that shit about Vietnam true we see on the TV?'

Nelson had his red eyes fixed on me. After a time he said, 'What I want to say is, Do you know where your wife is? Hah? I bet she's out with some dude and she be laying in his arms this minute. She be touching his nipples, pulling his pud for him while you sitting here big as life with your good friend. I bet she have herself a good friend too.'

'Nelson,' Benny said.

'Nelson nothing,' Nelson said.

Benny said, 'Nelson, let's leave these people be. There's somebody in that other booth. Somebody I told you about. Nelson just this morning got off a plane,' Benny said. 'Nelson—'

'I bet I know what you thinking,' Nelson said. He kept on with it. 'I bet you thinking, Now here's a big drunk nigger and what am I going to do with him? Maybe I have to whip his ass. Hah? That what you thinking?'

I looked around the room. I saw Khaki standing near the platform, the musicians working away behind him. Some couples were on the floor. People had piled into the booths and were listening to the music. I thought Khaki looked right at me, but if he did he looked away again.

'Ain't it your turn to talk now?' Nelson said. 'I just teasing you. I ain't done any teasing since I left Nam. I teased the gooks some.' He grinned again, his big lips rolling back. Then he stopped grinning and just stared.

'Show them that ear,' Benny said quickly. He put his empty glass on the table. 'Nelson got himself an ear off one of them little dudes,' Benny said. 'He carry it with him. Show them, Nelson.'

Nelson sat there. Then he started feeling the pockets of his topcoat. He took things out of the pockets. He took out a handkerchief, some keys, a box of cough drops.

Donna said, 'I don't want to see an old ear. Ugh. Double ugh. Jesus.' She looked at me.

'We have to go,' I said.

Nelson was still feeling in his pockets. He took a wallet from a pocket inside the suitcoat and put it on the table. He patted the wallet. 'Five thousand dollars there. Listen here,' he said to Donna. 'I going to give you two bills. Okay? Two one hundred dollar bills. I got fifty them. You with me? I give you two of them. Then I want you to French me. Just like his wife doing some other big fellow. You listening? You know goddamn well she got her lips around somebody's hammer this minute while he here with his hand up your skirt. Fair's fair. Two one hundreds. Here.' He pulled the corners of the bills from his wallet. 'Hell, here another hundred for your friend. So he won't feel left out. He don't have to do nothing. You don't have to do nothing,' Nelson said to me. 'You just sit here and drink your drink. Sit here and listen to the music. Good music. Me and this woman walk out together like good friends. And she walk back in by herself. Won't be long, she be back.'

'Nelson,' Benny said, 'this is no way to talk. Nelson, Nelson.'

Nelson grinned. 'I finished what I have to say.' Then he said, 'But I ain't joking.' He took the handkerchief and wiped his face. He turned to Benny.

'I always say my mind. Benny, you know me. You still my friend, Benny? Hell, we all good friends. But I want what I want,' Nelson said. 'And I willing to pay for it. Don't want something for nothing. I pay for it, or I take it. That simple.'

He found what he'd been feeling for. It was a silver cigarette case which he worked open. I looked at the ear inside. It lay on a piece of cotton. The ear was brown, like a dried mushroom. It was beginning to curl. But it was a real ear and it was attached to a key chain.

'God,' said Donna. 'Yuck.'

Benny and I looked at the ear.

'Something, hah?' Nelson said. He was watching Donna.

'I'm not going outside with you and that's that,' Donna said. 'No way. I'm not going and that's all there is to it.'

'Girl,' Nelson said.

'Nelson,' I said. And then Nelson fixed his red eyes on me. He pushed the hat and wallet and cigarette case out of his way.

'What you want?' Nelson said. 'I give you what you want.'

Benny closed his eyes and then he opened them and said, 'Thank heaven, here come Khaki. Nelson, Benny going to make a prediction. Benny predict that in thirty seconds Khaki going to be standing here asking if everything be all right, if everybody happy.'

Donna said, 'I'm not happy. I'm not one bit happy,' Donna said.

Khaki came over to the booth and put a hand on my shoulder

227

and the other hand on Benny's shoulder. He leaned over the table, his head shining under the lights. 'How you folks? You all having fun?'

'Everything all right, Khaki,' Benny said. 'Everything A-okay. These people was just fixing to leave. Me and Nelson going to sit here and listen to the music makers.'

'That's good,' Khaki said. 'Folks be happy is my motto.' He looked around the booth. He looked at Nelson's wallet on the table and at the open cigarette case next to the wallet. He saw the ear.

'That a real ear?' he said.

Benny said, 'It is. Show him that ear, Nelson. Nelson just stepped off the plane from Vietnam with this ear. This ear has travelled halfway around the world to be on this table tonight. Nelson, show him,' Benny said.

Nelson handed the case over to Khaki.

Khaki examined the ear. He took up the chain and dangled the ear in front of his face. He looked at it. He let it swing back and forth on the chain. 'I heard about these dried up ears and cocks and such things, but I ain't really believed it. Or I believed it, but I never really believed it till this minute.'

'I took it off one of them little gooks,' Nelson said. 'He couldn't hear nothing with it no more. I wanted me a keepsake.'

'My God,' said Khaki. He turned the ear on its chain. 'I guess I seen everything.'

Donna and I began getting out of the booth.

'Girl, don't go,' Nelson said.

'Nelson,' Benny said.

Khaki was watching Nelson now. I stood beside the booth with Donna's coat. My legs were crazy.

Nelson raised his voice. He said, 'If you go with this fucker, let him put his face in your sweets, you going to fry in hell with him!'

We started to move away from the booth. People were looking.

'Nelson just got off the plane from Vietnam this morning,' I heard Benny say. 'We been drinking all day. This been the longest day on record. But me and him we going to be fine, Khaki.'

Nelson yelled something over the music. He yelled, 'You fixing to plow that, son of a bitch, but it ain't going to do no good! It ain't going to help none!' I heard him say that, and then I couldn't hear any more. The music stopped, and then it started again. We didn't look back. We kept going. We got out to the sidewalk.

I opened the door for her and went around to my side. I drove us back to the hospital. Donna stayed over on her side of the car. From time to time she'd use the lighter on a cigarette, but she wouldn't talk.

I tried to say something. I said, 'Maybe I should have taken *his* ear for a souvenir. Look, Donna, don't get on a downer because of this. I'm sorry it happened,' I said.

'Maybe I should have taken his money,' Donna said. 'That's what I was thinking.'

I kept driving and didn't look at her. I couldn't say anything that would help.

'It's true,' she said. 'Maybe I should've taken the money.' She shook her head. 'I don't know. I don't know what I'm saying. I just shouldn't have been there.' Donna began to cry. She put her chin down and cried.

'Don't cry,' I said. There was nothing else to say.

'I'm not going in to work tomorrow, today, whenever it is the alarm goes off,' she said. 'I'm not going in. I'm going to quit. I'm leaving town. I take what happened back there as a sign.' She pushed in the lighter and waited for it to pop out.

d killed the engine. I scanned the old Chrysler drive into the lot with hands on the wheel for a minute, I didn't want to touch Donna. She hed either. The hug we'd given each he kissing we'd done at the Off- mebody else's life now, not my life. o do?' But right then I didn't care. a heart attack and it wouldn't have meant anything.

'Maybe I could go up to Portland,' she said. 'There must be something in Portland. Portland is on everybody's mind these days. Portland's a drawing card. Portland this, Portland that. Portland's as good a place as any. It's all the same.'

'Donna,' I said. 'I'd better go.' I started to let myself out. I cracked the door and the overhead came on.

'For Christ's sake turn off that light!'
I got out in a hurry. 'Night, Donna,' I said.
She nodded.

I left her staring at the dash and went to my car. I saw her move over behind the wheel. Then she just sat there without doing anything. She looked at me. I waved. She didn't wave back. So I started the car and turned on the headlights. I slipped it in gear and fed it the gas. Donna would get herself home okay.

In the kitchen I poured scotch, drank some of it, and took the glass into the bathroom. I brushed my teeth. Then I pulled open a drawer. Patti yelled something from the bedroom that I couldn't understand. She opened the bathroom door. She was still dressed. She'd fallen asleep with her clothes on.

'What time is it?' she screamed. 'I've overslept! Jesus, oh my God! You've let me oversleep, goddamn you!'

She was wild. She stood in the doorway with her clothes on. She could have been fixing to go to work. But there was no sample case, no vitamins. She was having a bad dream, that's all. She began shaking her head back and forth.

I couldn't take any more tonight. 'Go back to sleep, honey. I'm looking for something,' I said. I knocked stuff out of the medicine cabinet. Things rolled into the sink. 'Where's the aspirin?' I said. I knocked down more things. I didn't care. 'Goddamn it,' I said. Things kept falling.

GRANTA

MARIO VARGAS LLOSA
LA ORGÍA PERPETUA
AN ESSAY ON
SEXUALITY AND REALISM

Criticism would be simplified if, before setting forth, the critic declared his tastes. Every work of art is informed in a particular way by the 'person' of the artist, that, independent from considerations of execution, manages to charm or alienate us. Thus, the works we end up admiring are inevitably those that satisfy the twin demands of our intellect and our individual temperament. The failure to address these two distinct concerns has rendered so many aesthetic discussions inadequate.

Louis Bouilhet

'The death of Lucien de Rubempré is the great drama of my life,' Oscar Wilde is said to have remarked about Balzac's character. I have always regarded this statement as being literally true. A number of fiction characters have affected my life more profoundly than most of the real people I have known. In the heterogeneous, cosmopolitan circle of my literary imagination, a handful of friendly ghosts regularly come and go—today, for instance, I might casually include d'Artagnan, David Copperfield, Jean Valjean, Prince Pierre Bezukhov, Fabrizio del Dongo, the terrorists Cheng and the Professor, and Lena Grove. But no character has been more persistently and passionately present than Emma Bovary.

My first memory of *Madame Bovary* is derived from a film. It was 1952, a stifling hot summer night, at a recently opened cinema in Piura, on the Plaza de Armas with its swaying palm trees. James Mason played Flaubert; the lean Louis Jourdan was Rodolphe Boulanger; and Emma Bovary appeared through the nervous energetic gestures of Jennifer Jones. I could not have been terribly impressed, because afterwards—during a time when, as a voracious reader, I was staying up nights to devour novels—I was not compelled even to track down a copy of the book.

My second memory is academic. On the hundredth anniversary of the publication of *Madame Bovary*, the University of San Marcos in Lima organized a ceremony to honour the occasion. The critic André Coyné was impassively questioning Flaubert's reputation as a realist when his arguments suddenly became inaudible amid the cries of *'Viva Algeria Libre!'* and the shouting of more than a hundred San

Marcos students, armed with stones, making their way through the hall toward the platform where their target, the increasingly pale French ambassador, awaited them. Part of the celebration in honour of Flaubert was the publication, in a little booklet whose ink rubbed off on our fingers, of an edition of *Saint Julien l'Hospitalier*, translated by Manuel Beltroy. That was the first work by Flaubert I read.

In the summer of 1959, with little money and the promise of a scholarship, I arrived in Paris for the first time. One of the first things I did was buy a copy of *Madame Bovary* in the Classiques Garnier edition, in a bookshop in the Latin Quarter. I began reading it that afternoon, in a small room in the Hôtel Wetter near the Cluny Museum. It was at that point that my story begins. From the first lines, the book began to work on me, charming my mind like a potent magic. It had been years since any novel had captivated my attention so immediately and so exclusively, blotting out my surroundings and sinking me so deeply into its narrative. As the afternoon wore on, as night fell, as the sun then began to rise, the novel's literary magic increased, subordinating my real world to the authority of the imaginary one. It was morning—Emma and Léon had just met in a box at the Rouen Opera—when, dizzy with fatigue, I put the book down and went to bed. During my curiously troubled sleep, the book continued to exist and above its various scenes—the Rouaults' farm, the streets of Tostes, good-natured and stupid Charles, Homais and his ponderous pedantry—was the face of Emma Bovary, like an image anticipated in childhood dreams or obscurely prophesied through the many books of my adolescence. When I woke up to resume reading, I was struck by two incontrovertible realizations: I then knew the writer I would have wanted to have been; and I then knew that I was to develop a special relationship with Flaubert's creation: until my death I would be in love with Emma Bovary. Informing virtually everything I would then go on to do, she would be for me, as for Léon Dupuis at the beginning of their affair: 'l'amoureuse de tous les romans, l'héroïne de tous les drames, le vague *elle* de tous les volumes de vers.'[1]

Since then, I have read *Madame Bovary* a dozen times, and, unlike so many other cherished works, it has never disappointed me; on the contrary, rereadings always seem to reveal more of it. A novel becomes part of a person's life for a number of reasons related to the book and the individual. I would like to investigate, in this particular case, why *Madame Bovary* has succeeded in affecting me unlike any other narrative I have come across.

I am obsessed with form, and surely much of my admiration for *Madame Bovary* derives from my preference for works rigorously and symmetrically constructed—completed, perfect, finished—over those that are carefully and deliberately left open-ended, suggestive of the indeterminate, the vague, the 'process'. What I have sought (and what pleases me to find) in books, films, and paintings is not infinite incompleteness—however faithfully it might image one aspect of our continuous, always unfinished existence—but the opposite: the 'totalizations' which, with their bold, arbitrary but convincing structures give the illusion of *felt* experience and come closest to the comprehensive representation of it. My appetite was fully satisfied by *Madame Bovary*, the exemplar of the closed work, the perfect circle. But, more important, *Madame Bovary* defined for me what I value in literature: reading the book, that is, taught me how to read. I am, I discovered, attracted more by action—in a very conventional sense—than reflection; more by 'objective' representations of experience than the subjectively expressed responses to it; I prefer Tolstoi to Dostoevski; invention grounded in real experience to that originating in fantasy; and, among unrealities, what is closer to the concrete than to the abstract. I prefer pornography, for instance, to science fiction, and sentimental stories to horror tales.

In his letters to Louise Colet, while writing *Madame Bovary*, Flaubert was confident he was writing a novel of 'ideas' instead of one of 'action'. The terms are problematic and have led a number of critics to maintain that *Madame Bovary* is a novel in which nothing happens except on the level of language. *Madame Bovary is* rich linguistically; but it is also rich dramatically, and is virtually as busy and as varied as generically determined adventure novels, even when the many events it develops turn out to reveal the petty or the sordid. True, most of this appears to us through the subjectively organized and articulated perceptions of the individual characters, but because of Flaubert's maniacally materialistic style, the subjective reality in *Madame Bovary* possesses a solidity, a physical weight, as palpable as the objects of lived experience. That thoughts and feelings could convey the authority of *facts*, that they could be, it seemed, almost touched impressed and dazzled me, revealing an important aspect of my literary disposition.

For me, literary satisfaction is directly correlated to the emotions a work is able to elicit and manipulate. In *Madame Bovary* my admiration is evoked on a number of levels, one of which is derived from Emma's determined, morally reckless rebellion. Her conduct is motivated not by an ethic or an ideology but by appetites and dreams, her fantasies and her body—for the uninhibited expression of which she suffers, lies, commits adultery, steals, and ultimately kills herself. Her defeat is not, in the novel's context, morally significant, proving for instance that her end is a kind of ethical punishment, as Maître Sénard claimed as the attorney for the defence at the trial of *Madame Bovary* (his defence of the novel contributed to the legal travesty as much as the accusation against it brought forth by Fiscal Pinard, the Public Prosecutor, a clandestine composer of pornographic verse); instead, her defeat merely reinforces our sense of her particular solitary struggle. Emma is, in every possible way, alone; impulsive, sentimental, and indulgent, she is fundamentally a-social.

What matters most, of course, is not the defiance but its causes, originating in an attitude that she and I share intimately: our incurable materialism, our predilection for the pleasures of the body over those of the intellect, our respect for the senses and the instincts, our commitment to an unequivocally earthly existence. The pleasure Emma craves is sexual; her sensuality will not be inhibited or repressed, unlike Charles who fails to satisfy it because he fails to recognize its existence. The pleasure she craves is also aesthetic: she wants to surround her life with pleasing, superfluous things—the manifestations of elegance, refinement—to 'objectify' and 'externalize' the appetite for the beautiful cultivated through her imagination and inculcated through her reading. Emma's world is a romantic's, organized by the senses, and crowded with adventure, risk, and theatrical gestures of generosity and sacrifice. Her rebellion constitutes a rejection of everything but the physically urgent, the here and now; her aspiration, that is, is politically irresponsible: no society could tolerate this existential license, forever moving past those limits the transgression of which Georges Bataille describes, simply and unequivocally, as Evil. Emma, however, is a being not of society but

Mario Vargas Llosa

humanity, defending what virtually every religion, philosophy, and ideology disavow: the unrepressed satisfying of desire.

I remember reading, in the opening pages of a book by Maurice Merleau-Ponty, that violence is almost always an image of beauty. The statement was tremendously reassuring. I was seventeen then, and it disturbed me to note that despite my peaceful nature, violence—implicit or explicit, refined or raw—was absolutely necessary for a novel to persuade me of its reality and its power. Those works that lacked any suggestion of the violent seemed unreal, and unreality I find 'mortally' tedious. The narrative of *Madame Bovary* is organized by violence, manifest on a number of levels, ranging from the purely physical one of pain (the operation, gangrene, Hippolyte's amputation, Emma's poisoning) to the spiritual one of ruthless rapine (the merchant Lheureux), or selfishness and cowardice (Rodolphe, León), to its social forms in the exploitation of human labour (old Catherine Leroux) or the exploitation in interpersonal relationships: the violence, at its most generalized, inherent in prejudice and social envy. Emma's fantasy, in this context, her longing to be separated from the debilitating environment around her, stands out as special and important. And, appropriately, the most violent scene—in which Emma kills herself—is the most moving. The chapter, ineluctably etched in my memory, plays and replays in my mind, as Emma walks to Rodolphe's chateau at dusk, the last manoeuver that may save her and keep her from having to change, until the next day when she, overcome by the vision of the Blind Man crossing Yonville humming his vulgar song, enters death like a nightmare. For me, these pages—painful, sadistic, and terribly cruel—constitute one of the most satisfying and pleasing passages in literature.

Madame Bovary is a novel of a peculiar sexual cruelty; it is also, importantly, an extraordinarily indulgent book, given to instances of dramatic overstatement. Emma is sentimental, coarse, vulgar and, in each excess, undeniably attractive. My attitude toward her is clear; my attitude toward melodrama in general—and *Madame Bovary* is certainly a specific example of it—is more ambivalent and requires explanation. In the novel, unqualified by literary pretense, the melodramatic is insupportable. In the cinema, curiously, there is nothing I'd rather witness—a weakness derived, I suspect, from the forties and fifties, when I regularly and depravedly spent my time watching the Mexican films that I still miss so much today. My vulnerability to the melodramatic does not develop, I should add, from the contemporary intellectual sport that through self-consciously sophisticated *reinterpretation* aesthetically reclaims the ignoble and the stupid—as Hermann Broch does, for instance, through his concept of *kitsch* and Susan Sontag through *camp*—but, rather, from an absolute, undetached, and *emotional* identification with the material of narrative. My difficulty here may largely be semantic, and *melodrama* may not convey enough of what I am trying to say, suggesting as it does a specific genre of artistic activity whereas I refer to what characterizes all emotional interaction, only one example of which is represented in artistic melodrama. I am speaking, really, of the careful perversion of what each era recognizes as 'good taste'—the rhetorical gesture and the affront. I am speaking of the disruptions of the refinements of the dominant social ideology. I am speaking of the mechanization and distortions to which so many emotional and ideational aspects of human relations are so regularly subjected; I am speaking of the intrusion of the comic in the serious, the grotesque in the tragic, the absurd in the logical, the impure in the pure, the ugly in the beautiful. This material does not interest me intellectually, but emotionally. A crude but typical example is in the popular Spanish film *El Último Cuplé*, which with all its elephantine stupidity attracts me not as an entomologist to a spider—as a phenomenon to be examined and scrutinized—but as a creature to the spider-web in which I find I'm unwittingly trapped. I am caught, lost in unintellectual identification, akin to what Emma recognizes in her experience of *Lucie de Lammermoor* in Rouen ('La voix de la chanteuse ne lui semblait être que le retentissement de sa conscience, et cette illusion qui la charmait quelque chose même de sa vie').[2] In *El Último Cuplé*, however, the engagement does not outlast what has occasioned it. Reality—as in other sentimental Spanish films, *El Derecho de Nacer* by Corín Tellado or *Simplemente María*—is available to us only as melodrama, to the exclusion of everything else.

Nevertheless my inclination for overstatement is no doubt symptomatic of my uncompromising commitment to realism: I am moved because melodrama approaches my conception of the real more adequately than drama, as tragi-comedy does more than pure comedy or pure tragedy. And for me, it is an achievement of the highest order when a work of art can admit, without detached, ironic statement, the sloppy and the sentimental, and persist to the completion of its depiction without having to draw back uneasily from its subject.

Madame Bovary seems to go out of its way to be heavy-handed—from the relentless series of premonitory signs that bode Emma's end to the ragged Blind Man covered with sores to, even, Justin, the romantic commonplace, secretly in love with the unattainable woman. *Madame Bovary* is peopled with stock characters: Lheureux the shopkeeper is greedy, anti-Semitic, and rapacious; the notaries and functionaries are, of course, wicked and sordid; and the politicians garrulous, hypocritical, and ridiculous. Emma herself, coldly planning her excesses, exists in the Quixotic world of the books she reads, dreaming of exotic countries with picture postcard scenes, and relying on the grandiloquence of a cliché rhetoric (giving the man she loves the signet *Amor nel cor*, asking him 'to think of me at midnight', and reminding him that 'Il n'y a pas de désert, pas de précipices ni d'océan que je ne traverserais avec toi').[3] I am delighted by all the cheap serial coincidences of the novel or the unapologetically stock scenes: Justin, alone, sobbing in the shadow of Madame Bovary's tomb, or Emma, as her world is collapsing, tossing her last five francs to a beggar, or the fiacre ride ending with the simple image of a woman's hand scattering in the wind the torn bits of the letter breaking with her lover.

On April 24, 1852, Flaubert, having just read a novel by Lamartine (*Graziella*), wrote to Louise:

> Et d'abord, pour parler clair, la baise-t-il ou ne la baise-t-il pas? Ce ne sont pas des êtres humains, mais des mannequins. Que c'est beau, ces histoires d'amour où la chose principale est tellement entourée de mystère que l'on ne sait à quoi s'en tenir, l'union sexuelle étant reléguée systématiquement dans l'ombre comme boire, manger, pisser, etc.! Le parti pris m'agace. Voilà un gaillard qui vit continuellement avec une femme qui l'aime et qu'il aime, et jamais un désir! Pas un nuage impur ne vient obscurcir ce lac bleuâtre! O hypocrite! S'il avait raconté l'histoire vraie, que c'eût été plus beau! Mais la vérité demande des mâles

plus velus que M. de Lamartine. Il est plus facile en effet de
dessiner un ange qu'une femme: les ailes cachent la bossa.

Any novel that excludes the sexual is as distorting as one that reduces
experience exclusively to it (although, given my predilections, I prefer
an absolute sexual obsession to its absolute exclusion). The treatment
of sexuality constitutes one of the most delicate problems in fiction,
and is rarely emancipated from the network of prejudice and
conviction that both author and reader sustain: more than a few
novels, in the familiar theological metaphor, have been sent to hell by
way of their trousers. But in *Madame Bovary*, the erotic is mastered
with intelligence and care. Sexuality is the dominant concern
informing the narrative (rivalled perhaps only by money, although it is
impossible to separate the sexual from the economic). Nevertheless,
sexuality is generally present only through oblique expression, a
sensuality shadowing the book's development (Justin contemplating
Madame Bovary's undergarments; Léon adoring her gloves; and, after
Emma's death, Charles acquiring the objects she would have liked to
have possessed), and surfaces explicitly only on isolated but significant
occasions: the unforgettable scene of Emma like a courtesan letting
her hair down for Léon, or preparing for making love with the
refinement that the Egyptian Ruchiuk Hânem must have possessed.
Sexuality occupies the dramatic centrality that it does in life, unlike
Lamartine, Flaubert does not eclipse the biological by the halo of
lyrical spiritualism; nevertheless, the biological does not dominate
only. Flaubert's depiction of love partakes of sensibility, poetry, and
gesture, and, concurrently, of erection and orgasm. On September 19,
1852, he wrote to Louise: 'Ce brave organe génital est le fond des
tendresses humaines; ce n'est pas la tendresse, mais c'en est le
substratum come diraient les philosophes. Jamais aucune femme n'a
aimé un eunuque et si les mères chérissent les enfants plus que les pères,
c'est qu'ils leur sont sortis du ventre, et le cordon ombilical de leur
amour leur reste au coeur sans être coupé.'[5] The *brave organe génital*
'motivates' the narrative development of *Madame Bovary*. The
hopelessness which little by little drives Emma into adultery originates
in her frustration as a wife, a frustration that is fundamentally sexual.
The *officier de santé* is no match for Emma, and her dissatisfaction
precipitates her end. Precisely the opposite happens to Charles, whose

appetite is sated and ambition destroyed by the introduction of Emma into his life. His blindness, his conformism, his stubborn mediocrity, I am suggesting, results largely from his sexual contentment.

In the same letter to Louise, Flaubert dismisses the traditional, feminine notion of sexuality: 'Elles ne sont pas franches avec elles-mêmes; elles ne s'avouent pas leurs sens; elles prennent leur cul pour leur coeur et croient que la lune est faite pour éclairer leur bourdoir.'[6] The complaint is, of course, applicable to men, whose regular dishonesty obscures their own sensuality, misrepresenting the penis for the heart. The development of Emma's character in contrast charts the conflict between an individual's conditioning and the determination to be liberated from it. It is impossible not to be moved by Emma's aptitude for sexual pleasure; once stimulated and educated by Rodolphe, she surpasses her teacher and her second lover, and from the ninth chapter of the second part the novel is enveloped in a passionate eroticism. Moreover, as in eighteenth century libertine literature—and Flaubert was of course an enthusiastic reader of the Marquis de Sade—love is linked to religion, or rather, to the Church and the trappings of worship. It is noteworthy that Emma's sexual awakening takes place in a school run by nuns, at the foot of an altar, amid the incense of a Catholic Mass (a fact that gave the Public Prosecutor fits), and her first rendezvous with Léon, preceding the erotic scene in the fiacre, takes place, at Emma's suggestion, in the cathedral at Rouen. Conflating the religious and the erotic, the seduction develops as the couple is guided through—and offered detailed descriptions of—the cathedral. Emma's sexuality, that is, occasions her transcendence, her escape from the relentlessly repressive bourgeois community of Yonville whose women—Madame Langlois, Madame Caron, Madame Dubreuil, Madame Tuvache, Madame Homais—exist, like a breed of tame animals, only to be domesticated. Emma's curiously religious sexual emancipation is offered, in the context of the novel, as the only available choice of conduct, even though this choice proves fatal. Instead of inhibiting the satisfaction of her desires, Emma indulges them, perceiving clearly the distinction between 'coeur' and 'cul', and understanding that the moon exists only to light her bedroom.

It is a curious feature characteristic of the history of sexual censorship cases that the defense (such as that, for instance, put forward by Maître Sénard in rebuttal to Pinard's requisitory) always distorts the actual erotic experience of the reader, invariably arguing that sexual scenes are really inventories or objective descriptions that exist to educate or edify (depicting sin in order to combat it); or that the beauty of the form has so sublimated the content that its sexual elements invoke only a spiritual or intellectual pleasure; or—assuming the authority of generic determinants—that only commercial pornography seeks to excite, a function incompatible with the genuinely literary. For me, no novel can engage my attention or enthusiasm unless it acts to some measurable extent as an erotic stimulant—expressed not necessarily exclusively but obliquely, integrated with experience: a book by Sade, for instance, where the obsession devitalizes the sexual, making it a putative not a physical act, excites and interests me less than the (very few) erotic episodes in Balzac's *Splendeurs et misères des courtisanes* (I remember especially the knees rubbing against each other in a carriage), or those found here and there in the pages of *The Thousand and One Nights*. In *Madame Bovary* the erotic element is fundamental, even though much was suppressed to avoid censorship (and not only official censorship: Flaubert's friend, the writer Maxime Du Camp, favoured the textual cuts made by *La Revue de Paris*). That the book's sexuality is implicit does not diminish either its presence or its power. The erotic climax, the interminable journey through the streets of Rouen in the fiacre, is an inspired hiatus, a sleight-of-hand trick of genius that contrives to give the material hidden from the reader the maximum possible charge. It is remarkable that the most imaginative erotic episode in French literature does not contain a single allusion to the female body or a single word of love, that it simply enumerates the names of streets and places, describing the aimless wandering through the town in an old coach for hire. But there is more to *Madame Bovary* than erotic silences. I recall for instance the Thursdays at the Hôtel de Boulogne, in the port district of Rouen, where the trysts with Léon take place, when Emma's intuition of imminent catastrophe appears only to heighten her sensuality. Many times I have waited for her in that yielding room. I have seen her arrive, each time 'plus enflammée, plus avide'. I have heard the hiss with which her corset-lace falls to the floor. I have spied her running to make certain that the door is locked. And then, I have watched her, as her clothes drop, and she, pale and serious, enters the arms of Léon Dupuis.

In Flaubert, sexuality underlies everything we touch, smell, see; sensuality emanates from the details of the physical objects that crowd our daily existence, until those objects acquire a significance many times greater than what we normally assign them. I want to examine more closely Flaubert's special relationship with his physical world, and want especially to look at his curious treatment of one particular object in it. This constitutes, I realize, something of a tangent, but it is such an extraordinary one that I feel it is entirely justified.

It is interesting that, amid all the critics and bibliographers of Flaubert's work, no addict has yet produced a paper entitled 'Flaubert and Shoe Fetishism'. There is an abundance of material. I offer a sample of what I have chanced to come across. Albert Thibaudet tells us that as a child Flaubert often fell into rapt contemplation of a woman's high buttoned shoes, and hence the scene in *Madame Bovary* in which Justin begs the maid's permission to polish Emma's shoes, which the boy touches reverently as though they were sacred objects, is more or less autobiographical. Sartre points out the passage in which, for the first time in Flaubert's works, the theme of footwear appears ('si important dans la vie et l'oeuvre de Flaubert,' he adds, though he has no more to say on the subject: one of the many loose ends never tied up in his Cyclopean essay) in the lines in Chapter IX of *Mémoires d'un fou* in which Flaubert delicately describes a beautiful woman's foot: 'son petit pied mignon enveloppé dans un joli soulier à haut talon orné d'une rose noire.'[8] It is a well-known fact, moreover, that Flaubert kept in a desk-drawer, along with letters from his mistress and certain garments belonging to her, the slippers that Louise Colet wore on their first night of love which, during the course of writing his correspondence with her, he often took out to caress and kiss.

Feet and footwear emerge in Flaubert's letters, often in a most curious fashion. In the letter to Louise of August 26, 1853, he mentions, casually, that if he were a professor at the College de France he would give 'un cours sur cette grande question des Bottes comparées aux littératures. "*Oui, la Botte est un monde*," dirais-je.'[9] This long letter, a *divertimento* on the subject, consists of pages of surprising, ingenious, and vaguely perverted ramblings on the shoe as a symbol of culture, civilization, and even historical epochs—the Chinese, the Greeks, much of the middle ages, and especially Louis XV figure prominently here—or on various types of shoes that serve as emblematic analogues for authors and their books—Corneille, La Bruyère, Boileau, Bossuet, Molière, and so on. All this is doubtless a game, and you must allow me the indulgence of charting it. It is also, though, a rather disquieting game, symptomatic of what amounts to a rather unusual inclination: these playful fantasies—elaborated with such erudition—reveal that in his readings and so many of his otherwise casual observations Flaubert was very much aware—perhaps obsessed?—with the appearance of this particular member, the foot, and its social envelope, footwear.

Another letter to Louise, written a few days before, provides an interesting corroboration. Having arrived at Trouville for a holiday, Flaubert went to the beach to 'watch the ladies swimming'. His letter (August 14, 1853) expresses his astonishment at seeing how ugly the women look in the shapeless sacks in which they hide their bodies and the bathing caps into which they stuff their hair; but the most distressing is the most visible: namely, their feet. 'Et les pieds! Rouges, maigres, avec des oignons, des durillons, déformés par la bottine, longs comme des navettes ou larges comme des battoirs.'[10] It is, I suspect, significant that the name of Restif de la Bretonne—the father of foot-fetishism whose voluminous autobiographical *oeuvre* is organized around this delicate feminine extremity and the footwear in which it is encased—is scribbled in the margins of Flaubert's manuscripts of *Madame Bovary* preserved in the Municipal Library of Rouen, and from whose work Flaubert took the picaresque melody that the Blind Man sings.

Throughout *Madame Bovary*, in fact, this special member exudes a special significance, emerging as one of the most important aspects of the erotic life of the male characters.[11] I have mentioned the spell that Emma's shoes casts over Justin. At another point the narrator mentions that Léon, wearied by Emma, tries to be liberated from her, but that 'au craquement de ses bottines, il se sentait lâche, comme les ivrognes à la vue des liquers fortes.' Maître Guillaumin, the notary sought to help clear Emma's debts, is sexually excited when his knee brushes against 'sa bottine, dont las semelle se recourbait tout en fumant contre le poêle.'[12] While Emma leaves, sickened by his display, the notary remains motionless, struck like an idiot, 'les yeux fixés sur ses belles pantoufles en tapisserie' that have been 'un présent de l'amour.'[13] The first time Léon sees Emma, who has just come to Yonville, she is standing in front of the fireplace tucking up her skirts so as to warm 'son pied chaussé d'une bottine noire.'[14] And on the day of the horseback ride together, that ends with their making love, Rodolphe notes admiringly 'entre ce drap noir et la bottine noire, la délicatesse de son bas blanc, qui lui semblait quelque chose de sa nudité.'[15] And later, at the height of her affair, Emma is described as characterized by that 'quelque chose de subtil qui vous pénétrait se dégageait même des draperies de sa robe et de la cambrure de son pied.'[16] In the early manuscript drafts of *Madame Bovary* even Charles was a connoisseur. In one passage, later discarded, the *officier de santé*, contemplating Emma's foot as she is dying, is suddenly overwhelmed by erotic memories, and sees himself again on his wedding day, undoing the laces of Emma's white shoes as 'il frémissait dans les éblouissements de la possession prochaine.'[14] And indeed, the first emotion that Charles displays is organized around this curious fetish, provoked by the wooden shoes that Père Rouault's daughter is wearing. The narrator is nothing if not explicit: 'il aimait les petits sabots de mademoiselle Emma sur les dalles lavées de la cuisine; ses talons hauts la grandissaient un peu, et, quand elle marchait devant lui, les semelles de bois, se relevant vite, claquaient avec un bruit sec contre le cuir de la bottine.'[18] The obsession is expressed on a number of different levels: sometimes on the sensual, and other times on the religious, as when the Abbé Bournisien puts the holy oils on 'la plante des pieds, si rapides autrefois quand elle courait à l'assouvissance de ses désirs, et qui maintenant ne marcheraient plus.'[19] What I cherish most, amid this gallery of multiple references, is the description of Emma's 'mignarde chaussure' ('dainty shoe')—a little pink embroidered satin slipper—that dangles from the instep of her foot as she hops into her lover's lap in that crammed, small room in the Hôtel de Boulogne.

But I go on too long, and, in dissociating the indissociable, feel I'm falsifying the book. What is important is not one object, but many, each of which is informed with multiple significances, often sexual, throughout the development of the narrative.

While still under the immediate sway of *Madame Bovary*, I proceeded to read, one after the other like episodes in a serial, all the other books by Flaubert in the yellow paper Garnier editions. Each moved me, to varying degrees, and reinforced my addiction. I remember a number of Olympian discussions I had, in that summer of '59, with friends who laughed when I heatedly asserted that '*Salammbô* is a masterpiece too'. Everyone agrees today that the book is dated and no one can help yawning uneasily on reading of the young woman committing the sacrilege of touching the veil of Tanit in a story crowded with operatic histrionics and a kind of technicolour 'antiquity' reminiscent of Cecil B. De Mille. I cannot deny that much of the novel proceeds from the worst sort of romanticism, centering on the hollow, commonplace story of the love of Mâtho and the daughter of Hamilcar. But another side of this work has lost none of its power and vigour: its epic dimension, the crowd scenes, the social *comprehensiveness* that no other novelist except Tolstoi has brought off as well as Flaubert. (In *Madame Bovary* there is the agricultural fair at which the entire town of Yonville is present, *and* almost every character who appeared in the earlier parts of the book.) The banquets; the fêtes; the battles; the ceremonies; the unforgettable, hallucinatory sacrifice of the children to Moloch exhibit a dynamism, a plasticity, an elegance rarely seen in literature.

I have enjoyed everything Flaubert has written, but nothing has impressed me as profoundly as *Madame Bovary* with the exception of *L'Éducation sentimentale*, which, for years, I considered the greatest of Flaubert's novels because it was his most ambitious: what in *Madame Bovary* is a woman and a town is, in *L'Éducation sentimentale*, a generation and a society. The scope is greater, the historical perspective broader, the representations more richly diversified. And yet, despite its comprehensive variety, *L'Éducation sentimentale* proffers no figure comparable to Madame Bovary. Neither the timid Frédéric Moreau nor the elusive, maternal Madame Arnoux, nor the bankers, artists, industrialists, courtesans, journalists, workers, aristocrats can endure comparison with Emma, for none of them constitutes a human type in the Cervantean or Shakespearian sense that Flaubert defined so well: 'Ce qui distingue les grands génies, c'est la généralisation et las création. Ils résument en un type des personnalités éparses et apportent à la conscience du genre humain des personnages nouveaux.'[20] Like Don Quixote or, arguably, even Hamlet, Emma expresses, through the particularities of her tormented personality, an enduring, charmed relationship with the inflexible circumstances of her environment: the capacity to fabricate illusions and the mad determination to make them real. Salammbô, Saint Antoine, Bouvard and Pécuchet, Saint Julien l'Hospitalier also harbour extraordinary illusions and cultivate formidable wills bent on realizing their chimerical fantasies; but these fantasies ultimately originate with God or Science: Emma's utopia, by contrast, is rigorously human. On the morning of May 22, 1853, Flaubert wrote to Louise: 'Une âme se mesure à la dimension de son désir, comme l'on juge d'avance des cathédrales à la hauteur de leurs clochers.'[21] His greatest glory may have been to have created, in the vulgar, fickle, fictional figure of Emma Bovary, the best demonstration of this truth, one of the bell-towers that dominate the vast flat plain of human existence.

In 1962 I began to read Flaubert's *Correspondance*. I remember the exact date: I had just earned some money from a novel, and my first purchase was, in a bookstore in Tours, the thirteen volumes published by Conard. Apart from the interest in following step by step Flaubert's difficult life, retracing the gestation of his works, discovering at first hand his readings, his hatreds, his frustrations, entering his circle of intimates—Maxime, Bouilhet, Louise, George Sand, Caroline—Flaubert's correspondence provided the best possible friend for a budding literary writer. Those who know these letters—characterized by a gloomy, unrelieved pessimism and dominated by bitter curses against humanity in which its representatives appear, with very few exceptions (most of them writers), to be a grotesquely vulgar lot—will find my description curious, for I see these letters as unequivocally stimulating. While chronicling the rage and fatigue accumulated during the preceding ten or twelve hours of work, these letters also demonstrate the humanity of Flaubert's genius.[22] His talent emerges through a slow, slowly realized series of small conquests, during which we witness the aloneness of the writer as he confronts the limitations of his imagination and, through patience, persistence, and self-scrutiny, transcends them. It is, in the end, nothing less than inspiring to watch over the shoulder of this vociferous, provincial old bachelor who succeeds, after so much labour, in creating something that endures. When undergoing my greatest difficulties writing, I have often turned to Flaubert's letters, skipping about, elevated in every respect except for when I have occasion to notice the ridiculous and unfortunate cuts that his niece Caroline insisted be made in the *Correspondence*.

The end of 1960. A heated argument with a Bolivian friend who, disgusted, parted with the last words, 'You won't give an inch when it comes to Cuba or Flaubert.' Twenty years later, recalling that afternoon, I am infinitely more tolerant of criticism directed at the Cuban Revolution. On the other hand, I am as intransigent as ever in my defence of Flaubert. My devotion has led me through not only all of Flaubert's work, but most of the critical or parasitical literature that it has occasioned, and, not surprisingly I suppose, Flaubert has emerged as the standard by which I often measure other authors—or, if not the standard, an inflexible influence. I am certain, for instance, that my loathing of Barbey d'Aurevilly derives from his attacks on Flaubert, and that, for the same reasons, I have little interest in Valéry or Claudel (who dismissed the consummately beautiful opening of *Salammbô* as the dullest prose in the history of French literature), and that my complete revision of Henry James, whose novels had always tried my patience, originated with the discovery of his superb and forthright essay on Flaubert. Likewise, Baudelaire's article on *Madame Bovary* was the writing that confirmed by belief that imaginative authors ultimately offer far more illuminating perceptions about literature than either critics or literary journalists (a belief that was reconfirmed on coming across Pound's *ABC of Reading* in which he argues that, unlike the poet, who requires a long list of authors as preparation for his practice, the prose writer may simply begin with the author of *Bouvard et Pécuchet*).

Flaubert has sustained, of course, a curious relationship with writers. The critics of his day were alarmingly short-sighted. Even *Madame Bovary*, a popular success (due in large part to the trial), was mercilessly attacked by the Paris literary columnists (although Sainte-Beuve and a handful of others were perceptive enough to see its merits). Flaubert's other books, however, were universally misunderstood and regularly savaged (a dubious record was achieved by Barbey d'Aurevilly who declared *La Tentation de Saint Antoine* to be as indigestible as the second part of *Faust*). The following generation, on the other hand, claimed Flaubert as their patriarch, and though he refused to assume the lofty seat that Zola and the naturalists set aside for him Flaubert was certainly considered a master. But after this period, French littérateurs scorned Flaubert—Claudel no exception—and until the 1950s I have the sense that he was recalled only to be dismissed. (The existentialists, convinced that literature was a form for potential action not unlike a military weapon, were intolerant of Flaubert's fanatic concern for form, his haughty isolationism, his art-for-art's sake aesthetic, and his disdain for politics; Sartre's remarks about Flaubert in *Situations II* were the most brutally acerbic: it was, incidentally, an essay that I read and reread with fervour until the disquieting experience of coming across the hermit of Croisset for myself.)

During the 1960s, the French appraisal changed radically; scorn and neglect suddenly gave way to rescue, praise, and worship. The French became addicts at the same time I did, and half-pleased and half-jealous, I saw the passion for Flaubert spread in those convulsive years of Gaullism, the Algerian war, the OAS and, for me, between writing and preparing radio broadcasts (I was earning my living working for the ORTF), a schedule that kept me on the go from morning to night. I remember clearly the satisfaction—as though a member of my family or a personal friend had been the one thus honoured—with which I read François-Régis Bastide's preface to the new edition of *La Première éducation sentimentale*, published by Seuil, an early version of the novel that up to that time had been known only to university students and professors. I would not have hesitated a moment to post the last words of Bastide's preface on the door of my house: 'We already realized it, but now we realize it once and for all: the true *Patrón* is Flaubert.'

The *engagés* were of course succeeded by that heterogeneous group of novelists referred to by the general title of practitioners of the '*nouveau roman*'. Although each failed to engage my interest or support, with the exception of Samuel Beckett (included in the group as he was published by the same house), I was nevertheless always well-disposed toward all of them for their aggressive proclamation of the importance of Flaubert's influence on the modern novel. The first to provide the theoretical link was not a novelist, however, but the scholar Geneviève Bollème, who in 1964 published an essay, 'La Leçon de Flaubert', and pointed out the aspects already present in Flaubert's fiction which were currently being cultivated in contemporary writing: the concern for the aesthetic, the obsession with the descriptive, the autonomy of the text—in other words, Flaubertian 'formalism'. Her essay demonstrated a bold hypothesis: that in all of Flaubert, particularly *Madame Bovary*, what matters is the description, the foregrounding, that deliberately destroys the narrative. The bridge between Flaubert and the New Novelists was—albeit a little *too* cleverly—constructed. Subsequently, in interviews, articles, and lectures, Alain Robbe-Grillet, Michel Butor, Claude Simon recognized Flaubert as the precursor of modernity. But it was Nathalie Sarraute, in a brilliant and tendentious article entitled 'Flaubert le précurseur' published in the review *Preuves* (February, 1965) who crowned him officially as master of the *nouveau roman*. As I read it in a bistro in Saint-Germain, I was thunderstruck. I was pleased by the authority Flaubert had suddenly assumed ('At this moment, the master of us all is Flaubert. As to this name the consensus is unanimous: it is that of the precursor of today's novel'), but stunned by the reason occasioning it; I thought, literally, that I was dreaming. Taking a paragraph out of context from a letter to Louise ('Ce qui me semble beau, ce que je voudrais faire, c'est un livre sur rien, un livre sans attache extérieure, qui se tiendrait de lui-même par la force interne de son style, comme la terre sans être soutenue se tient en l'air, un livre qui n'aurait presque pas de sujet ou du moins où le sujet serait presque invisible, si cela se peut'), Nathalie Sarraute, allowing one intention *among many* to obscure the ultimate reality of the work created, arrives at the following extraordinary programme for Flaubert: 'Books about nothing, almost without a subject, free of characters, plot, and all the old props, reduced to the sort of pure movement that make them akin to abstract art.'[23] It would be difficult to distort Flaubert any more drastically; Borges' phrase, that every author creates his precursors, has never been truer: Sarraute, admittedly exercising every reader's privilege, has discovered in Flaubert only what she has put there herself.

Her Flaubert quote is from a letter written during the labours of *Madame Bovary*, letters which demonstrate the care with which he worked out every detail—scenes, background, characters, peripeteias—and the meticulous obsessiveness with which he mapped out his narrative strategy: that is, his *plot*. A number of passages from the *Correspondance* come to mind demonstrating the importance of the subject (what he called 'the ideas'), evident, for instance, from his opinion of Lamartine's *Graziella*. The desire to write a 'book of nothing', liberated from referentiality, derives surely from an enthusiasm for literary style and, secondly, from a belief in the autonomy of fiction: everything in a novel, its truth and its falsehood, is determined by its form; what a novel 'houses' is derived from its authority as a linguistic construct not from its fidelity to the world it ostensibly represents. But, while internally coherent, fiction nevertheless partakes of the outside world if only because it relies upon the shared language from it: the same language and the same referents that the reader brings to the text. Moreover, the letter Nathalie Sarraute cites actually argues in favour of the integrity of narrative—a concern entirely different from what she expresses. If she had continued reading she would have come across another letter taking up precisely the same idea (books about nothing):

> Je voudrais faire des livres où il n'y eût qu'à écrire des phrases (si l'on peut dire cela), comme pour vivre il n'y a qu'à respirer de l'air. Ce qui m'embête, ce sont les malices de plan, les combinaisons d'effets, tous les calculs du dessous *et qui sont de l'Art pourtant, car l'effet du style en dépend, et exclusivement.*[24]

For Flaubert the achievements of the imagination did exist dominantly on the level of language—in aspects of style. The world of 'facts' clearly occasioned less enthusiasm—the 'tricks of plotting', the 'combination of effects', the 'basic calculations' participate in the organization of a subject within a temporal system—but the concern for facts, this artistic ordering, was not less important. On the contrary, he states that 'the effectiveness of style' depends on these concerns, and adds, categorically: *and on them exclusively.*

An author of course can never know the full significance—or significances—of his work, and it is possible that Flaubert, aspiring to write novels that were simply words, books without the weight of narrative, contributed to our conception of modern fiction by way of inventions that have as much, or perhaps even more to do with technique—the 'montage' for instance—than with language. But it is clear, I hope, that the case is far more complex than it has been made out to be in recent years. Flaubert, a born story-teller, developed a specific conception of the value and function of fictional narration, and considered that the effectiveness of prose depended 'exclusively' on it. The pleasure that this quotation provided when I first came across it was surpassed—for a devoted admirer of *Amadis de Gaule* and *Tirant le Blanc*—when I discovered that Flaubert also had once written:

> Tu sais que c'est un de mes vieux rêves que d'écrire un roman de chevalerie. Je crois cela faisable, même après l'Arioste, en introduisant un élément de terreur et de poésie large qui lui manque. Mais qu'est-ce que je n'ai pas envie d'écrire? Quelle est la luxure de plume qui ne m'excite!'[25]

Not all distortions of Flaubert have come from the formalist contingent, I should add in passing. At about the same as Sarraute's article—what I'll call rightist deviationism—I read in *Recherches Soviétiques* in 1956 the translation of an essay by A. F. Ivachtchenko, a member of the Academy of Sciences of the Soviet Union, who offered a leftist deviationist interpretation: Flaubert, he argued, was the father of critical realism!

It was also at this time that Sartre began work on his laborious and monumental autocriticism. Sartre's attitude towards Flaubert is complex, and, through the history of his writing, changes considerably. From the summary judgment in *Situations II* to the later determination (*Critique de la raison dialectique*) to situate Flaubert in his historical milieu through a 'totalizing' interpretation that addresses the social and the individual aspects of literary creation, Sartre has provided a number of views on Flaubert's work, moving slowly from one of scorn to one of respect. This transition culminates in the three volumes of *L'Idiot de la famille* (a fourth volume, dedicated to *Madame Bovary*, was once announced but to my knowledge remained unfinished), the apotheosis of an interest in

Mario Vargas Llosa

Flaubert that characterized French literature of the sixties and seventies. This tremendous enterprise is a tremendous curiosity: a 'case' study of three thousand pages, claiming twenty years of labour from one of Flaubert's most intransigent critics, opposed to everything that Flaubert's conceptions of history and art represent, which ultimately acknowledges that the master of Croisset was, with Baudelaire, a founding father of modern sensibility. On a personal level, Sartre's floppy, sprawling monster provided me with an intellectual reconciliation of sorts, Sartre being, along with Flaubert, one of my most important literary debts.

I am not, however, an overly enthusiastic admirer of *L'Idiot de la famille*. After the two months needed to read it, the essay leaves a sense only of incompleteness, a tremendous task dwarfed by its even larger ambition: to account completely for the social and ideological context out of which Flaubert's novels emerged, and to do so through an interdisciplinary investigation incorporating Marxism, psychoanalysis, and the precepts of existentialism. The study, obviously, is not simply 'about' Flaubert, but, rather, 'about' as much of man generally as it is humanly possible to express. It is, without a doubt, an extraordinarily uneven book, inconsistent in its methodology, uneven in its results, and disproportionate in its treatment of the very objects it sets out to investigate. With the exception of a number of passages (such as the brilliant analysis of the social and ideological origins of Flaubert's family or the examination of the social classes during the Second Empire), the greatest part of *L'idiot de la famille* is taken up by a rigorous (and orthodox) psychoanalysis expressed through a regular patter of existentialist jargon. The Freudian approach does lead, however, to a number of exciting discoveries, as in the explanation of the 'Pont-l'Evêque crisis', the endlessly debated question about the precise nature of Flaubert's illness—epilepsy? hysteria?—to which Sartre contributes a solid, imaginative, even if complex theory of neurosis. There are of course a number of sections the brilliance of which is obscured slightly by the massive text into which they have been sunk: the discussion entitled 'Névrose et programmation chez Flaubert: le Second Empire', for instance, a critically ground-breaking discussion in the otherwise unfocused third volume; or the last section, developing a comparison between Flaubert and Leconte de Lisle, or the intriguing analysis of the relations between Flaubert and the Second Empire.

The book, however, ends with tremendous abruptness, as though exhaustion had overtaken its author and he could not find the strength to reach a goal so distant. In the end, it is disheartening to realize that the only texts Sartre managed to analyze in detail have been those from Flaubert's childhood and adolescence, and that the effort expended in scrutinizing these relatively insignificant works ended up destroying the critic. All these thousands of pages, that is, constitute an error in planning, which, failing even to study the first novel Flaubert published, amount to what in Sartre's original scheme would have been merely preliminary considerations, a prologue before the task proper. Unlike the character in Camus' *La peste* who could never write a novel because he could never decide how to phrase the first sentence of it, Sartre has written with such fury and has dealt in such detail with so many adventitious subjects that he loses sight of the book he set out to write. The result is a monstrous progeny, a monumental child, and a brilliant failure: falling far short of its aim by aiming too high, *ailes de géant qui empêchent de marcher.*

The similarities between Sartre's last book and Flaubert's are too obvious to neglect. Have there ever been two such equally admirable failures- -caused by such equally idealistic reasons—as *L'Idiot de la famille* and *Bouvard et Pécuchet?* Both are impossible undertakings, enterprises destined to miscarry because, aimed at the unattainable, both were, even in conception, more than any one mind could achieve. To represent in a novel the totality of the human condition was as unrealistic, even if inspiring, a dream as aspiring to capture in an essay the totality of a life, explaining the individual by reconstructing all the sources—social, familial, historical, psychological, biological, linguistic—contributing to what we understand him to be. In each case, the author has dared to unravel a tangled skein that has a beginning but no end. But in each case we recognize the victory, the grandeur emanating from the inevitable failure. For to have persisted in an adventure so reckless and so irrational—to have succumbed to Lucifer's crime—is to have redefined our conception of language and literary representation and to have projected entirely new standards to which our fiction and our criticism must aspire.

Translated by Helen R. Lane

1. 'The beloved of every novel, the heroine of every play, the vague *she* of every volume of verse.'

2. 'The soprano's voice seemed to her to be merely the echo of her own consciousness, and this illusion charmed her part and parcel of her own life.'

3. 'There is no desert, abyss, ocean that I wouldn't cross with you.'

4. 'And first of all, to put the matter bluntly, does he fuck her or doesn't he? The pair of them aren't human beings, they're mannequins. How beautiful a thing these love stories are where the principal thing is so surrounded by mystery that one doesn't know what in the world is going on, sexual intercourse being systematically relegated to the shadow along with drinking, eating, pissing, etc.! This partiality irritates me no end. Here's a healthy youth living with a woman who loves him and whom he loves, and never a desire! Not a single impure cloud ever appears to darken this pale blue lake! O hypocrite! Had he told the real story, it would have been even more beautiful! But truth demands hairier males than Monsieur de Lamartine. It is easier in fact to draw an angel than a woman: the wings hide the hunched back.'

5. 'The honest sex organ is the basis of human affection; it is not itself affection, but rather it is the *substratum*, as philosophers would say. No woman has ever loved a eunuch, and if mothers cherish their children more than fathers do, it is because they are the fruit of their womb and the umbilical cord of their love remains attached to their hearts without being severed.'

6. 'They are not honest with themselves; they do not acknowledge their sensuality; they confuse their cunts with their hearts and think that the moon's reason for being is to light their bedrooms.'

7. *Gustave Flaubert* (Paris, 1968), p. 115.

8. 'Her adorable, tiny foot sheathed in a pretty high-heeled shoe trimmed with a black rose'—cited in *L'Idiot de la famille: Gustave Flaubert de 1821 à 1857* (Paris, 1971), vol. II, p. 1525.

9. 'A course on the important subjects of boots in comparative literature. "*Yes, a boot is the world*," I would say.'

10. 'And their feet! Red, skinny, with corns and bunions, deformed by their button boots, feet as long as shuttles or as broad as

washerwomen's paddles.'

11. Not only in *Madame Bovary*, of course, but here I want to limit myself to speaking only of this book. Traces of this same special interest can be glimpsed all through Flaubert's works. We need only recall the moving meeting, after so many years, of Madame Arnoux and Frédéric in *L'Éducation sentimentale*. After recalling his extraordinary and impossible love, Frédéric falls to his knees and endeavors to reawaken his desire of yesteryear. He is on the point of succeeding in doing so when he spies 'la pointe de sa bottine' (the tip of her button shoe), '[qui] s'avançait un peu sous sa robe' ('peeking out from beneath her dress'). On the point of fainting, Frédéric murmurs in a faltering voice: 'La vue de votre pied me trouble' ('The sight of your foot disturbs me').

12. Léon: 'on hearing the creak of her button shoes, he felt his resolve weaken, like drunkards at the sight of strong drink.' Maître Guillaumin: 'her shoe, the sole of which was curling and smoking as it rested against the stove.'

13. 'His eyes staring at his handsome carpet-slippers' that have been a 'love-gift'.

14. 'Her foot sheathed in a black button shoe.'

15. 'Between the black cloth and the little black boot, her delicate white stocking, that seemed like a bit of her naked flesh.'

16. 'A subtle, penetrating aura that emanated even from the folds of her dress and the arch of her foot.'

17. 'He trembled at the dizzying thought that he would soon possess her.'

18. 'He liked the sound of Mademoiselle Emma's little wooden shoes on the scrubbed stone flags of the kitchen; their thick heels made her just a bit taller, and, when she walked in front of him, the wooden soles, clacking swiftly along, hit against the leather of her shoe [inside] with a sharp slapping noise.'

19. 'The soles of her feet, which once ran so quickly to satisfy her desires, and which now would never walk again.'

20. 'What distinguishes great geniuses is generalization and creation. They sum up scattered personalities in a type and bring new characters to the awareness of mankind'—from the letter to Louise Colet of September 25, 1852.

21. 'The measure of a soul is the dimension of its desire, as we

might form our conceptions of a cathedral by the height of its bell-tower.'

22. These fits of rage at times moved him to unexpected rash decisions, setting himself time limits for proving his talents. After having worked for a number of weeks on the scene of the agricultural fair, he suddenly wrote to Louise: 'I give myself two weeks more to be done with it. At the end of this time, if nothing good has come of it, I'm abandoning the novel indefinitely.' The twenty-nine page episode was in fact to cost him four months of work.

23. 'What seems beautiful to me, what I would like to do, is a book about nothing, a book with no attachments to the outside world, which would be self-sustaining thanks to the internal force of its style, as the earth holds itself in the air without being supported, a book that would have almost no subject, or where the subject would at least be almost invisible, if that is possible.'

24.'I should like to compose books in such a way that the only thing necessary would be to write sentences (if I may put it that way), just as in order to live the only thing necessary is to breathe. I don't like having to bother with the tricks of plotting, the combinations of effects, all the basic calculations, *and yet they are Art, for the effectiveness of style depends on them . . . and on them exclusively*'—from 'Letter at Daybreak', June 26, 1853; my italics.

25. 'You know that it has long been one of my dreams to write a romance of chivalry. I think this could be done, even after Ariosto, by introducing an element of terror and sweeping poetry that is missing in him. But is there anything I don't yearn to write? Is there any lust of the pen that does not excite me!'

GRANTA

PATRICIA HAMPL
THE BEAUTY DISEASE

Over the maroon horse-hair sofa in my grandmother's house where, as a child, I took my afternoon nap, there was a picture of a girl with black hair. She wore the kind of garment that is not so much dress as drapery. It folded in dozens of deep creases, and was a dark, hypnotic green. In her arms she held a lute. One hand was draped over the strings near the sounding board's hole; the other hardly seemed to exert any pressure on the frets. Her hair was rich and heavy, like the dress; it was curled and tangled beautifully, alluringly. She was an art nouveau figure, relaxed in what looked to me like extra flesh, the arms just round enough to suggest sausages and in that association to attach her and her beauty to the plain earth, in spite of the fantasy of her hair. She looked, except for the upholstery fabric of her dress, like my grandmother in the wedding picture I had seen.

The girl's mouth was parted slightly. She might have been meant to be singing, but I always thought the song had just ended. Her gaze was not directed at me as I lay on the sofa, looking up at her in the mid-afternoon half-light of the parlour. Her gaze was higher, above me, pure and direct, undeflected. I thought she was beautiful.

Beauty, for my grandmother and my aunts, was divided like a territory into estates, each part governed by a different seignior. There were no alliances among the fiefdoms. A woman was not 'beautiful', not even 'pretty'. It was more complicated than that. She had perfect skin, but her hands were bad; she had lovely brown eyes, but she was fat; her legs were good, but what are legs if your teeth are crooked? The body was a collection of unfederated states, constantly at odds with each other, recognizing no sovereign to sort out the endless clan feuds.

Only one kind of woman lived outside this feudal world. 'Gertrude is a plain woman,' one of my aunts would say musingly. And no discussion of parts took place. They stirred their tan coffee-and-cream, and fell silent for a moment in the grip of the ineffable. Gertrude's slate was wiped clean. Homeliness was a ticket to freedom, to a no-nonsense world where you walked around in a sober suit of sad flesh—the less said the better. You were out of the running in some absolute way, but you were free. The way a child feels when sent to bed with a cold: away from the bustle of the house, hardly human in the usual way.

The striving for beauty is a way to feel powerful, to control the world. It is completely engrossing; it breaks the world up, as my grandmother and aunts and I did, into morsels that can be attended to one at a time: fingers, nails, toes, eyebrows, eyelids (eyelid creme: I have a tiny jar, yellowing like rancid mayonnaise), on and on, tirelessly, over the vast steppes and plains of the body, through its tangled hair, over the distressing angles and bulges of elbows and stomach. It is a sweet slavery, beauty itself rising beyond like the gorgeous mirage cities pioneers used to see quivering on the horizon of their desolate homesteads. It is a frontier that is never broken, where one is always, everlastingly, riding one's starving horses over the same endless prairie, the huge task still beyond.

I gathered very early on that beauty might fade, but never a woman's allegiance to beauty. No one in our family spoke about sex, but beauty was discussed endlessly. The body was an endless topic and, as far as you could tell from our conversations, the body's purpose was beauty, not sex.

The pursuit of beauty and beauty itself hold a ghostly power over most women (even youth—'a younger woman' is usually translated to mean a more beautiful one). The rituals of beauty are confused rituals of self-love and purification. The shaving of one's legs is an example of this double-edged ritual: one must rid oneself of hair, of that coarse, unruly *growth*; this is purification. But one is also paying the greatest attention to the intimate body, to the care of detail, the sensuous, stroking touch; this is self-love.

But above it all is the sense of striving for perfection, a world that is static and yet not dead. Like family pictures from the past where history allows us to live and yet be fixed in something beyond mortal flesh, beyond self, the pursuit of beauty attempts to turn self-absorption itself into an impersonal form.

The different kinds of beauty got mixed up in my mind, confused. There was first the beauty of the female face and body which was a cruelty that neither I nor any woman (especially girls) troubled by its elusiveness can believe is lodged democratically in the eye of the beholder. Then there was the sheer beauty of the natural world, and the made beauty of art, and the comforting, familiar beauty of one's own culture—if you could find it, if it existed. Finally, there was the beauty that was method, that wasn't actually beauty at all but the deep craving caused by the lack of the other kinds, the willingness to be enslaved by sensibility: the life sentence of the bourgeois woman.

The confusion of these different sorts of beauty, which I tried (unsuccessfully, largely unconsciously) to unsort, I now see as the point of my obsession rather than a mess to be cleared up. How *do* such things get confused? How has female physical beauty, the metaphor women have been required to embody, been confused by me (in me) with art, or even with the traditional American greed and the recent acknowledgement of our ruin of the natural beauty of the continent, and with the American insecurity over culture? My sources are odd, sometimes trivial, but they embody the obsession, the confusion.

I have even made lists, rudimentary charts, looking for the relation among these different strands, reasons for the confusion, for the root of the obsession that has connected these things in my mind. Did it begin with Sister Mary Patricia, who taught us Modern European History (which was not modern: the textbook stopped with the end of the Hapsburg Empire, and was itself bound in a green watery moiré, a book not only about but from a former time). Sister told us one day that Hans Christian Andersen, the fairy-tale man, was supposed to have driven through the streets of Prague, hanging love-sick out his carriage window, smitten with the beautiful Czech girls, crying, 'Pretty maiden, pretty maiden, let me kiss you!' In passing, Sister mentioned that Bohemian women were considered the most beautiful in Europe. She was a history teacher who could be counted on for this kind of satisfyingly useless remark.

I raised my hand.

'Yes, Patricia,' she said.

I stood up—we had to rise to recite, giving our class rooms a churchy up-and-down quality—and I said, as if in a dream, fatally unconscious, 'I'm Bohemian.'

Everyone hooted. Even Sister, kindly poker face, smiled and said, 'Well, is that so.' As I sat down, almost before the room filled with laughter, I came to myself out of that momentary ethnic trance. I couldn't believe I'd actually stood up—braces, pointy glasses, pimples—and said what I'd said.

As a rule, I thought of myself as monumentally ugly. Was I in fact as homely as I thought? Impossible. But the mere thought of my looks inflamed my imagination and caused me to see myself as a freak—for no particular reason, simply because I had a physical existence. Like many people obsessed by their appearance, I had no idea what I actually looked like. I was afraid of photographs as if they were evidence brought forward by the prosecution. I studied the mirror solemnly and then, minutes later away from its image, was dismayed to realize I could not remember what the girl in the glass looked like. It was a typical adolescent self-consciousness, but it seemed to last forever. In fact, can I truly say it finished? Writing about it as an adolescent preoccupation only seems to place it in the past.

I was probably—to use my mother's sane phrase—nice enough looking. My mother was not obsessed by beauty and thought a woman had done her level best if she 'put on her face', kept her hair decently combed, and manicured her nails once a week. Perfume, lipstick, nail polish were not, for her, rituals of self-love; they were the spit-and-polish discipline of a good soldier who kept to the forms. She spent no time worrying about the face and body fate had dealt her; they were 'nice enough'. Beauty was another realm, something that, like inherited wealth, struck rarely—and to other, stranger, beings. Unlike my grandmother and aunts, my mother did not ponder the elusive qualities of beauty, did not ache to be gorgeous—at least, not as far as I knew. Why bother—she looked nice enough. Those who *were* beautiful were, in my mother's cosmology, a joy for the rest of us to behold, not our competition. And in our family it was my father who, everyone agreed, was the beauty. 'Handsome as a movie star,' my mother's friends would sigh. For a while in first grade I was under the impression that he was president of the United States (he was president of the church Men's Altar Guild that year, I believe). It seemed natural that someone so handsome should run the country.

My father was not only handsome. As a florist he was, to me, somehow in charge of beauty. A man, 'handsome as a movie star', whose business was beauty. In second grade, when we were given an assignment to find out how our fathers' work 'helped the community', I went home with foreboding, sensing that my father's work did not help the community in any way, that in fact it was superfluous to the community. As I saw it, children whose fathers were doctors or house-painters, for instance, were home free. But my father's occupation struck me as iffy, light-weight, positively extraneous, and therefore (to my Catholic puritan logic) not useful to the community.

I felt this foreboding in spite of the fact that I loved the green-house and often played in the palm-house (which was Africa). I once saw a rabbit give birth to her babies in the root cellar, and in the summer I trailed my finger teasingly across the low pool in the back lot where the goldfish—some of them alarmingly large—and the water plants were kept. In winter I wandered through the moist houses, as each glassy room was called, watching the exotic trick my father played on the Minnesota weather. I read the labels on the huge, ancient rose trees and great geranium plants in expensive pots, which wealthy matrons had left in the green-house to be cared for while they went to Florida or Arizona, or, the really ethereal ones, to Italy.

The odour of crushed evergreen, the intense little purple berries of juniper, the fans of cedar, and the killing hard work of the Christmas rush *were* Christmas to me. I preferred this market-place Christmas, full of overworked employees and cross tempers and the endless parade of 'gift plants' and boxed cut flowers, to our own family Christmas with its ordinary tree and turkey like everybody else's.

But was any of this of use to the community? Did it do any good? I did not want to put my father on the spot. Still, I had the assignment and I asked my question, beginning first with the innocuous part: what, exactly was his job? He answered at great and technical length; he loved his work.

Then the real question: 'Is your job of any use to the community?' I had decided to word it this way, rather than asking *how* it was useful, sensing as I did that it was of no use whatever. I thought that he could simply say, as painlessly as possible, no. And then we'd just drop the subject. My handsome father, who had been enjoying the interrogation, the opportunity to explain his place in the world, frowned. 'What do you mean—is it of any use to the community?' he asked sharply.

'I mean, does it do any good—to the community?' I was flustered and was losing hold of what community meant. I was only eight and the whole thing was beginning to unravel as I saw my movie-star father frowning at me.

'Who asked you to ask that?'

'Sister. Sister said,' I practically cried, falling back on the Catholic school child's great authority.

'Sister,' my father said. He was angry. It was as I had thought: he served no use to the community. He was silent for some time, not weighing his words, but apparently deciding whether to speak at all.

'You tell Sister,' he finally said, coldly, as if he were talking to an adult, 'I do the most important thing for the community. Do you think people can live without beauty? Flowers—do they kill anybody? Do they hurt anybody? Flowers are beautiful—that's all. That's enough. So they're sending you home to find out what's the *use!* You tell her they're beautiful. Tell her I bring beauty to the community.' He said the final word with regal contempt, as if he only used the grimy jargon of Sister and her band of philistines for purposes of argument.

It was less than ten years after the Second World War; the Korean 'conflict' was just ended. My father wasn't talking to me, not to an eight-year-old, and probably not to a nun with a 'unit on work' in her social studies class. He spoke, I think, to himself, in a cry for values, dismayed that the use of a red rose had to be explained, as if my question were proof that the world had been more brutalized than he had known.

The confusion I had about the types of beauty might have come a little later, in 1966, when I wrote my first published book review, for the university newspaper. The book was *Ariel* by Sylvia Plath. I didn't know that this was not just a book, but a legacy that I—and practically every woman writer of my generation—was about to claim, disclaim, 'relate to', and 'deny'. A few years later, in Women's Literature classes, people were saying, 'If only feminism had happened sooner . . .'. This meant in effect: Sylvia Plath would not have killed herself. Whether or not this was believed, it was said and mused over at least during the coffee breaks of these—at the time informal—classes. Plath's suicide didn't interest me much, not deeply. Maybe because suicide itself did not fascinate me, as it does some people. I was untouched by what A. Alvarez calls the savage god. To me, suicide was, simply and bluntly, hurting oneself—something I went to lengths not to do.

But suicidal or not, women identified with Sylvia Plath. Women poets especially, but not only poets: Plath was a figure for the mass of educated American women and, beyond that, a figure for all women touched by feminism as an idea. The greatest dynamism of feminism, in fact, has had to do with its cultural vitality. The economic and

Patricia Hampl

political implications of the movement are important, of course. But in a country where even people who consider themselves not only educated but literary don't read poetry and have said to me cheerily, as if I will appreciate their candour, that they 'just don't understand poetry' and therefore 'just don't read it', when a group bands together to discuss the work of a poet like Plath who is undeniably obscure at times and definitely difficult, they are acknowledging, against the grain of the culture, that her work contains essential information they *must* have and that it can be had only by cracking the rind of poetic difficulty. And this, in our country, is revolutionary and is eloquent of a ravenous cultural appetite. Sylvia Plath's work, coming at the time it did, created this focus. People—women—who did not read poetry, read poetry. And they understood it; they bothered to.

Beyond Plath's poems there was a novel, letters, more poems, memoirs by those who had known her, critical studies. In a word, fascination. The allure included the works, but went beyond it into biography. For me, the most poignant of these biographical lures was not, as it was for others, the suicide, nor even the brilliance of her mind or the pluckiness of her ambition. It was the period of her life that is the major background of her autobiographical novel, *The Bell Jar*: her time as a guest editor at *Mademoiselle* magazine.

The summer internships of college seniors on a fashion/beauty/general interest magazine (which publishes poetry and fiction) aimed at college women is an odd American literary institution. It is a distinctly female tradition, in spite of the fact that there are a few men in the program each year. The women are the focus, the would-be writers, the winners of fiction or poetry contests, women with talent, with some sort of accomplishment behind them and, probably, some ambition ahead of them. They are brought to New York to get experience working on a national magazine; they live for a few weeks in the city, hanging out at least on the fringes of publishing. And they get a make-over: hair-cuts, make-up consultations, fashion tips, wardrobe counselling. They are reminded of their primary allegiance: to beauty. In the midst of work, they are reminded of self, of their sexual self.

It may seem a small thing, but it glares at me, out of the biography of Sylvia Plath. The absurdity of it, the hopelessness of the mixture of beauties—the female body's old rituals in honour of the

264

ideal form and the duty any artist assumes toward beauty in art are brutally tossed together for a woman in a way they are not for a man. The first compliment that women began to turn over and over, wondering of its insidiousness, was, 'You think like a man, you write like a man.' The statement meant vaguely, imprecisely, that one wrote without frills, without sentimentality. More precisely, the statement 'You think like a man' probably means simply 'You think'. Perhaps it *is* easier to think ('like a man') if the apparatus of thinking is not split, deflected, even as it goes about what everyone agrees is business.

Sylvia Plath had gone to Smith College. I wrote my book review for the student newspaper of a land-grant institution. Plath came from New England, and I was in the Midwest. She was a figure of success, of accomplishment for me (the suicide was beyond me, or maybe in a romantic way, even her suicide seemed grander than any gesture I could command). Her ambition soothed me somehow and made ambition seem less wrong. I read the rules for the *Mademoiselle* fiction and poetry contests. I think I entered once or twice; at least, I intended to enter. But in 1966, by the time I wrote my review and heard for the first time my own opinions (for that was the puzzling relationship I discovered I had with writing: I wrote to find out what I thought), I realized that I was ashamed that Sylvia Plath had been a guest editor on the magazine. I recoiled and I didn't know why—I hadn't read *The Bell Jar* yet, didn't even know of it. I was humiliated (if I had recognized my confused feelings) by this mixture of fashion and art. I felt, obscurely, that *Mademoiselle* guest editors were, like the Miss Americas are to other young women, representatives for me. The contest was *my* contest. It didn't matter that I didn't win or perhaps wasn't even a contestant: that was my world. And I was humiliated in absentia that even here—in art, poetry, thinking and doing, 'the world of the mind', I'd thought—here too, everything still rested on the premise that women must pursue beauty, that we must be made over.

The desire to cut the bond with beauty has been intense. It is one of the cultural currents of feminism, the reason everybody was suddenly dressing in overalls, wearing combat boots (this was a war, this was work), and didn't own lipstick. The best, most astonishingly powerful motto of the times was Black Is Beautiful. And suddenly they *were* beautiful, knocking the country over with raw superiority, genuine style, not only with a cause that was just. But our motto, if we were to find a cry to express the freedom we wanted, would have to have been something ungainly and negative like We Aren't Beautiful, Lovely Is Lousy, Female Is Ugly. But we didn't mean that either. We meant . . . but that is the suicidal part: it is hard to sever the cords that tie us to our slavery and leave intact those that bind us to ourselves.

I could not think of beauty in a usefully diagrammatic way, each type in its slot. In front of me now I have a picture of Keats, given to me by a friend; it has printed beneath it, deadpan, 'A poet who considered beauty the most important thing in the world.'
He knew what it was:

'Beauty is truth, truth beauty',—that is all
Ye know on earth, and all ye need to know.

It's because of those lines that the inscription on the picture strikes me as so funny: the donkeyish prose parses, solemnly, the famous last lines of the grand ode.

Keats, to my mind, is the model of the modern lyric poet. But it is the blunt sentimentality of a copy-writer below the (arty, not authentic) picture that I find myself brooding about. I believe it: beauty for Keats was the most important thing in the world. And for me. But it is not the same thing. Anyway, I do not think that I mean truth. And it will take me a long time to extend my sympathies and unify my sense of what beauty is to feel that the equation between truth and beauty is all I need to know. My sense of beauty is troubled, clouded, confused. Like my sense of the past, it is splintered, part of the longing I feel and which is placated and deflected from the real search by my willingness (society's willingness) to live in a consumer culture with its array of consolation prizes for the middle class. Keats wasn't a consumer. Beauty, I suppose, was not an equivocal word to him. And it is *him*. The history of women is the history of beauty. Our bodies have been the metaphor for an entire aspect of life, a deep layer of consciousness: the beautiful woman, even to women, is the image of beauty itself. It is the word made flesh.

I would like beauty, like the past, to be something that can be traced, a theme, as my English-student self would have it. The word, unfortunately, is a touchstone for too many things: *beauty* has become a switchboard through which I route and connect the various desires and disappointments of my own life and also what I sense more confusedly are those of the culture. I persist in believing that the perception of beauty, the hunger for it, is somehow (but how?) all of a piece, or at least related, no matter how different the meanings are behind the uses of the word itself. It's an old trust in language and I can't shake it: if we use the same word for vastly different subjects, I believe in their relation before I can prove it, even before I entirely sense it. My desire to *be* beautiful (a woman's desire), to create beauty (as an artist), to live surrounded by beauty (a citizen's sense, which is both aesthetic and, in the entirely public sense, cultural) are connected only by the word. They are in themselves quite different things. I have sought the agility of mind that could find their relation. For I sensed that if I could find a relation to beauty in which beauty is truth, I might also discover a relation to history that is generative. It is the old American quest, perhaps the first heritage of white people in the New World: to stand on the new, beautiful continent and decide where to put the first mark. This is the work of history and of creation.

Technicians speak of making a beautiful bomb. And I suppose that has meaning. We are most outraged morally not at the absence of beauty in life but in its ironic presence: Mozart quartets in Terezin, the 'model' concentration camp, for example. Beauty misplaced in this way is obscene. During the Vietnam War my friends and I, young poets, shuddered to learn that McNamara read poetry—or was it religious philosophy—on those long nights at the Pentagon. Rilke or Teilhard de Chardin—someone like that. Whoever it was—and whether or not the story was true—we found it eloquently horrible and its power came from our sense of the dislocation of beauty.

To be a woman of taste and sensibility is the accepted way (for those in the middle class) to bind the self together, to make the fragmented, frustrated parts a working whole. My fashionable Aunt Lillian, who devoted her life to shopping in the largest department store in Minneapolis like a knight on quest, was my first instructor. Later, when I had the money in my pocket from my first job as a copy-editor at the St Paul paper, I embarked on my own mad career as a consumer (the word itself was just beginning to be used; Ralph Nader was just being mentioned here and there as a possible presidential candidate). I lost pay-cheque after pay-cheque to the soft fantasy of fashion. I threaded my way through the maze of boutiques that cleverly, phonily, evoked the colour and brio of a street bazaar, although every cash register was wired up to the single credit department above. I knew and didn't care. I spent and spent.

Our country had become a consumer nation, but it is strange that this sad, greedy noun we chose for ourselves did not instantly make clear that beauty is our problem, our lack, even in an introverted sense, our obsession.

There were other figures of the romantic quest in my life. Orna Tews was one. She was an artist and was invited by the nuns every year to give one of the weekly 'assembly speeches' at our school. To most of the girls she was a plain woman wearing aggressively homely clothes, shod in sensible shoes like our own uniform Girl Scout oxfords. How lucky we were to be wearing them, too, we were always told. How happy we would be years later when our metatarsal bones were straight and true, unlike the deformed and painful feet of foolish public school girls who wore penny loafers or—worse—moccasins.

Here in this holding-pool for ugly ducklings who, one fine day, would give geese-like cackles when they turned into the swans that were Catholic wives-and-mothers, Orna Tews, spinster artist, was invited by the Sisters to address us. To me Orna Tews with her odd and faintly elderly name and her aggressive disregard for fashion (a far cry from Aunt Lillian), was the epitome of a spinsterishness that was positively glamorous. I hung on her every assembly hall word (I believe she had an accent) as if she were a missionary only briefly returned to the tepid homeland before rejoining, drab herself, the world of macaws and jaguars and savage religion to which she belonged. An artist, speaking of art.

She said to observe everything. Actually, she said *Observe perpetually*. I went around for a week with my head on a swivel, eyes popping, looking so diligently for 'the significant detail' that I was in a state of chronic peevishness. I could hardly fall asleep at night because of my earnest attention. I was an exhausted, querulous wreck. But I was observing—perpetually.

Fifteen years later when I found that Orna Tews's dictum was the final entry in Virginia Woolf's *Writer's Diary*, a line itself quoted from

Henry James, I didn't feel deceived. In fact, I was often drawn to people who lived only the shell of life in our measly present, in St Paul, Minnesota, where God had absent-mindedly dropped them, speaking in their own unauthentic, timorous voices. They lived, actually, in literature. The first boy who kissed me, a French horn player who soon after explained that he had to be careful of his lip, held me in a long embrace and said, 'My God, you're fun to kiss!' Scott Fitzgerald, *Tender Is the Night*, book II, chapter 9, spoken by Dick Diver to Nicole: *their* first kiss. My French horn player didn't care if I found out his magic line was not his own; it was he, soon after, who loaned me the novel and said I ought to read it. The language of the art crazed is rarely our own, almost never in youth. Orna Tews quoting from Virginia Woolf's diary, the boy of my first kiss copping an exclamation from Fitzgerald—we spoke the same language though it wasn't ours. It was the alluringly aged, dusty voice of an author. It was prose. We bowed our heads and spoke in quotation, excising the citations for the sake of the moment.

Miss Tews talked about art in life, the beauty of dailiness. I was all agog. She was a sort of arty Aunt Lillian, the next step; an intellectual providing theory where my aunt had been all wonderful praxis. Her message seemed to be that art was made of nothing. Or perhaps that nothing—that is, everything—was art. She dwelt at length on the art that went into baking a *truly beautiful* cake, the care in sifting, the delicate folding of egg whites into batter, the attention to preheated ovens and well-creamed butter and sugar mixtures. Details, details, the art of the tiny could fill a lifetime. Our mothers were artists! Our fathers, oiling a creaking hinge on a door, were artists! Our grandmothers were artists ('the fine old American art of darning—how many of you girls have ever thought of darning as an art?'). The well-driven bus, the carefully plowed street in winter, the beautifully set dinner table, the diligently written history theme: art, art, all art!

I wanted to sign up for the whole package: the lifetime of oxfords, the doughy resilience of a belief in the beauty that resided in all things, the fanatic's ecstasy as she toiled her way through the art of cakes and pastries, the itty-bitty harmlessnesses that, translated into what Miss Tews called at the end of her speech 'formal art', were the business of perpetual observation. And perpetual observation was the first tool of any questor. Which is what, though she stayed at home to practise her formal and informal arts in her manic way, Orna Tews was.

Though deeply unbeautiful, she had further involved me in this pursuit of beauty. I didn't know it, I only knew what attracted me. But now I see her, and Aunt Lillian (who was beautiful), and my grandmother (who also was) as the triumvirate they were: my figures for the pursuit of what I felt I did not possess myself but which, I sensed, the world might provide: beauty, the loveliness I was willing to seek, to make, if I could not *be* it, as I understood was woman's way.

There were kindred spirits my own age too. A girl in our parish fascinated me, and although I didn't know her well—she was two or three years older—I was always aware of her. Her name was Helen. I can remember with unusual clarity our few conversations. Helen looking directly at me as we talked, curious, so curious to hear what I would say next. She was genuinely interested in other people. She was the ugliest girl I had ever seen, ugly beyond her years, with an elderly witch-like angularity that thrilled me and made me shy as if it were love I was feeling. It was pity, though, and it made my heart move toward her. She loved to read and was very intelligent; this somehow consolidated her homeliness. She was a heroine, I thought, in the best mode: brilliant, original mind, hopelessly unbeautiful, like Jane Eyre, my great favourite.

The last time I saw Helen, the summer before she began the university, she told me, 'I tested out of freshman English. I can go straight ahead and take literature courses.' We had met by chance on the St Clair bus, she coming home from the University of Minnesota, I from the St Paul library downtown. I was deeply impressed. I resolved, when the time came, to test out of freshman English myself, a thing I hadn't known was possible.

We sat in the darkened St Clair bus, the forest-green upholstery worn smooth and almost grey, the two narrow bands of yellowish light running along both sides of the interior above the windows. Romantic, gauzy light, even then. The light of our town with its buttery streetlights, the softened light of memory and dream. Helen's face that night is one of the clearest pictures I have of any human being. She sat in the shadowy glow, all the angularity of her strange face and attenuated body throwing their own shadows. 'Hey, that's great,' I said. It was somehow only fair that such homeliness should at least pass out of freshman English. The thing about her that took my breath away was the poise of her ugliness. She was smiling, a perfectly natural and yet somehow alarming smile. It dawned on me: she doesn't know she's ugly.

How this had occurred—the vast deception of a brilliant mind, a mind that could test out of freshman English at the university—I couldn't begin to understand. She was not troubled, she was not downcast, she was not even self-conscious. She didn't care that she wasn't pretty. Apparently, she didn't think about it. Beyond the ugliness, which she hadn't registered, she was simply a very eager girl. Eager to live. Passing out of freshman English was just another stroke that cleared away the intervening dross, a little leap that brought her nearer to experience. Like me, she was literary and she 'wanted to experience life'. I wanted to ask her . . . so many things. But mainly, how she had received this inoculation against beauty? Like the women of my grandmother and aunts' coffee conversations on the subject, she was plain: she was free. She had tested out of freshman English, she had tested out of the rougher course, the college of good looks from which the rest of us sensed we would never graduate.

But who asks questions, who even knows, staring fascinated at another person and absorbing her mystery, that these things are *questions* that beat their wings on just the other side of consciousness? I asked nothing. Yet I felt our kinship was complete. I'd always felt the sisterhood of gawky homeliness was ours and that, just as she was smarter than I, she was homelier. Not essentially different, just *more* ugly, *more* undesirable. But twins, all the same. Two homely girls who liked to read long novels about English governesses.

She left the bus before I did, getting off at Victoria Street, queenly and unaffected, stunning me again with a mystery that I finally understood was grace. She waved gaily from the curb as I, a lit face in a darkened rectangle, passed down St Clair Avenue toward home.

A couple of years later, when I was at the university (where I had not passed out of freshman English and had failed on my first theme: 'didn't follow directions', the notation said), I heard Helen had gone to Paris to study. She got married there. She's settled down in Paris, my mother said, who liked Helen's mother and liked Helen and likes life, I sometimes think, because she likes fiction. She is always trailing after somebody's dénouement, keeping track of her old friends, my old friends, the deaths of other people's relatives, reading to the end of everybody's book to see how things turn out. It's because of my mother that I know what happened to Helen.

I was living in a different state when my mother sent me a clipping from the *Pioneer Press*, which she reads every morning with her X-acto knife in hand. It was an article from the Women's Page, as it used to be called and as my mother still calls it, though the title now is Trends.

The article was about Helen who had come home to visit her family. Home from Paris. The picture was huge, a three-column portrait of a beautiful woman, her elegant head looking from atop the languid frame, looking not at the camera, not at anything in particular, absorbed apparently in her thought: selfless, *thinking*. The expressive hands were held out slightly in some gesture of thought, grasping her idea.

What was she explaining, this enigma of my girlhood, this proof of the mystery and transformative power of time? It didn't matter. She had become gorgeous, utterly, utterly beautiful.

Helen had become a fashion model in Paris after she married. You're just right for my clothes, Coco Chanel had told her. She was on the cover of *Elle*, *Vogue*, and whatever the rest of them are called. She only worked part-time, here and there. It wasn't a career so much as a lark. 'Clothes are toys,' she said in the article. She explained it wasn't a matter of beauty. She said she saw girls all the time, everywhere, to whom she wanted to say, 'You could be a model if you want to.' It wasn't beauty, she said. All you needed was to have high cheekbones and be skinny.

The reporter wrote that Helen seemed *unable* to gain weight, that she ate what she wanted—according to the reporter, a whole bag of Tom Thumb donuts just that morning—yet kept her bony beauty, throwing her stylish shadows from the planes of her high cheekbones.

She had taken a professional name. She had chosen the name of our bus line: to Coco Chanel, to the editors of *Vogue* and *Elle*, she was Helen St Clair. Helen of St Clair, of the shabby and romantic St Clair bus, poised on the hills of our town, as Helen, that night, had been poised on the curb, waving, our emissary to the light, to the City of

Light.

'You've got the beauty disease,' a friend of mine said a few years ago, exasperated with me—the flowers, the attention to detail, the domestic fussing with myself and the materials at hand, the stark neediness and extravagance of wanting to be beautiful or, failing that, wanting beauty around me. We were living, five of us, in a farmhouse in the middle of the Minnesota nowhere, near the South Dakota border, in a vaguely communal arrangement. We were supposed to be living cheaply (the rent was ten dollars a month per person) and writing (that was more iffy, especially when one of the group came up with the idea that writing was implicitly sexist because discipline was macho; I cannot begin, now, to explain this reasoning or why it made sense at the time). We were also considering the idea (pretty abstractly, in our case) of non-exclusive relationships. We were casting about after university years of protesting the Vietnam War, seeing how far we could push our new idea, feminism.

It didn't last. We spent most of our time being appalled by each other. One of my insupportable traits as a room-mate turned out to be the beauty disease, my infuriating habit of plunging a bouquet of wildflowers not into a milk bottle but into the Waterford decanter I'd hauled with me like the willowware a pioneer wife wrapped in cotton wool and put defiantly into a barrel, even if the tallow had to be left behind. My too-suave hand with a Mornay sauce got on everybody's nerves. When we woke one morning to find that the mice, whose home the place really was, had eaten a rounded bite out of the Linzertorte I'd made from scratch the day before, I don't think anybody really felt sorry for me. I was their embarrassing revisionist. 'You remind me,' my fellow communard said, trying to get a handle on the beauty disease, pausing for the worst, 'of . . . of my *mother*.'

Woman as aesthete; the 'civilizing sex', as we have always been honoured, burdened, as if the true female heritage were a handing down of certain obsessive-compulsive genes that are not simply house-keeperly traits but the very essence of the sex. The beauty disease as a way of feminine life. The phrase has stayed with me because, except for the brief, easily forgotten introduction to decadence and Dorian Gray in high school, this was the first time it had occurred to me that there was anything odd—pathological, even—about wanting to be beautiful. Feminism had made me feel vaguely uncomfortable (everybody was starting to wear combat boots and overalls . . . but it was still fashion), but the ideas of the women's movement were so many and so grand that in contemplating them during those first years I flitted around from one to another, so free in my mind that I hardly considered my habits.

But here it was, harshly spoken: I had the beauty disease. And I felt shame, a female shame—because I had registered my identity most deeply as an aesthetic, not as a sexual, being. Many women do. Beauty is women's work. Male homosexuals, for example, are stereotyped most nastily as 'not men' when they are seen as beings obsessed with appearance, interior decorators, hair-dressers. And they are held in greatest contempt for just that quality, perhaps because beauty is designated, in the unexamined part of the mind, as peculiarly female, and therefore *queer*. Erma Bombeck, whose columns my mother slashes out for me with her X-acto knife (my mother thinks I have the beauty disease too), is the renegade philosopher of sloth and disregard in this matter. But she must adopt a silly tone; she must always make fun of herself, the slob. Like the Polack jokes we as a nation of unconscious greenhorns keep telling on ourselves, her humour is based on a sophisticated problem whose roots are so essentially unfunny that she has material for a lifetime of columns.

Beginning with *Seventeen* magazine, the popular women's magazines have plotted out a woman's life in progressive publications whose single theme is beauty. From *Seventeen* on to *Mademoiselle* (college) and *Glamour* (first job) and then, somewhere in the late twenties, into the pure ether of *Vogue* where beauty leaves prettiness and the beginner thrills of 'looking your best' far behind with their good intentions (that vapid theme is carried forward, as an occasional motif, in magazines for housewives, such as *Redbook*, just as the overt sexual uses of beauty are relegated to *Cosmopolitan*). In *Vogue*, beauty becomes abstract, the way art did after the Second World War. Looking in *Vogue* at the spacy models and their minimal bodies, the aloof streaks of their facial features and sculpted heads, we see the inevitable destination of the *Seventeen* girl: the beautiful body is not a possibility—just as my grandmother and my aunts mused over their cream-and-sugar coffee. But they spoke of the body as fragmented, a series of endless patch jobs; the high-fashion model is a whole, she is the figure. Here, in the models of *Vogue*, we are given actual bodies whose extremity—of thinness, of mouth, of coiffure, of expression, of make-up—has rendered them indivisible.

Never mind that we shiver at the obvious analogy of these figures: the model is reminiscent of the vacant, starved face of a just-liberated prisoner of Auschwitz. Never mind the blasphemy. Never mind the fascination. We have, unconsciously and hesitantly, claimed the beauty that must be ours, as if it were a historical, even an evolutionary inevitability. There in the swank fashion magazines is the sexless (or androgynous, as the word is carelessly used now, to mean either both sexes or none at all) figure, thin to the point of horror, looking out from the page with the bewildered vacuity of a refugee. Thin, thin beyond flesh. *All you need is high cheekbones and you have to be thin.* You must be thin beyond health or hope. There is no thinness, no disappearance of flesh extreme enough to satisfy our idea of beauty—for we call it beauty, this bruised sacrilege of the body. The human figure changed with the Second World War. The spontaneous image clouded and came back in that horrible way, the skeleton in its gruesome pajamas.

The female fatale, which had been at the beginning of this century such a woman—the generous flesh and the insistent metaphor of all that glorious (or diabolical) hair in the portraiture of the pre-Raphaelites and of the art nouveau, in Burne-Jones and in Klimt and Mucha—became now as it had also after the slaughter of the Great War, masculine, the hair short, slicked back, cropped, the body just a backbone. The women that look out of the pages of *Vogue* in these extreme gestures of the figure are femmes fatales still, but their poison seems not for men, or not only. They are fatal now to themselves, not empowered as those earlier prewar (both wars: it started with the First) witches, but simply sick with their own malignancy. Another aspect of the beauty disease. The fashion model of this sort, the ultra-sophisticated mannequin peering from the high-fashion magazine with her alarming cheek-bones and professional concave body, is the dead risen to life, the ghost in our idea of beauty.

The beauty women perceive for themselves as the ideal—as opposed to that designed to appeal to men—is startlingly desexed. It is the beauty of the flat surface, the breastless, buttless set of bones upon which clothes are best hung. Two distinct models come to mind:

Marilyn Monroe and Audrey Hepburn. Opposites, reigning figures at about the same time in the fifties and early sixties. Monroe, about whom so much has been written, her life having become as eloquent in its way as Sylvia Plath's in hers, is a body, a femme fatale of the old art nouveau school, a man's idea of a woman. She was not, for me or the girls I grew up with, an ideal. This was partly because adolescent prudery is ferocious and Monroe was too frank a sexual symbol. But why was everyone so crazy to look like Audrey Hepburn? She played roles that involved a lot of costume changing: *Funny Face*, for instance, in which she is 'discovered' (as a dowdy clerk in a book store, no less) and made into a top Paris fashion model, Fred Astaire snapping the camera; and, later, in *Breakfast at Tiffany's*, a movie that influenced school-girl style in much the same way as, more recently, Diane Keaton's Annie Hall has. The body we sought was the body for clothes, for fashion, for the remotely physical, not the sensual. The thinner the body, the better because to be thin was to be less—less woman. It is the simultaneous appearance of both these figures that suggests the significance of their differences. It doesn't matter that Monroe is a monumental figure and Hepburn minor. Perhaps she is minor because her power and allure remained within women's minds (and *young* women's, girls') and like much that influences women (and not men) she was simply not taken seriously. And of course there was no suicide. She was, really, a representative of the fashion magazine, not of movies. Her power was that of a *Vogue* model brought to movie life, given a story, given lines. But the allure remained that of the high-fashion mannequin. Therefore, beyond the typical adolescent prudery that made Monroe an ideal for only the rare ('fast'!) girls, Audrey Hepburn was given pride of place in our minds for other, more telling reasons. It was her aloofness from the female figure that we longed for.

Like modern architecture and Scandinavian design with its rectitude, this minimal female body (Twiggy, Penelope Tree, the other nameless ones) delivers its lean message beyond its fashion statement. The 'boy look', the flat chest and curveless body, is not the result of feminism or any version of the women's movement. This stark body is the image of the slaughter of war in our country. The appearance of such figures as fashionable coincides eloquently with the end of the century's first European mass war. Women have been thin or fat, generous or lean, down through the ages: it is the *fashion* in body types that is indicative, a fashion for extreme thinness coming hard on the heels of the quite opposite image of the pre-Raphaelites and art nouveau. My grandmother with her little lipstick kiss of a mouth, like a heroine on the silent screen, was art nouveau and did not sigh to be skinny. One of the most striking aspects of the cheesecake pictures predating the First World War, especially the Belle Epoque photos of French music hall actresses (there's a wonderful one of Colette), is the relaxed flesh—not just big breasts, but a generous plumpness. You can tell those thighs are *soft*.

The fashion for fashion (consumerism) that has recently been noted, principally by Christopher Lasch, as an indication of the narcissism of our culture is something different; it concerns the clothes. I am looking, for the moment, at the mannequin. The current craze, male and female, gay and straight, to 'dress', to spend a lot of money on clothes, is probably not much different from the phenomenon that Thorsten Veblen analyzed in *The Theory of the Leisure Class*. This phenomenon has everything to do with restlessness and insecurity, change and fear, greediness and high spirits. There is not an excessive emphasis in the current stylishness (which is part of consumerism) on the thin body. The clothes of Calvin Klein or of anyone else hang better on a not-fat person, but these styles are not geared for extremity. They are for, precisely, everybody. They are the middle range, and as part of the marketplace, they change endlessly, causing us to desire fitfully. That is consumerism, that is fashion, that is big business, that is the clothes. But how steady and unwavering the mannequin has remained. The haute couture figure has not changed, decade after decade since the Great War when, in our cruelly timed emancipation, she cropped her hair to bedevil the Edwardians: a gesture of freedom and life, all those bobbed heads after the First World War. Or perhaps more unconsciously, the ancient way women have always keened for their dead. The essence of fashion may be the feverish marketable *change* that not only creates an appetite for personal gratification but leaves no time for anything else. But the one steadfast image is the mannequin, the body that is the background for all the busyness. Strange and telling that there—and so unguardedly— we should meet the figure of our haunted history, the recently interred shapes of Europe: the camp prisoner with the bones that can be counted with the eye. This is our grotesque ideal. Like all metaphoric

Patricia Hampl

emblematic figures, there is no mistaking its historic resonance. There, a scant generation ago, are the concentration camp bodies and here, a world away, are the gaunt anorexic girls in American hospitals, starved and suicidal over the horrible blubber they imagine they are dragging repulsively through the world. Rich girls mostly, sick, truly, with the beauty disease, dreaming of perfection, wanting to disappear.

Memed My Hawk SUMMER

YASHAR KEMAL *translated by Edouard Roditi*

In the impoverished Taurus highlands of Anatolia, a young lad, Slim Memed, is driven by the savage cruelty of the Agha or local landowner to rebel against the injustice he sees around him. Still a youth, he does battle against his Agha, takes to the hills as a bandit, and becomes the fugitive scourge of corrupt oppressors. This wild and haunting saga of Memed, champion of the landless poor, has become a living legend in contemporary Turkey.

An international best-seller, at last available in paperback. . .

"It has that insider's feelings for man, the oppressed, labouring animal, almost a ghostly projection of the soil, that you might find in Tolstoy, Hardy, or Silone." *The Guardian*

"Here is that directness and that fierce poetry which one knew in the old heroic stories, and a hero in whom one can have such faith and trust that one can bear to read of his torments knowing that he is strong enough to endure them." *Glasgow Herald*

Kemal "is trying to find, to create, in his own country, a language for millions and millions of people whom no one's ever heard of, whom no one has ever spoken for, and who cannot speak." James Baldwin

Now an author of international repute, several times nominated for the Nobel prize,

The Georgia Review

Winter 1980

- James Guimond's *Toward a Philosophy of Photography*
- William J. Free's *Beckett's Plays & the Photographic Vision*
- Peter Stitt's *Robert Penn Warren: Life's Instancy & the Astrolabe of Joy*
- Marjorie Perloff's *The Man Who Loved Women: The Medical Fictions of William Carlos Williams*
- William F. Van Wert's *Holes: The Idea of an* Entr'acte
- Charles Baxter's *In the Suicide Seat: Reading John Hawkes's* Travesty

FICTION by Murray Baumgarten, Hilary Masters, & Joyce Carol Oates.

POETRY by Robert Bly, Christopher Bursk, Geraldine Connolly, Daniel Hoffman, William Matthews, Linda Pastan, Tony Petrosky, Stanley Plumly, Bin Ramke, Arthur Smith, David Wagoner, Robert Penn Warren, & David Weiss.

BOOK REVIEWS by Michele Bogart, William E. Cain, Diane Cole, Frederick Ferré, Joseph Parisi, Peter Stitt, & Benjamin Taylor.

"A quantity of quality" . . . "The best bargain in American publishing today." Now distributed to bookstores nationally by B. DeBoer, Inc., Nutley, N. J.

Please enter my subscription to *The Georgia Review* (4 issues per year):

___ 1 yr/$6 ___ 2 yrs/$10   (outside U.S. add $2/yr—U.S. funds only)

Begin subscription with the _____ issue.

Name: _____

Address: _____

City _____ State _____ Zip _____

The Georgia Review is published by the University of Georgia, Athens, Georgia 30602

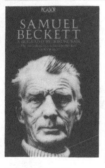

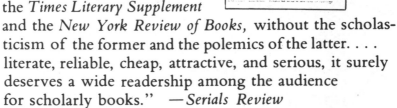

New Fiction Spring 1981

Günter Grass
THE MEETING AT TELGTE
June   £5.95

Italo Calvino
IF ON A WINTER'S NIGHT A TRAVELLER
June   £6.95

Carlos Fuentes
BURNT WATER
January   £6.50

Walker Percy
THE SECOND COMING
January   £6.95

Siegfried Lenz
THE HERITAGE
June   £7.95

John Banville
KEPLER
January   £5.95

from
Secker & Warburg

THE INFERNO

**The Divine Comedy of
DANTE ALIGHIERI
A Verse Translation with
Introduction and
Annotations by
ALLEN MANDELBAUM**

This first volume of *The California
Dante, The Inferno,* with en face
English and Italian text, has
prompted a sequence of forty-two
graphic "meditations" by Barry
Moser. The accord of remarkable poetic, scholarly, graphic,
and typographic gifts makes
this a unique edition, one that
can only confirm Burton Raffel's
judgement in *The Denver
Quarterly:* "We are about to have,
at long last, an Englished
Dante . . . which should satisfy
Italianists, and medievalists, and
readers of poetry."

    The California Dante will contain an intro-
duction and facing text and verse translation,
with a separate volume devoted to each *cantica*
of *The Divine Comedy.* It will also include, under
the General Editorship of Allen Mandelbaum,
a separate volume of commentary for each *cantica*. The three
commentary volumes will constitute the California Lectura
Dantis. In these volumes, each canto will be the subject of an
essay/reading by one of an international group of participating
scholar-critics. The thirty-three—or in the case of *Inferno,*
thirty-four—canto readings in each volume will be
supplemented by a comprehensive index-glossary and
synoptic appendixes.

336 pages, £15.00

 University of California Press
Ely House, 37 Dover Street, London W.1.

Acclaim for a remarkable new novel set in India
during the time since Independence.

MIDNIGHT'S CHILDREN
by Salman Rushdie

'I haven't been so continuously surprised by a novel since I first read
One Hundred Years of Solitude.' Elaine Feinstein, *The Times*

'This massive extravaganza, certainly unlike anything else I have ever
read, has something to tell the British reader about India that he will
not be able to obtain from anywhere else: a record of how a diverse
culture has broken up (or is breaking up), and yet of how, in a certain
sense, it has endured.' Martin Seymour-Smith, *Financial Times*

'A magnificent book. Rushdie's narrative, jocose, expansive, daring,
brilliantly minute, glitters with redundant stories, important
parenthises, witty similitudes and outrageous red herrings. He takes as
much care over small colloquial details—a note on a fortune-teller's
wall, "Spitting during Visit is Quite a Bad Habit".' Hermione Lee,
Observer

'A new kind of fiction of the highest order: magical, artistic, urgently
political ... emerging as many times larger than the critical terms we
might use to describe it.' Bill Buford, *New Statesman*

'Brilliant piece of writing. He swings between a variety of styles as the
narrative swings between politics, sex, clothes, furniture, clothes,
jewels, animals, crowds, loneliness, magic ... in all senses a fantastic
book—and, I think, an important one for Europeans to read.' Victoria
Glendenning, *Sunday Times*

JONATHAN CAPE   **£6.95**

NOTES ON CONTRIBUTORS

Poet, translator, and author, **Guy Davenport** has written several books including *Da Vinci's Bicycle*, a collection of short stories published last year by the Johns Hopkins University Press, and two new works with the North Point Press: *Eclogues* (fiction) and *The Geography of the Imagination* (essays). He has just been awarded the Morton Dauwen Zabel Prize by the American Academy and Institute of Arts and Letters. **Brigid Brophy's** novels include *Flesh, Hackenfeller's Ape, Snow Ball,* and *Palace without Chairs.* She is a frequent contributor to the *TLS* and the *London Review of Books.* **John Sutherland's** *Bestsellers* was published this spring by Routledge and Kegan Paul. He is a Reader of English Literature at University College, London. **David Caute** was, until recently, the Literary Editor of the *New Statesman.* He is member of the Writers' Guild and is currently writing a book on Zimbabwe. **Blake Morrison** is Poetry and Fiction Editor of the *TLS.* His book *The Movement, English Poetry and Fiction in the 1950s,* was published last year. **Per Gedin** is Director of the Swedish publishing house Wahlström & Widstrand, and is the author of *Literature in the Marketplace.* **Eric Burns** is a recent graduate of Jesus College in Cambridge. **Walter Abish** was born in

Vienna, grew up in Shanghai, served in the Israeli army, and is currently living in New York City. His novel *How German Is It?* has just won the first PEN/Faulkner Award for Fiction. Part of this book originally appeared in **Granta**. **Lisa Zeidner's** 'Lucy' is taken from *Customs*, her first novel, to be published this October by Jonathan Cape. **Nicole Ward Jouve** is a lecturer in literature at the University of York. 'The Drawer' is included in a collection of stories entitled *Shades of Grey*, translated from French, and published this month by Virago at £2.95. **Martin Amis** is the author of four novels. *Other People*, published this spring, is his most recent. **Kenneth Bernard** was one of the winners in the recent Arvon Foundation Poetry Competition. His fiction and essays have appeared in a number of literary magazines. **Raymond Carver** is a poet and author of four collections of short fiction. His most recent book, *What We Talk about when We Talk about Love*, was just published by Knopf. **Mario Vargas Llosa's** books include *Conversation in the Cathedral* and *Captain Pantoja and the Special Service*. He has taught at the University of London and was recently a Fellow at Churchill College in Cambridge. He is currently living in Lima, Peru. **Patricia Hampl's** poems and short fiction have appeared in the *New Yorker*, the *Paris Review*, and a number of little magazines. 'The Beauty Disease' is from *A Romantic Education* which has just won the Houghton Mifflin Literary Fellowship Award.